READING ACROSS CULTURES

READING ACROSS CULTURES

TRANSLATING ROMANCES, FABLES, AND POETRY IN MEDIEVAL ASHKENAZ

CAROLINE GRUENBAUM

CORNELL UNIVERSITY PRESS
Ithaca and London

First published 2025 by Cornell University Press

Library of Congress Cataloging-in-Publication Data

Names: Gruenbaum, Caroline, 1990- author.
Title: Reading across cultures : translating romances, fables, and poetry in medieval Ashkenaz / Caroline Gruenbaum.
Description: Ithaca : Cornell University Press, 2025. | Includes bibliographical references and index.
Identifiers: LCCN 2024040248 (print) | LCCN 2024040249 (ebook) | ISBN 9781501782411 (hardback) | ISBN 9781501782428 (pdf) | ISBN 9781501782435 (epub)
Subjects: LCSH: Literature, Medieval—Translations into Hebrew—History and criticism. | Literature, Medieval—Appreciation—History—To 1500. | Jews—Intellectual life—History—To 1500. | Ashkenazim—History—To 1500. | Judaism—Relations—Christianity—History—To 1500.
Classification: LCC PN671 .G78 2025 (print) | LCC PN671 (ebook) | DDC 809/.02—dc23/eng/20250101
LC record available at https://lccn.loc.gov/2024040248
LC ebook record available at https://lccn.loc.gov/2024040249

Contents

Acknowledgments

I am grateful for the support of many individuals and institutions throughout this decade-long process. I began this project at New York University (NYU), after Maud Kozodoy introduced me to *Sefer ha-Maʿasim* during a casual chat. That text and our chat sparked my entire research trajectory. I am very thankful to Maud for her ideas and encouragement along the way. While I am not sure if it was coincidence or foresight that caused us to overlap at Brown, NYU, and Posen, I feel lucky to have been her student for so many years. Maud's even-keeled and no-drama attitude has made research-related frustrations much more palatable. I have learned so much from her.

Thank you to my mentors and professors at NYU, including Bob Chazan (*z"l*), Hasia Diner, David Engel, Marion Kaplan, Sarah Pearce, Jeffrey Rubenstein, Elisha Russ-Fishbane, Martha Rust, and Kathryn Smith.

This book took its final shape at Yale's Institute for Sacred Music, which gave me the flexibility to write and edit the manuscript, and to continue teaching and publishing in the field. This would not have been possible without the support of Martin Jean and Eben Graves, and my fellow fellows.

It takes a village to write a book about medieval literature across cultures. Thank you to colleagues close and far who provided feedback along the way: Emilie Amar-Zifkin, Elisheva Baumgarten, Ilana Ben-Ezra, Tovi Bibring, Shamma Boyarin, Mathilda Bruckner, Sarah Kay, Rella Kushelevsky, Eyal Levinson, Ivan Marcus, Annegret Oehme, David Shyovitz, David Wacks, Anna Waymack, Adrienne Williams Boyarin, and Eli Yassif. The Medieval Academy sent me a windfall when it paired me with Annegret and David Wacks for a mentorship program at Kalamazoo in 2019. Their advice has been invaluable.

At Cornell, Mahinder Kingra has been a wonderful editor for this project. The input from him, the two anonymous reviewers, and editorial boards, and initial insights from Anne Lester and Cecilia Gaposchkin, have greatly improved the final version of this book.

I acknowledge gratefully the Posen Library for Jewish Culture and Civilization for making a warm and comfortable workplace atmosphere, where grammatical discussions are encouraged and where my personal and professional interests are always celebrated.

Thank you, finally, to my family: my parents and parents-in-law for their encouragement; my siblings for their unfeigned interest in my work; and, of course, to Benji and the girls for their unwavering support and love.

Introduction

On Jewish Knights

A pair of caparisoned horses prance in the bottom margin of a thirteenth-century manuscript, their riders decked in armor, carrying shields and vigorously brandishing swords. Painted in bright colors, these knights seem to gallop off the page. In the bottom margin of another page, a single golden knight sits atop his steed, also colored in shiny gold; he too holds his sword above his head. These vivid illuminations come as little surprise in the thirteenth century, which saw a significant rise in the number of decorated manuscripts and indeed holds a place in the collective Western imagination as the quintessential era of knights and courtly entertainment.[1] What may be a shock, though, is that the text in which these particular knights appear is a copy of Moses Maimonides' Hebrew legal code, the *Mishneh Torah*.[2]

The *Mishneh Torah* was originally written circa 1170 in Egypt and contains a summary of Jewish law pertaining to all aspects of life, including

1. Malachi Beit-Arié, *Unveiled Faces of Medieval Hebrew Books: The Evolution of Manuscript Production—Progression or Regression?* (Jerusalem: Hebrew University Magnes Press, 2003).

2. The knights appear in Library of the Hungarian Academy of Sciences, Budapest, Kaufman MS A 77, fols. 2r and 16v. The manuscript has been digitized and can be found at http://kaufmann.mtak.hu/en/ms77a/ms77a-coll1.htm.

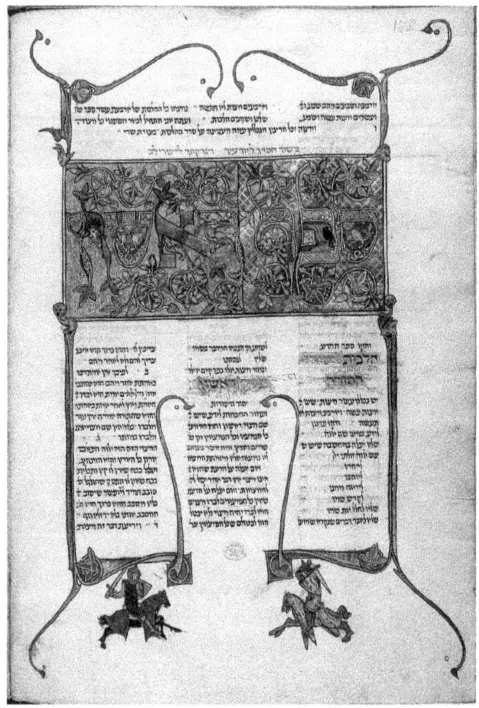

FIGURE 1. Moses Maimonides, *Mishneh Torah*. Northern France, 1296. Hungarian Academy of Sciences, Kaufman MS A 77, fol. 16v. Courtesy of the Library and Information Centre of the Hungarian Academy of Sciences.

philosophical and ethical principles; dietary laws; Sabbath and holiday observance; temple sacrifices; marriage and divorce; the sabbatical year; and much, much more (see figures 1 and 2). The page with the fighting knights is the first page of the first chapter, "On the Basic Principles of the Torah," and begins with an exhortation to believe in God before affirming the centrality of the Torah and its missives. Knights are nowhere to be found in the content of this chapter or in any other chapter in his book.

The illustrations of that *Mishneh Torah*, copied in northern France in 1296, present a microcosm of the interplay among religious observance, non-Jewish culture, and rabbinic authority, none of which was monolithic and all of which varied across geographic, chronological, and generic boundaries; that interplay is at the heart of the arguments presented in this book. Even within the relatively narrow chronological focus of this book, namely, twelfth- and thirteenth-century Europe, diverse rabbinic opinions about the types of cultural expression that

FIGURE 2. Moses Maimonides, *Mishneh Torah*. Northern France, 1296. Hungarian Academy of Sciences, Kaufman MS A 77, fol. 2r. Courtesy of the Library and Information Centre of the Hungarian Academy of Sciences.

Jews were intended to enjoy and produce proliferated. While some rabbis rejected engagement with non-Jewish culture, such as stories of knights and other forms of courtly culture, medieval Jews nevertheless read and wrote Hebrew texts, meant for Jewish audiences, that incorporated non-Jewish ideas, characters, and plots. This book addresses the relationship between medieval Jews and literature with non-Jewish origins that they produced, filled with, among other secular oddities, jousting knights, illicit affairs, and talking animals.

In the medieval Jewish world, translation, usually into the characteristically Jewish language of Hebrew, was a main conduit for moving non-Jewish culture into the Jewish fold. In a now lost thirteenth-century Hebrew version of a romance featuring Alexander the Great from Southern Italy or Spain, its translator writes:

> Not because I see myself as wise, nor because of my skill with language, have I decided to translate this book from Latin, into

> Hebrew, for I am most ignorant and unwise. Indeed, I wished to translate it after I saw it written in the book of the Christians and painted with nice figures and different colors, and with silver and gold, because of their great love for it. And most people believe its contents, and I am not one of them (even though everything is possible, and maybe I will find some benefit from them). Its translation and composition are sound.[3]

In this passage, the translator refers to the Latin sources that inspired his Hebrew Alexander romance. The translator outlines his reasons for performing a translation from Latin (literally, "the language of the Christians") to Hebrew. He denies the historical accuracy of Alexander's legends, admitting that he does not believe them. His decision to translate then is purely for the great popularity and pomp that Christians give its contents. In the Middle Ages, important books bore ornate illuminations and bindings, and the ornamentation of the Latin version of the Alexander romance leads the translator to think it is worthy of translation. Unfortunately, this is the only part of the manuscript that exists, copied in a nineteenth-century scholarly article. It is possible that this manuscript was used as a source for an extant Alexander romance penned by the Jewish author Immanuel Bonfils (ca. 1300–1377), whose Hebrew text shows evidence of Latin and French sources.[4]

This translator emerged from the literary culture of medieval Sepharad, encompassing the Iberian Peninsula and parts of southern Europe. In Sepharad, Jewish authors such as Judah ha-Levi and Moses Ibn Ezra frequently engaged in literary translation and borrowing from Arabic. Between the tenth and thirteenth centuries, they wrote secular poetry that was based on Arabic poetics but consisted of biblical Hebrew language. Hebrew prose narratives, inspired by Arabic short stories and non-Jewish folktales, appeared in the thirteenth century in southern Spain and France. Scholars have long acknowledged and celebrated this culture of translation in Sepharad and the close relationship between

3. Israel Lévi, ed., *Le roman d'Alexandre: texte hébreu anonyme* (Paris: Librairie A. Durlacher, 1887), xiii–xiv; Shamma Boyarin, "Hebrew Alexander Romance and Astrological Questions: Alexander, Aristotle, and the Medieval Jewish Audience," in *Alexander the Great in the Middle Ages*, ed. Markus Stock (Toronto: University of Toronto Press, 2016), 100n5.

4. The extant copy is Paris, Bibliothèque Nationale Héb. 750.3. and edited with translation in Israel Kazis, ed., *The Book of the Gests of Alexander of Macedon*, trans. Israel Kazis (Cambridge: Medieval Academy of America, 1962). See also Kazis, *The Book of the Gests*, 40, 79, 203–22.

Hebrew and Arabic literary cultures.[5] This scholarship is made possible in part by the thousands of fragments of the Cairo Geniza, an abandoned storeroom filled with medieval Jewish manuscripts from several communities around the Mediterranean, comprised of documents, literary sources, letters, and liturgical texts. This storeroom was discovered in the nineteenth century, and its cataloguing process is still ongoing. This treasure of literary endeavors stands in stark contrast to the contemporaneous Jewish communities of Ashkenaz, the region of Jewish communities encompassing northern Europe, especially in England, northern France, and Germany along the Rhineland. For many reasons, including its lack of a hidden storeroom filled with thousands of local and regional medieval documents, we do not have a comparable documentary and literary trove from medieval Ashkenaz. The relatively few treasures of Ashkenazi literature are in a continuous process of discovery and publicization. This book aims to change the narrative of medieval Jewish literature from Sepharad alone, in all its poetic and documentary glory, to include Ashkenaz.

In 1979, the eminent Israeli medieval literary scholar Dan Pagis outlined the state of the field of medieval Hebrew literature. In his "Trends of Medieval Hebrew Literature," he elucidates the stumbling blocks for the development of medieval Hebrew literary analysis. However, he focuses almost exclusively on poetry and poetics, especially in Sepharad, without mention of a single Ashkenazi author or text. This was not a conscious shunning of Ashkenaz but rather an organic oversight because of a lack of scholarship on Ashkenazi nonliturgical literature.[6]

5. Jefim Schirmann, "The Function of the Hebrew Poet in Medieval Spain," *Jewish Social Studies* 16, no. 3 (1954): 235–52; Raymond P. Scheindlin, *Wine, Women, and Death: Medieval Hebrew Poems on the Good Life* (Oxford: Oxford University Press, 1986); Rina Drory, *Reshit Ha-Maga'im Shel Ha-Sifrut Ha-Yehudit 'im Ha-Sifrut Ha-'Arvit Ba-Me'ah Ha-'aśirit* [The Emergence of Jewish-Arabic Literary Contacts at the Beginning of the Tenth Century] (Tel Aviv: Ha-Kibutz ha-Meuhad, 1988); Ross Brann, "The Arabized Jews," in *The Literature of Al-Andalus*, ed. Maria Menocal, Raymond P. Scheindlin, and Michael Sells (Cambridge: Cambridge University Press, 2000), 435–54.

6. An early scholar of medieval Hebrew literature, Moritz Steinschneider tentatively acknowledged that translations from non-Jewish sources took place in Ashkenaz. See Moritz Steinschneider, *Die hebraeischen Übersetzungen des Mittelalters und die Juden als Dolmetscher* [The Hebrew Translations of the Middle Ages and the Jews as Translators] (Berlin: Kommissionsverlag des Bibliographischen Bureaus, 1893). See also a new edition of Steinschneider's work with editorial notes and introduction in Charles H. Manekin, Y. Tzvi Langermann, and Hans Hinrich Biesterfeldt, eds., *Moritz Steinschneider: The Hebrew Translations of the Middle Ages and the Jews as Transmitters* (Dordrecht: Springer Netherlands, 2013). It is also important to note the contributions of Joseph Dan, who took important steps toward understanding medieval Jewish literature across Europe, not solely in Ashkenaz. Joseph Dan, *Ha-sipur ha-'ivri*

The field of Ashkenazi literature is still catching up to its Sephardic counterpart fifty years later. In an updated encyclopedic analysis of the state of the field of medieval Hebrew belles lettres published in 2018, texts and authors from Ashkenaz are again absent.[7] Within the last two decades, however, more articles and some books propelled the study of Ashkenazi literature forward. This scholarship analyzed specific texts or authors from Ashkenaz, with special focus on influence from non-Jewish sources, just as Sephardic literary analysis highlighted influence from Arabic. Scholars, including Eli Yassif, Rella Kushelevsky, Tovi Bibring, Ruth Nisse, and Jerold Frakes, have focused exclusively on Ashkenazi literature and pinpointed many French, German, and Latin sources that underlie this body of Hebrew and Yiddish material.[8]

The influence of non-Jewish literature on Ashkenazi texts cannot be overstated. Simply put, the combination of non-Hebrew text with Jewish languages (whether Hebrew, Yiddish, or vernaculars such as Hebraico-French) created a vitally important body of literature between the twelfth and the fifteenth centuries in Ashkenaz. Despite the dozens of folktales, prose narratives, songs, and stories, no comprehensive literary study of medieval literature from Ashkenaz exists.[9] This book heeds

---

bi-yeme ha-benayim: 'iyunim be-toldotaẏ [The Hebrew Story in the Middle Ages] (Jerusalem: Keter, 1974).

7. Jonathan P. Decter, "Belles-Lettres," in *The Cambridge History of Judaism*, ed. Robert Chazan (Cambridge: Cambridge University Press, 2018), 787–812.

8. The following represents a selection of influential articles and books on the topic of medieval Ashkenazi literature, especially in the context of external, non-Jewish influence and translation. Eli Yassif, "The Hebrew Narrative Anthology in the Middle Ages," *Prooftexts* 17, no. 2 (May 1997): 153–75; Eli Yassif, *The Hebrew Folktale: History, Genre, Meaning* (Bloomington: Indiana University Press, 2009); Rella Kushelevsky, *Tales in Context: Sefer Ha-Ma'asim in Medieval Northern France* (Detroit, MI: Wayne State University Press, 2017); Tovi Bibring, "'Would That My Words Were Inscribed': Berechiah Ha-Naqdan's 'Mišlei Šu'alim' and European Fable Traditions," in *Latin-into-Hebrew: Texts and Studies*, ed. Resianne Fontaine and Gad Freudenthal (Leiden: Brill, 2013), 309–29; Ruth Nisse, *Jacob's Shipwreck: Diaspora, Translation, and Jewish-Christian Relations in Medieval England* (Ithaca, NY: Cornell University Press, 2017); Jerold C. Frakes, *The Emergence of Early Yiddish Literature: Cultural Translation in Ashkenaz* (Bloomington: Indiana University Press, 2017); Tamás Visi, Tovi Bibring, and Daniel Soukup, eds., *Berechiah Ben Natronai Ha-Naqdan's Works and Their Reception: L'oeuvre de Berechiah Ben Natronai Ha-Naqdan et Sa Récéption* (Turnhout: Brepols, 2019); Caroline Gruenbaum and Annegret Oehme, eds., *Medieval and Early Modern Jewish Romance* (Kalamazoo, MI: Arc Humanities, 2023).

9. Although they do not focus exclusively on Ashkenaz, two comprehensive studies by Eli Yassif have shaped scholarship on medieval Hebrew literature, providing in-depth analyses of many different genres of literature from several different regions. He emphasizes the impact of outside literature on nearly all facets of medieval Jewish literature. See Yassif, *The Hebrew Folktale*; Yassif, "The Hebrew Narrative Anthology in the Middle Ages."

the call to explore the literary history, cultural underpinnings, and thematic variations that make Ashkenazi literature worthy of study.

My focus here is on the emergence of medieval Ashkenazi literature through processes of translation, and the relationship between translation and the religious identity of its authors and readers. In other words, I explore how and why literature made its way from non-Jews to Jews, examining how texts changed during this movement and how this movement reflects the authors' cultural and religious milieus. Not every text surveyed here comes from Ashkenaz directly. All of them, however, show a familiarity among the Jews of Ashkenaz with themes from non-Jewish sources.

This book explores the culture of translation in medieval Ashkenaz as a combination of unique factors, as a result of both internal cultural and religious institutions, and external literary influence. In chapters 1 and 2, the book begins with a discussion of institutional and cultural processes of learning and access to stories in non-Jewish languages both written and oral, and chapters 3–5 move into an exploration of the content of translated texts. Chapter 1 introduces the process of education and literacy in medieval Ashkenaz, exploring the places where literate men may have been exposed to non-Jewish literature and engaged in textual translation. Men in Ashkenaz traditionally learned to read (and write) Hebrew through rabbinic establishments as part of a religious education. I argue that this education ably prepared them for the ability to read non-Jewish literature as well. Chapter 2 analyzes the linguistic realities of diglossic Jews living in medieval Ashkenaz: speaking the vernacular of French or German but writing and reading almost exclusively in Hebrew. When they translate, they do so from the vernacular into a language usually reserved for devotional material. In medieval literature, the emergence of a vernacular literary culture allowed wider access to material for readers who did not know Latin. But in medieval Jewish culture, translations restricted the readership by restraining it to Hebrew, the "high" register language of the male elite.

The second half of the book focuses on the content of the translated texts and their proposed reception by medieval Jewish audiences. Chapter 3 considers the translated Hebrew texts that borrow and translate from non-Jewish sources that espouse non-Jewish wisdom, especially Berechiah ha-Nakdan's *Mishle Shu'alim* (Fox Fables). Rather than reframe their material into biblical and rabbinic terms for its new Jewish audience, the translators choose to present their ethical instruction almost exactly as it appeared in the source text. Chapter 4 argues that medieval Hebrew texts used stories borrowed from medieval French romance in order to promote ideas about marriage, centering largely around the Hebrew text *Melekh Artus* (King Arthur). These ideas did not necessarily contradict the source texts, and the Jewish authors did not feel obligated to add elements of Jewish piety to make their arguments. The source texts are generally acceptable as they are, with only slight editorial emendations to promote a new type of Jewish story not necessarily based on religious observance or biblical exegesis. Chapter 5 discusses exceptions to this trend of acceptance of non-Jewish material through translation by exposing the literary boundaries that medieval Jews could not cross, specifically focusing on literature that they did not borrow or translate from non-Jewish literature. I argue that the only Jews who could write in the literary spheres of poetry and autobiography were those who crossed over the boundary themselves as converts to Christianity.

Translated Texts in and from Ashkenaz

Throughout this book, I analyze (or mention) every translation produced in Ashkenaz in the medieval period, a group of about half a dozen texts (see the appendix for the full list of literary texts from Ashkenaz, including translations). While my corpus of translated texts is small, it is mighty. It represents several types of nonrabbinic literature—literature that is not liturgical or exegetical, or does not deal with rabbinic law—including fables, exempla, songs, romance, and more. Each text is unique in its authorship and origin, and they differ in how they refer to their source texts (if they do at all), but all share an undeniable link to non-Jewish literature that they translate. These variations point to the complexity of identifying a corpus of this literature when no two authors approach their translations in the same way. The similarities are compelling enough to permit the application of the word "corpus," and the texts are disparate enough that there is no single suitable translation or literary theory that can possibly account for each text. In this book, I celebrate the diversity of the corpus through an analysis that considers each text individually within its specific genre, chronology, and geography.

Before seeing how the lines between Jewish and non-Jewish linguistic and literary output are blurred, a definition of Jewish literature is necessary. We turn to the pioneering Jewish folklorist Dov Noy's simple yet striking definition of what makes a Jewish folktale Jewish. He reckoned that a Jewish folktale needed four ingredients: a Jewish time (such as a holiday), Jewish place (i.e., a prayer hall or Jewish city), Jewish characters (a rabbi or known Jewish figure), and a Jewish moral or message.[10] By this reckoning, however, several of the tales analyzed in this study are not Jewish. Instead, I propose a single criterion that applies to all medieval Jewish stories or tales: a Jewish folktale or story was intended for a Jewish community. That criterion alone, although we have disregarded the others, is established through the unique linguistic reality of medieval Jewish life, in which only Jews communicated with texts written in Hebrew or in the Hebrew script. The act of turning a text "Jewish" rests in the author's decision to translate it into a Jewish language or script.[11]

Jewish texts follow several trends captured by medieval translation theory, although these theories are, unfortunately, not often applied to Hebrew literature. Medieval Jews generally adhered to a literary polysystem, with both Hebrew and the vernacular language appearing in various ways in their work. Although the bulk of the literary material by medieval Jews was written in Hebrew, vernacular phrases, transliterated into Hebrew letters, often come into play. For Jews under Islam, their written language was often Judeo-Arabic, Arabic written in Hebrew characters, with many Hebrew words sprinkled in. Jews of medieval Europe were much more covert, however, about their linguistic choices. They never acknowledged their literary sources, but the art of translation becomes obvious when we compare the Jewish texts to non-Jewish texts within the medieval Jewish sphere of influence.

I use the term "translation" throughout this book, knowing that the process of moving a text from one culture or language into another can take many forms.[12] In Ashkenaz, medieval Hebrew texts generally fall into two groups: creative translation that relies on "borrowing," as seen in romance and other belletristic Hebrew literature, with ideas transmitted from the source language rather than individual words. This group

10. Dov Noy, "What Is Jewish about the Jewish Folktale?," in *Miriam's Tambourine: Jewish Folktales from around the World*, ed. Howard Schwartz (Oxford: Oxford University Press, 1988), xv–xviii.

11. Translating texts into Jewish languages can be considered an act of Judaization, although I generally avoid that term. See, for example, Raphael Patai's entry on Dov Noy and a summary of the scholar's definition of Judaization, which included several elements: changes to the beginning and end of the tale, the addition of biblical verse and allusions, Hebrew wordplay and poetics, and Jewish folklore set in Jewish place and time. Raphael Patai, *Encyclopedia of Jewish Folklore and Traditions* (London: Routledge, 2015), 394–96.

12. For a brief foray into medieval translation theory, see Emma Campbell and Robert Mills, eds., *Rethinking Medieval Translation: Ethics, Politics, Theory* (Cambridge: D. S. Brewer, 2012); Peter Burke and R. Po-chia Hsia, eds., *Cultural Translation in Early Modern Europe* (Cambridge: Cambridge University Press, 2007).

represents the bulk of the corpus. The second group is literal, word-for-word translation, which often occurs in medieval scientific and medical translations and which appeared less frequently.

One of the earliest examples of translation in Ashkenaz is Berechiah ha-Nakdan's collection of over one hundred animal fables in rhymed prose, *Mishle Shu'alim*.[13] Berechiah ben Natronai ha-Nakdan (Berechiah the Punctator, son of Natronai) practiced in Normandy in the late twelfth century or first quarter of the thirteenth century, probably in Rouen.[14] The author of the last fable in the edition of *Mishle Shu'alim*, published by A. M. Haberman, is not Berechiah but a certain Crescia the Punctator, who writes in the first person. The only known punctator by this name was Crespia (or Cresbia) the Punctator ben Isaac, who lived in Rouen around 1240 and who copied and annotated various books there.[15] In his codex of Pentateuch and prophetic writings, Berechiah's son, Elijah ben Berechiah, also refers to himself as living in Rouen by 1233.[16] Although previous scholarship placed Berechiah in England, newer research suggests that he only traveled there and worked mainly in Normandy and Provence.[17] This research bases its theory on the likely dedication of another of Berechiah's texts, *Sefer musar haskel* (Book of the Discipline of Wisdom), to Meshullam ben Jacob of Lunel and its composition in Provence as well.[18] *Sefer musar haskel* and another of Berechiah's philosophical works, *Ha-Matsref* (The Refiner), shows Berechiah's familiarity with Judeo-Arabic philosophy and ethics, with clear influence from Se'adya Ga'on (ca. 882–932) and Abraham Ibn Ezra. His *Mishle Shu'alim* contains some works only known in Provence but also emerges from a northern cultural background, placing Berechiah at a crossroads between a variety

13. Berechiah ben Natronai Ha-Nakdan, *Mishlei Shualim*, ed. A. M. Habermann (Tel Aviv: Schocken, 1946); Berechiah ben Natronai Ha-Nakdan, *Fables of a Jewish Aesop: Translated from the Fox Fables of Berechiah Ha-Nakdan*, trans. Moses Hadas (New York: Columbia University Press, 1967). Haim Schwarzbaum produced a summary of the fables and a detailed analysis of the origin of each. He emphasizes the importance of universal folktale motifs and oral retellings that informed the Hebrew author. Haim Schwarzbaum, *The Mishle Shu'alim (Fox Fables) of Rabbi Berechiah Ha-Nakdan* (Jerusalem: Institute for Jewish and Arab Folklore Research, 1979).

14. Albert C. Friend, "The Tale of the Captive Bird and the Traveler: Nequam, Berechiah, and Chaucer's Squire's Tale," *Medievalia et Humanistica* 1 (1970): 64.

15. Norman Golb, *The Jews in Medieval Normandy: A Social and Intellectual History* (Cambridge: Cambridge University Press, 1998), 439.

16. Golb, *The Jews in Medieval Normandy*, 328–33.

17. Tamás Visi, "Berechiah Ben Naṭronai Ha-Naqdan's *Dodi ve-Neḵdi* and the Transfer of Scientific Knowledge from Latin to Hebrew in the Twelfth Century," *Aleph* 14, no. 2 (July 2014): 14.

18. Visi, "Berechiah Ben Naṭronai Ha-Naqdan's *Dodi ve-Neḵdi*," 16–20.

of literary spheres.[19] Besides its dozen extant Hebrew manuscripts, *Mishle Shu'alim* exists in four Hebrew editions, and one Latin and one Yiddish edition printed prior to 1850, attesting to a multilingual early modern reception.[20] He produced several other works, including liturgical and secular poetry, and a translation-paraphrase of Adelard of Bath's *Quaestiones naturales*.[21] Scholars have attributed a lapidary and a commentary on Job to him as well.[22] His secular poetry is one of only a handful of known examples of the genre from a northern European author.

A second source, a thirteenth-century folktale anthology that scholars have named *Sefer ha-Ma'asim* (Book of Tales), contains several tales of interest, with components translated or borrowed from contemporary non-Jewish French sources. The collection appears in the manuscript Oxford, Bodl. Or. 135 alongside rabbinic legends, medieval stories, and medieval philosophical works. The manuscript dates to the late thirteenth century in Champagne.[23] Many of the tales appear for the first time in this manuscript, while others have rabbinic origins. The first complete English translation with a new Hebrew edition was published in 2017.[24] *Sefer ha-Ma'asim* relies on borrowing and reframing stories rather than direct textual translation from its non-Jewish source material, but it remains a vital resource to understanding the ways that medieval Jews engaged with their surrounding culture.

A third source is *Melekh Artus*, a Hebrew Arthurian romance with an extant manuscript from 1279 that was written (or copied) in northern

19. Bibring, "Would That My Words Were Inscribed"; Golb, *The Jews in Medieval Normandy*, 339–42.

20. Magdaléna Jánošíková, "Fox Fables in the Early Modern Era: The Fables That Ashkenaz Read in Hebrew," in *Berechiah Ben Natronai Ha-Naqdan's Works and Their Reception*, ed. Tovi Bibring, Tamás Visi, and Daniel Soukup (Turnhout: Brepols, 2019), 190.

21. Some editions and translations of these texts exist. Berechiah ben Natronai Ha-Nakdan, *Dodi Ve-Nechdi*, ed. and trans. Hermann Gollancz (Oxford: Oxford University Press, 1920); Berechiah ben Natronai Ha-Nakdan, *The Ethical Treatises of Berachya Son of Rabbi Natronai Ha-Nakdan, Being the Compendium and the Masref*, ed. and trans. Hermann Gollancz (London: D. Nutt, 1902); Berechiah ben Natronai Ha-Nakdan, *A Commentary on the Book of Job: From a Hebrew Manuscript in the University Library, Cambridge*, trans. S. A. Hirsch (London: Williams & Norgate, 1905).

22. Gad Freudenthal and Jean-Marc Mandosio, "Old French into Hebrew in Twelfth-Century Tsarfat: Medieval Hebrew Versions of Marbode's Lapidary," *Aleph* 14, no. 1 (January 2014): 11–187. The commentary on Job is likely misattributed.

23. Eli Yassif, "Sepher Ha-Ma'asim: The Character, Origins and Impact of the Collection of Stories at the Time of the Tosafists [Heb.]," *Tarbiz* 53, no. 3 (April 1, 1984): 409–29; Malachi Beit-Arié, "Ms Oxford, Bodleian Library, Bodl. Or. 135: On the Margins of the Article by E. Yassif [Heb.]," *Tarbiz* 54, no. 4 (July 1, 1985): 631–34.

24. Kushelevsky, *Tales in Context*.

Italy with French source material. Although the existing manuscript survives in only a few folios, this fragment shows that northern Italian Jews, undoubtedly of Ashkenazi origin, translated from contemporaneous French Arthurian stories, including the *Merlin* and the *Mort Artu* (Death of Arthur) from the *Lancelot-Grail Cycle*.[25] During the periodic expulsions of Jews from France in the thirteenth century (and in a great wave after the expulsion of 1306), French-speaking Jews migrated to northern Italy, bringing their literary traditions and memories of France with them.[26] Therefore, *Melekh Artus* is a product of Ashkenazi culture that moved to northern Italy by the late thirteenth century. Little reception history of this story can be traced, but several Yiddish Arthurian stories attest to the awareness and interest in this genre among medieval Jews.

A fourth source, briefly discussed throughout the book, is the Jewish romance *Dukus Horant* (Duke Horant), written in Middle High German in Hebrew characters (some argue, an early form of Yiddish) in 1382.[27] The text was discovered in the Cairo Geniza, the documentary treasure trove from Mediterranean Jews, but in very fragmentary form and missing its end. In verse, *Dukus Horant* tells a story of a bridal quest in keeping with the Germanic tradition of romance and based directly or indirectly on figures that also appear in the medieval German epic *Kudrun*. Although not a translation into Hebrew, *Dukus Horant*, like *Sefer ha-Ma'asim*, borrows its narrative from vernacular culture and "translates" it into a Jewish script intended for a Jewish audience.

In addition, I will discuss other relevant texts, including a thirteenth-century Hebraico-French wedding song, and other texts that do not fit neatly into categories, such as a thirteenth-century tale from the same manuscript as *Sefer ha-Ma'asim*.

---

25. Caroline Gruenbaum, "The Quest for the 'Charity Dish': Interpretation in the Hebrew Arthurian Translation Melekh Artus (1279, Northern Italy)," *Medieval Encounters* 26, no. 6 (February 2021): 517–42.

26. Susan L. Einbinder, *No Place of Rest: Jewish Literature, Expulsion, and the Memory of Medieval France* (Philadelphia: University of Pennsylvania Press, 2008), 1–14.

27. The text appears on folios 41–84 of Cambridge University Library "Codex C-Y," T-S 10 K. 22, along with several other early Yiddish texts. The entire codex was first edited by Layb Fuks. See Lajb Fuks, *The Oldest Known Literary Documents of Yiddish Literature (c. 1382)* (Leiden: Brill, 1957), http://archive.org/details/oldestknownliter0002fuks. A more recent edition and analysis appears in Jerold C. Frakes, ed., "Dukus Horant," in *Early Yiddish Texts 1100–1750: With Introduction and Commentary* (Oxford: Oxford University Press, 2004), 33–43. It was translated by Frakes as well: Jerold C. Frakes, trans., "Dukus Horant," in *Early Yiddish Epic* (Syracuse, NY: Syracuse University Press, 2014).

Most of these texts might be described as "secular." However, the term is highly problematic and anachronistic for medieval Jews, for whom religion and daily life could not be separated. When I use the term "secular," I do not mean devoid of Jewishness, as we will see that many nonrabbinic texts nonetheless incorporate aspects of piety. Instead, "secular" simply designates the material generically by exclusion: it describes literature that is not liturgical, exegetical, or halakhic (dealing with rabbinic law).[28]

Although we lack any other information about the anonymous, southern European author of the Alexander romance who spoke about translation, his words apply to many texts produced and circulated in medieval Ashkenaz. I suggest that the Ashkenazi authors also found worth in the texts that they read from non-Jewish sources, translating them for purposes of entertainment or wisdom. The texts explored in this book belong to a complex and multifaceted literary culture in Ashkenaz, a culture that merges vernacular source material with Jewish tradition. Each chapter will prove that nonrabbinic Jewish texts of northern Europe merit special focus for their innovations, distinctive from genres that preceded or paralleled them. By virtue of the communities who wrote and read these texts, however, these texts follow the path of a continuous Jewish literary tradition.

28. The idea of aspects of premodern "secular" Judaism is not entirely revolutionary. Consider the argument made by David Biale that threads of secularism were present in Jewish culture even as early as the biblical period, even if an organized movement of Jewish secularism did not advance until the Enlightenment. David Biale, *Not in the Heavens: The Tradition of Jewish Secular Thought* (Princeton, NJ: Princeton University Press, 2010), https://press.princeton.edu/books/hardcover/9780691147239/not-in-the-heavens.

Chapter 1

Education, Literacy, and Intellectual Culture in Medieval Ashkenaz

In medieval Muslim Spain, a land fantasized in the scholarly and popular imagination as a place of religious freedom between the ruling Muslims and the subordinated Jews and Christians, secular literature burst out from the Jewish community as never before. Hebrew love poetry, inspired by Arabic literary modes, combined traditional biblical language with sensuality and themes of revelry.[1] In the thirteenth century, Jews in Islamic lands produced new rhymed prose narratives built on the foundations of the genres of the Arabic *maqama* and Eastern frametale story collections.[2] This literary output continued as the Jews of Muslim Spain emigrated (willingly and by expulsion) into Christian Spain and farther east to southern France and Italy.

1. For the most salient scholarship, see Jefim Schirmann, "The Function of the Hebrew Poet in Medieval Spain," *Jewish Social Studies* 16, no. 3 (1954): 235–52; Raymond P. Scheindlin, *Wine, Women, and Death: Medieval Hebrew Poems on the Good Life* (Oxford: Oxford University Press, 1986); Joseph Ṭobi, *Between Hebrew and Arabic Poetry: Studies in Spanish Medieval Hebrew Poetry* (Leiden: Brill, 2010).

2. See, for example, Rina Drory, "The Maqama," in *The Literature of Al-Andalus*, ed. Maria Rosa Menocal, Raymond P. Scheindlin, and Michael Sells (Cambridge: Cambridge University Press, 2000), 190–210; David A. Wacks, *Framing Iberia: Maqamat and Frametale Narratives in Medieval Spain* (Leiden: Brill, 2007); Ayelet Oettinger, "Maqama," in *Encyclopedia of Jewish Folklore and Traditions*, ed. Ḥaya Bar-Itzhak and Raphael Patai (London: Routledge, 2013), 352–53.

Raymond Scheindlin, in his compendium of Hebrew secular poetry *Wine, Women, and Death*, categorizes these innovative medieval Hebrew poets as belonging to a rabbinic courtier class. These literate, wealthy Jews knew Arabic literature and language but continued their pious observances and dedication to Jewish life. They held positions of authority within Islamic court systems, and writers relied on patronage from wealthy Jews. However, the Andalusian courter rabbis differed from communities of earlier Jews who similarly navigated secular culture with Judaism:

> What was unique about the Andalusian Jewish courtiers was the self-conscious way in which they synthesized the dominant Arabic-Islamic culture with Jewish religious and literary traditions. These men, who founded a new type of Jewish life, based on a novel educational program and geared to producing a new leadership, sought literary expression in a completely renovated poetry. For these Jews, religious commitment, cultural identification, and national loyalty were strong enough and flexible enough to permit them to enter openly into the life and style of the dominant culture while remaining Jews.[3]

The "novel education program" specifically catches our attention because this may be the most defining factor out of all the factors that distinguished Sephardic culture from Ashkenazi culture in the early Middle Ages.

Ashkenazi men, it is assumed, did not receive an education in French literary culture or Latin scholasticism like their Christian neighbors. They did not hold positions of economic, social, or intellectual authority among the majority culture as in Sepharad, and there was no system of patronage to encourage belletristic endeavors. But the extent to which Ashkenazi authors immersed themselves in French culture while maintaining Scheindlin's Jewish interests nevertheless parallels the situation in Sepharad. If we entertain the idea of an Ashkenazi courtier rabbi or an Ashkenazi intellectual elite, we find more parallels between literary culture in Sepharad and in Ashkenaz than have previously been identified. This chapter will explore the educational and intellectual systems that allowed medieval French and German Jews to acquire the literacy and literary historical knowledge required to produce nonrabbinic

3. Scheindlin, *Wine, Women, and Death*, 4.

literature. The gaps in our knowledge of how education and intellectual culture operated in medieval Ashkenaz are many; however, it is useful to employ a teleological approach using the translated texts from Ashkenaz as an endpoint. Because we know of several translated texts in Ashkenaz that rely on non-Jewish literary culture, it is worthwhile to examine how the Jewish authors had the literary background necessary to write these texts—and how their Jewish audience had the requisite background to understand the texts.

In medieval Ashkenazi literature, the unique combinations of Hebrew and traditional Jewish literary forms with secular themes attest to a highly educated yet innovative authorship. How that innovation might have occurred, from a systemic perspective, and why it was limited to only a few extant examples, is discussed in this chapter. To understand this range of literary expression, we will examine the foundation of intellectual culture in medieval northern European Jewish communities, which revolved around structures of rabbinic education. We will explore the dimensions of intellectual culture, identifying the existing educational systems and curricula in the geographical areas where our authors studied and wrote (mostly twelfth- and thirteenth-century northern France and Germany). From this, we can speculate how these authors ascertained their knowledge of non-Jewish literature.

To begin this chapter, a discussion of terminology is useful. Three terms will appear several times throughout this book: rabbinic culture, intellectual culture, and secular culture. The first, rabbinic culture, refers to the institutionalized program of rabbinic learning followed by several male elites in northern France and Germany. This particular program will be discussed below; it involved early education at home, followed by small learning groups with a tutor, and often ending with the yeshiva, a secondary school for which students often moved to different cities, depending on the rabbi whose yeshiva they wanted to join. The second, intellectual culture, describes a culture that existed both within and without the yeshiva, including poetry, philosophy, prose, and other literary and scholarly topics. This will be explored through the limited evidence we do have for cultural systems in Ashkenaz. Secular culture in this case refers to non-Jewish culture that makes its way into the Jewish milieu. In Ashkenaz, this consists of French, German, Arabic, and Latin literary themes, characters, plot, and genres that appear in Hebrew, Yiddish, and other Jewish languages and scripts.

The texts explored in this book often contain rabbinic motifs and biblical references, and they are usually written in Hebrew. Writing Hebrew, more so than reading, came about through institutionalized study, and rabbinic language from the Talmud and verbatim use of biblical verses were similarly learned in formal study as well (even if most Jews were familiar with the entire biblical corpus, not all would have been able to quote from it from memory). For example, the florid language that Berechiah ha-Nakdan employs in the prologue to his *Mishle Shu'alim*, as well as rabbinic allusions in a handful of his stories, points to a formal education in Hebrew and Judaism. In addition, although he wrote the bulk of *Mishle Shu'alim* in rhymed prose, short sections at the end of each fable are in more formal verse. In colophons and brief mentions, later Jewish authors have referred to Berechiah as a biblical commentator (although only one commentary tentatively attributed to him, on the Book of Job, is extant and is possibly misattributed).[4] He writes in the prologue to his fables, with biblical verse in italics: "But *he who walks in righteousness and speaks uprightly* [Isaiah 33:15] is *in the shadow of death, without order* [Job 10:22]. From the *noise* of the scornful *archers* [Judges 5:11] my twigs have burgeoned and I make bold to direct my pen to a parable against falsehood."[5]

The three biblical quotations in these several lines attest to the embeddedness of canon in medieval Jewish writing in a process called *shibbutz*. Shibbutz is a process of combining new Hebrew text with interspersed biblical verses and can be compared to *florilegia*.[6] The biblical references

4. Norman Golb, *The Jews in Medieval Normandy: A Social and Intellectual History* (Cambridge: Cambridge University Press, 1998), 333–38; Menachem Banitt, ed., *Le Glossaire de Leipzig* (Jerusalem: Académie nationale des sciences et des lettres d'Israël, 1995), 3:416–17; Jordan S. Penkower, "The End of Rashi's Commentary on Job: The Manuscripts and the Printed Editions," *Jewish Studies Quarterly* 10, no. 1 (2003): 40–46; Tamás Visi, "Introduction," in *Berechiah Ben Natronai Ha-Naqdan's Works and Their Reception*, ed. Tamás Visi, Tovi Bibring, and Daniel Soukup (Turnhout: Brepols, 2019), 14.

5. הלך צדק ודבר מישרים, צלמות ולא סדרים ומקול מחצצים חמתלוצצים, סעפי בי נצים ואצים, לנטות עטי למשל על השקר אשר משל לשבת על מרומי קרת, ותהי האמת נעדרת וסר מרע משתולל ורשע על תאותו הלל ומלאו פני תבל ריקים אושי תבל.

Berechiah ben Natronai Ha-Nakdan, *Fables of a Jewish Aesop: Translated from the Fox Fables of Berechiah Ha-Nakdan*, trans. Moses Hadas (New York: Columbia University Press, 1967), 3; Berechiah ben Natronai Ha-Nakdan, *Mishlei Shualim*, ed. A. M. Habermann (Tel Aviv: Schocken, 1946), 4. I have made silent emendations to Hadas's translations when necessary.

6. In medieval Hebrew poetry, *shibbutz* "consisted of an adroit and fluent weaving together of biblical quotations from a short phrase to an entire verse. The quotation could be verbatim, slightly altered or elliptical; it could create a broad spectrum of effects by assuming an altogether different and even contradictory meaning in its new setting. At times an entire poem is chequered with quotations from a specific and relevant biblical passage. In such cases, the strands of quotations and allusions cease to be an ornamental device and become the very fabric of the poem, a sustained metaphorical texture." T. Carmi, *The Penguin Book of Hebrew Verse* (London: Penguin, 1981), 27.

sometimes reinforce the meaning of the Hebrew text it complements, but elsewhere, the biblical references are neutral, with no discernible relationship to its context besides the use of similar words.[7] Words and phrases from the Hebrew Bible would be easier for the average Jew to recognize because portions from it were recited in the synagogue several times per week.

The Talmud and rabbinic legal manuals would have been inaccessible, however, for most. Despite using only one fable culled from the Talmud, Berechiah shows his knowledge of the rabbinic context of the fable through his conscious dismantling of its original content.[8] *Melekh Artus* (King Arthur) displays a similar familiarity with rabbinic material and plays with this source material through innuendo and puns.[9] *Sefer ha-Ma'asim* (Book of Tales) generally contains more rabbinic and biblical material because of its more pious tone than many of the other texts explored here. Much of its content—especially the stories that do not have a secular origin—were inspired by rabbinic stories.[10]

These and other references to rabbinic law and language suggest that the authors of medieval nonrabbinic literature in Ashkenaz had a thorough command of the intricacies of rabbinic and biblical Jewish tradition. The intellectual foundation for the authors explored here was Talmud and Torah study, including reading ability in Hebrew (and rabbinic Hebrew and Aramaic) as well as writing proficiency. We find in medieval Ashkenaz that rabbinic and intellectual culture were closely linked, largely because of the close relationship between literacy and formal education. Education, including literacy and the ability to write, and rabbinic scholarship existed hand in hand. A Jewish building in medieval Rouen, for example, may have existed as both a synagogue and a yeshiva.[11] The very idea that a debate exists over the use of the building

7. See the translator's introduction to Solomon Ibn Saqbel, "Asher in the Harem," in *Rabbinic Fantasies: Imaginative Narratives from Classical Hebrew Literature*, ed. Mark Jay Mirsky and David Stern, trans. Raymond P. Scheindlin (New Haven, CT: Yale University Press, 1990), 255. Also note the process of *shibbutz* to establish a courtly tone in the early modern Hebrew translation *Amadís de Gaula*. See David A. Wacks, *Double Diaspora in Sephardic Literature: Jewish Cultural Production before and after 1492* (Bloomington: Indiana University Press, 2015), 203–4.

8. Eli Yassif, "Storytelling and Meaning: Theory and Practice of Narrative Variants in Religious Texts," in *Religious Stories in Transformation: Conflict, Revision and Reception*, ed. Alberdina Houtman, Tamar Kadari, Marcel Poorthuis, and Vered Tohar (Leiden: Brill, 2016), 6–20.

9. See chapter 4.

10. Eli Yassif, "Sepher Ha-Ma'asim: The Character, Origins and Impact of the Collection of Stories at the Time of the Tosafists [Heb.]," *Tarbiz* 53, no. 3 (April 1, 1984): 409–29.

11. Susan L. Ward, "Visual Environment of Jewish Learning in Twelfth-Century Rouen," *IMAGES: A Journal of Jewish Art and Visual Culture* 11, no. 1 (December 5, 2018): 43–56.

also attests to the inseparability between the two institutions—it is not easy to determine which was its use.

Girls had no recourse for formal education but nonetheless found ways to attain a level of Hebrew ability. The only educational venues for Jewish girls were in the home, although Jewish women did know enough Hebrew to recite the prayers and teach them to one another in informal learning settings. They also had economic acumen, often running the household's business while their husbands were away for business or religious study.[12]

Jewish men, meanwhile, had opportunities for education both within the house in their youth and outside the home in formal educational systems as young men. A specialized ritual in medieval France and Germany marked a young boy's first foray into Jewish education, which involved a teacher reciting Hebrew phrases with the young boy and ingesting of food with biblical verses written on it.[13] In the rabbinic French sources, the time to begin schooling depended on the individual child's maturity; the German sources, however, state that during the holiday of Shavuot is when the rite should occur.[14] Although it is not clear what sort of education happened throughout the child's youth, the Tosafists (northern French commentators) note that schooling at home with a boy's father should begin at age five and more formal schooling with a teacher, who was a surrogate for the father, at age six.[15]

Documents from the Jewish communities under Islam found in the Cairo Geniza suggest that schoolchildren attended formal elementary school where they learned writing and reading, often using individual wooden boards and exercise books to practice.[16] Although scant records detailing Jewish youth education exist from Ashkenaz, one page from the early thirteenth-century French rabbinic legal compendium *Maḥzor Vitry* resembles an elementary primer. It contains the first verses of Leviticus, the Hebrew alphabet written forward and backward and in

12. Judith R. Baskin, "Some Parallels in the Education of Medieval Jewish and Christian Women," *Jewish History* 5, no. 1 (1991): 41–51; Judith R. Baskin, "Dolce of Worms: The Lives and Deaths of an Exemplary Medieval Jewish Woman and Her Daughters," in *Judaism in Practice: From the Middle Ages through the Early Modern Period*, ed. Lawrence Fine (Princeton, NJ: Princeton University Press, 2001), 429–37.

13. Ivan G. Marcus, *Rituals of Childhood: Jewish Acculturation in Medieval Europe* (New Haven, CT: Yale University Press, 1996).

14. Marcus, *Rituals of Childhood*, 25–33.

15. Marcus, *Rituals of Childhood*, 44.

16. S. D. Goitein, *A Mediterranean Society: The Jewish Communities of the Arab World as Portrayed in the Documents of the Cairo Geniza* (Berkeley: University of California Press, 1967), 2:171–210.

other patterns, and numerological sequences.[17] Ephraim Kanarfogel has argued against the theory that northern French Jews had institutionalized forms of elementary education, suggesting instead that young male children learned from their fathers or in a small group with a paid tutor.[18] After this early education, students attended group lectures delivered by a local teacher or traveled to an academy (yeshiva) in another city. They chose academies based on the reputation of the rabbi who headed the school and occasionally would move to a new town for the academy, living with the rabbi or with family members nearby.[19] The Tosafist academies hosted only about a dozen students each, and these students may have belonged to the same few families.[20] The institution of formal education represented elite intellectual society.

At the academies of northern France and Germany, these older students would primarily learn Talmud (including dialectic, at least for the scholars of northern France), and occasionally they studied the biblical books themselves.[21] Knowledge of biblical verse is evident through the production of liturgical poetry (*piyyut*) that involved interspersing biblical verses and original Hebrew lines to produce poetic stanzas. Students learned to read Hebrew at a young age, but there is no evidence of grammatical study of the language or of poetics or literary study.[22]

The engagement with philosophy among some twelfth- and thirteenth-century European Jewish rabbinic circles suggests, however, that there were opportunities for in-depth and well-rounded scholarship. Scholars have begun to investigate the many layers of intellectual engagement of German and French medieval rabbis in the realms of philosophy, medicine, and literary creativity, in contrast with previous views of Ashkenazi rabbinic culture as rejecting those forms of scholasticism.[23] The scholarly pursuits of twelfth- and thirteenth-century northern European

17. *Mahzor Vitry*, France, 1204. Jewish Theological Seminary, MS 8092, fol. 165a; Marcus, *Rituals of Childhood*, 39.

18. Ephraim Kanarfogel, *Jewish Education and Society in the High Middle Ages* (Detroit, MI: Wayne State University Press, 2007), 15–32.

19. Kanarfogel, *Jewish Education and Society*, 65–67.

20. Kanarfogel, *Jewish Education and Society*, 66–70.

21. Irving A. Agus, *Urban Civilization in Pre-Crusade Europe: A Study of Organized Town-Life in Northwestern Europe during the Tenth and Eleventh Centuries Based on the Responsa Literature* (Brill: New York, 1965), 730–49.

22. Kanarfogel, *Jewish Education and Society*, 79–83.

23. Ephraim Kanarfogel, *The Intellectual History and Rabbinic Culture of Medieval Ashkenaz* (Detroit, MI: Wayne State University Press, 2013); Ephraim E. Urbach, *Baʿale ha-tosafot: toldotehem, ḥiburehem, shṭṭatam* (Jerusalem: Mosad Bi'aliḳ, 1968); Avraham Grossman, *The Early Sages of Ashkenaz* (Jerusalem: Magnes, 2001); Israel Ta-Shma, *Creativity and Tradition: Studies*

rabbis including R. Jacob ben Meir Tam (Rabbenu Tam), R. Samuel ben Meir (Rashbam), R. Moses of Coucy, and R. Meir of Rothenburg show a surprising amount of engagement with nonexegetical writings, including liturgical poetic compositions, and mystical-philosophical dimensions that underlie their writings.[24] These elements of literature that appear in medieval northern European rabbinic exegesis suggest that rabbis and their students appreciated and learned from a variety of literary art forms.

In addition to the exegetical texts penned by prolific northern French rabbis, especially in the Tosafist school of biblical interpretation, Ashkenazi authors also produced works inspired by the late antique rabbinic tradition of midrash that proliferated throughout the Middle Eastern Jewish communities in Babylonia and Persia and into North Africa. Midrash usually refers to narrative material that acts as exegesis for biblical or rabbinic verses, often incorporating a variety of exegetical models from different sources or relying on intertextuality, the use of "prooftexts" that contain parallel words or phrases to explicate the original material.[25] The classical and late midrashic collections followed a similar model: a biblical citation followed by its explication in narrative form for each of its stories. By the medieval period, midrashic anthologies or compilations appeared in northern Europe as well, featuring retellings of classic midrash and often organized by a new type of chronological framework.[26] Medieval anthologies, in comparison with earlier models, incorporated more narrativity and literary creativity.[27]

---

in Medieval Rabbinic Scholarship, Literature and Thought (Cambridge, MA: Harvard University Press, 2007).

24. Kanarfogel, *Intellectual History and Rabbinic Culture*, esp. chapters 5 and 6. Kanarfogel devotes more time to the question of magic and mysticism in the northern European rabbinic writings in Ephraim Kanarfogel, *Peering through the Lattices: Mystical, Magical, and Pietistic Dimensions in the Tosafist Period* (Detroit, MI: Wayne State University Press, 2000).

25. James L. Kugel, *In Potiphar's House* (San Francisco: Harper, 1990); Daniel Boyarin, *Intertextuality and the Reading of Midrash* (Bloomington: Indiana University Press, 1990).

26. Jacob Elbaum, "Yalqut Shim'oni and the Medieval Midrashic Anthology," in *The Anthology in Jewish Literature*, ed. David Stern (Oxford: Oxford University Press, 2004), 159–75; Eli Yassif, "The Hebrew Narrative Anthology in the Middle Ages," *Prooftexts* 17, no. 2 (May 1997): 153–75.

27. Itamar Drori, "The Power of the Tongue: A Medieval Hebrew Story from Midrashic Literature," *Fabula* 58, no. 3–4 (January 10, 2017): 319–34; Rachel S. Mikva, "'Midrash vaYosha' and the Development of Narrative in Medieval Jewish Exegesis" (PhD diss., Jewish Theological Seminary of America, 2008); Jeffrey L. Rubenstein, "From Mythic Motifs to Sustained Myth: The Revision of Rabbinic Traditions in Medieval Midrashim," *Harvard Theological Review* 89, no. 2 (April 1996): 131–59.

The educational study of the Bible, the Talmud, and midrash could have been learned orally without the need to rely on physical texts. This would support a theory that any knowledge of nonrabbinic writing also happened orally. There is much evidence to suggest, however, that a Jewish reliance on literacy and on material textual culture allowed for Jewish engagement with literary materials that included writing in non-Jewish languages such as French, German, and Latin. Many aspects of Jewish religious education became textualized in the early medieval period, both in Sepharad and in Ashkenaz.[28]

The case for Jewish literacy in medieval northern Europe in general is well established. In twelfth-century France, a student of the famed Christian theologian Peter Abelard praises Jewish literacy: "A Jew, however poor, even if he had ten sons would put them all to letters, not for gain as Christians do, but for the understanding of God's law, and not only his sons but his daughters."[29] The student here implies widespread literacy among Jewish men—not only for pragmatic, business purposes but out of religious devotion. He even notes that literacy need not apply to just the wealthy because even poor Jews teach their sons and daughters.

The rise in academic centers in medieval Ashkenaz in the twelfth century brought with it a need for more Hebrew manuscripts, leading to a "cultural revolution."[30] From 1251 to 1300, the number of dated Italian and Sicilian Hebrew manuscripts rose fiftyfold, from one produced between 1200 and 1250, to forty-nine in the second half of the century. Ashkenazi dated manuscripts in the same period climbed from fifteen to fifty-four.[31] Although these statistics reflect only dated manuscripts,

28. Stefan C. Reif, "Aspects of Mediaeval Jewish Literacy," in *The Uses of Literacy in Early Medieval Europe*, ed. Rosamond McKitterick (Cambridge: Cambridge University Press, 1990), 134–55; Malachi Beit-Arié, "Publication and Reproduction of Literary Texts in Medieval Jewish Civilization: Jewish Scribality and Its Impact on the Texts Transmitted," in *Transmitting Jewish Traditions: Orality, Textuality, and Cultural Diffusion*, ed. Yaakov Elman and Israel Gershoni (New Haven, CT: Yale University Press, 2000), 225–47; Geoffrey Khan, "Learning to Read Biblical Hebrew in the Middle Ages: The Transition from Oral Standard to Written Standard," in *Jewish Education from Antiquity to the Middle Ages: Studies in Honour of Philip S. Alexander*, ed. George J. Brooke and Renate Smithuis (Boston: Brill, 2017), 269–95; Talya Fishman, *Becoming the People of the Talmud: Oral Torah as Written Tradition in Medieval Jewish Cultures* (Philadelphia: University of Pennsylvania Press, 2011), esp. chapter 5.

29. Kanarfogel, *Jewish Education and Society*, 16.

30. Denis Levy Willard, *Le Livre Dans la Société Juive Medievale de la France du Nord* (Paris: Editions du Cerf, 2008), 43.

31. Colette Sirat, *Hebrew Manuscripts of the Middle Ages*, ed. and trans. Nicholas de Lange (Cambridge: Cambridge University Press, 2002), 11.

the increase in manuscript production likely remains the same if we factor in undated manuscripts and ones that did not survive.[32]

We have little information about the scribes who produced such books, other than the information that colophons reveal about commissions and patrons.[33] Nearly one-third of all dated thirteenth-century manuscripts lack this information, which leaves us with unsubstantiated theories about the remainder. Some scribes, like Berechiah ha-Nakdan, also engaged in punctuating books; his nickname "ha-Nakdan" means "the Punctuator."[34] Nearly all medieval Hebrew books were commissioned privately, either written by a scholar himself or, less often, by a trained scribe, and if synagogues owned books or Torah scrolls, they were donated by a private individual.[35]

In response to the rise of manuscript production and scribal culture, questions on the sanctity of the book, scribal activities, and reading methods proliferate in late medieval rabbinic discussions.[36] *Sefer Ḥasidim* (Book of the Pious), a pietistic manual from the twelfth and thirteenth centuries, particularly emphasizes the book as a material object.[37] In one instance, the text advises, "He who has a book in his hand should not show his anger by pounding his hand against it or hitting another with the book. A teacher who is angry with his student should not hit him with a book, nor should his student shield himself with the book

---

32. The number of extant, dated manuscripts is only a portion of the manuscripts that likely circulated in these circles. It is not in itself entirely indicative of the entire manuscript culture, but it gives us a relative population size that we can then use for extrapolation. It should not be used as the final determinant for production of manuscripts, let alone popularity and transmission.

33. Malachi Beit-Arié, *Hebrew Codicology: Historical and Comparative Typology of Hebrew Medieval Codices Based on the Documentation of the Extant Dated Manuscripts in Quantitative Approach* (Jerusalem: National Library of Israel, 2017), http://web.nli.org.il/sites/NLI/English/collections/manuscripts/hebrewcodicology/Pages/default.aspx.

34. The association of Berechiah with punctuating appears in a colophon written by his son in 1223, in which his son writes, "I am the scribe and punctator Elijah, son of the Master . . . Berechiah the punctator, the scholar of holy writ and rabbinic lore, expert grammarian, most wise man, the counsellor." References to Berechiah as a punctuator also appear in other contemporaneous writings. Golb, *The Jews in Medieval Normandy*, 329, 334–36. See also the references to punctuation that appear frequently in Elijah's annotations. Elodie Attia, *The Masorah of Elijah Ha-Naqdan. An Edition of Ashkenazic Micrographical Notes*, Open Access, Materiale Textkulturen 11 (Berlin: De Gruyter, 2015).

35. Malachi Beit-Arié, "Book Production," in *The Cambridge History of Judaism*, ed. Robert Chazan (Cambridge: Cambridge University Press, 2018), 535–54, https://doi.org/10.1017/9781139048880.021.

36. Fishman, *Becoming the People of the Talmud*, chapters 5 and 6.

37. Talya Fishman, "The Rhineland Pietists' Sacralization of Oral Torah," *Jewish Quarterly Review*, no. 1 (2006): 9.

unless the blows are very dangerous."[38] This reverence may have financial implications in addition to sentimental ones because books were expensive. R. Asher b. Yeḥiel (the "Rosh," 1250–ca. 1327), who was active in both northern Europe and Spain, admonished sharply against a student who refused to lend his books, writing that he "is ordered to pay a fine of 10 *zehuv* each day for not wanting to lend his books. Because, given the lack of books in his town, he is impeded from studying."[39] While this example appears to highlight the lack of books, the existence of at least some private collections in each town implies accessibility of textual traditions. Extant book lists from the fifteenth century and beyond reveal that some Jews, including the Finzi family of Mantua and the physician Judah Leon Mosconi in Majorca, had libraries with hundreds of books in Hebrew and Arabic. Unfortunately, book lists from medieval Ashkenaz have not survived.

Elsewhere in *Sefer Ḥasidim,* the pietistic leader Judah he-Ḥasid emphasizes the importance of the scribe and writing process by giving instructions to scribes. He also opposes manuscript illumination in the twenty-four books of the Bible, writing, "If one were to make illustrations, how would it seem?"[40] In his view, illustrations detract from the sanctity of the text. Meir ben Barukh of Rothenberg (the Maharam, active in France and Germany in the late thirteenth century) also discourages the use of decorations in prayer books. In a response to a query about

---

38. Parma 3280 H, paragraph 662:

מי שיש ספר בידו לא יראה כעסו בידו
להכות על הספר או להכות אחד מן
הספר הרב שכועס על תלמידו לא יכנו
בספר והתלמיד לא יגן בספר לקבל הכאות
אלא אם כן יש בהכאות סכנת נפשות

39. Rosh, no. 663, chapter 93. Quoted in Willard, *Le Livre Dans la Société Juive Medievale de la France du Nord*, 43.

40. Parma 3280 H, paragraph 709:

מי שמשכיר סופר לכתוב מסורת
לעשרים וארבע ספרים יעשה תנאי
עם הסופר שלא יעשה המסורת ציורים עופות
וחיות או כאילו ולא שום צייורין מה שהתחילו
המסורת לכתוב בספר עשרים וארבעה ספרים
כי הראשונים היו בקיאין במסורת לכך כתבו
בספרים ואם יעשה צייורים איך יראה ועוד
לא יכתוב בצידי הדף כי כשיראה בדף לא יראה
מה שבצידי הדף פונה לעומת פניו אלא צריך
להפנות הצד אליו ומה שבדף לא יהא מול
פניו

illuminating *maḥzorim* (prayer books), he notes that the viewer would become engrossed in the pictures of animals, diverting his attention from God.[41]

But who read these books the rabbis mention? We have several clues about the literate Jewish populations. Bigger sacred books, like Torah scrolls, had a liturgical function because they were large enough to be seen throughout a synagogue audience. Individual readers used smaller books for personal use, implying a private readership population.[42] A rabbinic story included in *Sefer ha-Maʿasim* tells of a learned Jewish boy who must read the book of Genesis out loud in Hebrew for a non-Jewish king who cannot learn the language. The story moralizes the boy's literacy and subsequent reward as a positive reflection of his parents.[43] This literate body may have included women.[44] Book production, and specifically manuscript illumination, often involved collaboration between Jews and Christians—scribes and illuminators incorporated motifs present in Christian manuscripts, and members of both faiths produced illuminated manuscripts together.[45]

We still know very little, however, about which books existed because of a lack of extant manuscripts (from loss over time, and from mass burnings, confiscations, and censorship of Jewish books in the late medieval period) and from a lack of book lists.[46] While we can be sure that scholars learned the Talmud, especially in northern French academies, and knew the biblical texts by heart once they reached adulthood, we have no sense of which, if any, nonrabbinic texts they studied. Unlike

41. Meir ben Barukh of Rothenberg, *Shaarei Teshuvot*, ed. Moses Bloch (Berlin: Itskovski, 1891), 134.

42. Sirat, *Hebrew Manuscripts of the Middle Ages.*

43. Rella Kushelevsky, *Tales in Context: Sefer Ha-Ma'asim in Medieval Northern France* (Detroit, MI: Wayne State University Press, 2017), 300, Hebrew 302.

44. Beit-Arié, *Hebrew Codicology*, 89.

45. Bezalel Narkiss, *Hebrew Illuminated Manuscripts* (New York: Encyclopedia Judaica, 1969); Eva Frojmovic, "Jewish Scribes and Christian Illuminators: Interstitial Encounters and Cultural Negotiation," in *Between Judaism and Christianity: Art Historical Essays in Honor of Elisheva (Elisabeth) Revel-Neher*, ed. Elisabeth Revel-Neher, Katrin Kogman-Appel, and Mati Meyer (Leiden: Brill, 2009), 281–306.

46. Simcha Emanuel, "The Lost Halakhic Books of the Tosaphists [Heb.]" (PhD diss., Hebrew University of Jerusalem, 1993); Beit-Arié, "Publication and Reproduction of Literary Texts in Medieval Jewish Civilization"; Andreas Lehnardt, "'I Saw in a Town Violence and Strife': An Unknown Ashkenazic *Maqama* Found in a Binding Fragment," in *Berechiah Ben Natronai Ha-Naqdan's Works and Their Reception*, ed. Tamás Visi, Tovi Bibring, and Daniel Soukup, vol. 182 (Turnhout: Brepols, 2019), 163–85, https://doi.org/10.1484/M.BEHE-EB.5.117468; Andreas Lehnardt, ed., *"Genizat Germania": Hebrew and Aramaic Binding Fragments from Germany in Context* (Leiden: Brill, 2010); Andreas Lehnardt, ed., *European Genizah: Newly Discovered Hebrew Binding Fragments in Context* (Leiden: Brill, 2020).

in Sepharad, there is no evidence that Ashkenazi men learned poetics in a formal educational setting. Some grammar books and dictionaries in Ashkenazi manuscripts suggest some interest in the topic, however, which may have aided in development of an intellectual culture in the region. *Sefer ha-Ma'asim* is bound in the same manuscript, Bodl. Or. 135, as other folktale collections, as well as with a copy of *Mishle Shu'alim* (Fox Fables), but also with grammatical texts originating in southern French communities, including David Kimḥi (Radak)'s early thirteenth-century Provençal text *Sefer ha-Shorashim* (Book of [Hebrew] Roots) and Shlomo ibn Parḥon's late twelfth-century grammatical and biblical lexicon *Maḥberet he-Arukh* (Notebook of Comprehension) (a summary of earlier Hebrew grammars).[47] It also contains Moses ibn Ezra's *Sefer ha-'Anaq* (The Book of the Necklace), a Spanish Hebrew didactic poem on grammar. In addition, there are four extant Hebrew translations of French lapidaries, some of which may have originated in Ashkenaz and relied on Old French texts as a foundation for their Hebrew versions, in lieu of or in conjunction with Latin texts.[48] Some evidence suggests that a handful of Ashkenazi authors had access to Arabic, but most references to Arabic by Ashkenazi authors stem directly from Hebrew sources.[49]

The rise of Christian Hebraism also influenced Jewish engagement with Christian literatures and languages. In the twelfth and thirteenth centuries, certain learned Christians like Herbert of Bosham, Robert Grosseteste, and Roger Bacon embarked on explorations of biblical Hebrew and rabbinic texts.[50] Superscript Latin glosses appeared over

47. Ibn Parḥon was the first to edit and translate the linguistic texts of Ibn Hayyūj and Ibn Janāḥ from Arabic to Hebrew, bringing them from Spain to the European Jewish world. See Shimeon Brisman, *A History and Guide to Judaic Dictionaries and Concordances* (New York: KTAV, 2000), 25–27.

48. Judith Olszowy-Schlanger, "The Science of Language among Medieval Jews," in *Science in Medieval Jewish Cultures*, ed. Gad Freudenthal (Cambridge: Cambridge University Press, 2012), 359–424; Gad Freudenthal and Jean-Marc Mandosio, "Old French into Hebrew in Twelfth-Century Tsarfat: Medieval Hebrew Versions of Marbode's Lapidary," *Aleph* 14, no. 1 (January 2014): 11–187.

49. Visi, "Introduction," 8; Tamás Visi, "Berechiah Ben Naṭronai Ha-Naqdan's *Dodi ve-Nekdi* and the Transfer of Scientific Knowledge from Latin to Hebrew in the Twelfth Century," *Aleph* 14, no. 2 (July 2014): 58–63. The little-known author Solomon ibn Abun may be an exception because he was apparently of Ashkenazi origin but lived in Spain and engaged with Arabic culture.

50. For more on the Christian Hebraists of the twelfth century and their legacy, see Beryl Smalley, *The Study of the Bible in the Middle Ages* (Notre Dame, IN: University of Notre Dame Press, 1964); Deborah L. Goodwin, *Take Hold of the Robe of a Jew: Herbert of Bosham's Christian Hebraism* (Leiden: Brill, 2006); Deeana Copeland Klepper, *The Insight of Unbelievers: Nicholas of Lyra and Christian Reading of Jewish Text in the Later Middle Ages* (Philadelphia: University of

Hebrew Bibles, and Hebrew-Latin dictionaries emerged especially out of Oxford and Cambridge. To acquire this knowledge, Christian Hebraists worked directly with texts, shifting away from previous models of oral learning from rabbis and Jewish intellectuals (and, as will be seen in chapter 5, Jewish converts to Christianity). Through their newfound Hebrew knowledge, these Christian writers embarked on literary analyses of the Bible, offering new translations and insight based on the original Hebrew text. At the same time, Jews who interacted with Christian Hebraists and earlier Hebraic scholars presumably learned something about Latin and Christianity from the Christian perspective during those conversations.

In southern Europe, a rise in intellectual Jewish culture appeared in the middle of the twelfth century in Provence, prompted largely by emigration of Jews who brought Arabic learning with them from Muslim lands. These new forms of learning found a willing audience among Provençal Jews, who traditionally had been engrossed in Talmudic study like their neighbors to the north and the east.[51] The introduction of Arabic philosophy and poetics changed the face of southern Jewish culture.

Despite a lack of widescale immigration to northern France and Germany in the twelfth and thirteenth centuries, and limited access to Arabic, some nonrabbinic learning also reached those areas, as we will see in the literary evidence explored in this book. There is enough evidence to suggest an interest in secular learning, even without evidence of formal study. It is not unreasonable to propose that some literature, such as the texts from Bodl. Or. 135, appeared in Ashkenaz through the intermediary of itinerant individuals from Sepharad. Abraham Ibn Ezra, for example, is credited with bringing a culture of translation, especially of philosophy and medical texts, to Ashkenaz, where he completed some of his translations.[52] Although not operating in Ashkenaz, Doeg the Edomite,

---

Pennsylvania Press, 2010); Raphael Loewe, "The Mediaeval Christian Hebraists of England: Herbert of Bosham and Earlier Scholars," *Transactions* 17 (1951): 225–49; Raphael Loewe, "The Mediaeval Christian Hebraists of England: The Superscriptio Lincolniensis," *Hebrew Union College Annual* 28 (1957): 205–52.

51. Gad Freudenthal, "'Arav and Edom as Cultural Resources for Medieval Judaism: Contrasting Attitudes towards Arabic and Latin Learning in the Midi and in Italy," in *Late Medieval Jewish Identities: Iberia and Beyond*, ed. Carmen Caballero-Navas and Esperanza Alfonso (New York: Palgrave Macmillan, 2010), 52–53.

52. Gad Freudenthal, "Abraham Ibn Ezra and Judah Ibn Tibbon as Cultural Intermediaries: Early Stages in the Introduction of Non-Rabbinic Learning into Provence in the Mid-Twelfth Century," in *Exchange and Transmission across Cultural Boundaries: Philosophy, Mysticism and Science in the Mediterranean World = Yeda' Ḥotseh Gevulot Tarbut: Filosofyah, Misṭikah u-Mada' Be-Agan Ha-Yam Ha-Tikhon*, ed. Haggai Ben-Shammai, Shaul Shaked, Sarah Stroumsa, and Shlomo Pines

a convert who lived in southern France, is responsible for the vast majority of Latin to Hebrew translations in the medieval period.[53] Similarly, Berechiah ha-Nakdan received an education in philosophy during his travels through southern France.[54]

It is not possible to answer definitively how intellectual culture in Ashkenaz traveled in new directions, with its foundation of rabbinic learning and Hebrew literacy. We have no indication of a cultural system, like in Sepharad, that encouraged gatherings that focused on recitation of poetry and prose. Maimonides notes that even Jewish elders and pious men attended wine parties that featured recitations of secular poetic songs in Arabic and Hebrew.[55] We have no evidence of practices like this, however, or of any public performance at all outside life-cycle events like weddings from Ashkenaz. While they did not host wine and poetry parties like in the Sephardic communities, they could have emulated their Christian neighbors instead. By the fourteenth century, the literate read books, from the devotional to the secular, both out loud for entertainment and privately.[56] It is not unreasonable to assume that Jews also had similar reading practices, with private devotion in the form of small copies of the Book of Psalms (akin to the widespread Christian psalter) and prayer books for the holiday of Passover, as well as public recitation of secular books, although for this aspect of reading we lack sufficient manuscript evidence.[57] As will be obvious in chapter 2, written transmission is a highly possible source of information for our authors about literary motifs in French and German, in addition to any possible oral channels.

(Jerusalem: Israel Academy of Sciences and Humanities, 2013), 52–81; Mauro Zonta, "Medieval Hebrew Translations of Philosophical and Scientific Texts: A Chronological Table," in *Science in Medieval Jewish Cultures*, ed. Gad Freudenthal (Cambridge: Cambridge University Press, 2012), 17–73.

53. Gad Freudenthal, Michael McVaugh, and Katelyn Mesler, "Twelfth-Century Latin Medicine in Hebrew Garb: Doeg the Edomite as a Cultural Intermediary," *Medieval Encounters* 26, no. 3 (September 24, 2020): 226–84, https://doi.org/10.1163/15700674-12340072.

54. Visi, "Berechiah Ben Naṭronai Ha-Naqdan's *Dodi ve-Neḵdi*"; Visi, "Introduction"; Cyril Aslanov, "Can the Language of Mishlei Shu'alim Give Us a Clue about Berechiah Ha-Naqdan's Geographical Origin?," in *Berechiah Ben Natronai Ha-Naqdan's Works and Their Reception*, ed. Tamás Visi, Tovi Bibring, and Daniel Soukup (Turnhout: Brepols, 2019), 75–84.

55. Maimonides, *Commentary on the Mishnah*, Avot. 1.16. Quoted in Scheindlin, *Wine, Women, and Death*, 21.

56. For a small sample of works that explore reading practices in Europe, see Joyce Coleman, *Public Reading and the Reading Public in Late Medieval England and France* (Cambridge: Cambridge University Press, 1996); Suzanne Reynolds, *Medieval Reading: Grammar, Rhetoric and the Classical Text* (Cambridge: Cambridge University Press, 1996); Jessica Brantley, *Reading in the Wilderness: Private Devotion and Public Performance in Late Medieval England* (Chicago: University of Chicago Press, 2008).

57. Narkiss, *Hebrew Illuminated Manuscripts*, 29.

Chapter 2

Languages of Translation in a Diglossic Society

In *Dukus Horant* (Duke Horant), the fourteenth-century German-Jewish romance, its eponymous hero Horant sings out loudly from his ship during his journey, "Now, on this day, today, may He Who delivered the Jews on the sea come to comfort us. In God's name do we fare; His mercy do we desire."[1] At first glance, this praise of the God of the Jews is a strange exhortation for Horant, a swashbuckling hero firmly enmeshed in German courtly culture. It would be easy to attribute this line to the wit of the epic's Jewish author; tongue in cheek, he has his German hero wish to have the same amount of protection as God has given the Jews, in language that sounds pseudo-biblical. But these two lines do not come from a biblical prayer. Instead, they have been attributed to a Middle High German crusader song, heightening the author's irony and witticism.[2] *Dukus Horant* here knowingly plays with the concept that it is a Jewish text set, and written, in a German world. Its characters attend church and say their prayers, with

1. Jerold C. Frakes, trans., "Dukus Horant," in *Early Yiddish Epic* (Syracuse, NY: Syracuse University Press, 2014), 168.

2. "These last two clauses are quoted from a famous Middle High German Crusader song, the ironic wit of which usage here would not have been lost on the Jewish audience." Frakes, "Dukus Horant," 443. Unfortunately, I have been unable to identify the source of the "famous" song that Frakes mentions. Some doubts persist about the origin of the two lines.

time marked in relation to the courtly celebration at Pentecost.[3] By Dov Noy's definition of a Jewish folktale, this would certainly not qualify. However, by virtue of its Jewish script, it is intended only for a Jewish audience. The language of a medieval Jewish text has enormous power over its context, its intent, and its reception.

To contextualize the corpus of translation in medieval Ashkenaz, we need to understand the relationship between language and text among the medieval Jewish communities of northern Europe. In this chapter, I propose that these texts can help us understand the relationships forged between text and oral literary culture, made especially complex in a bilingual society. In other words, we can address the pathways through which Jews attained knowledge of vernacular texts and through which they transmitted their knowledge to a Jewish audience. I argue that text-based references to the vernacular demonstrate that Jews engaged in French literary culture not just through oral channels but through direct reading of French manuscripts. These learned Jews could read the Roman alphabet and copied directly from the non-Jewish literary tradition of their surroundings. The linguistic framework of these texts assists in understanding how and why medieval Jews engaged in translations of source texts far removed from a Hebrew literary sphere. However, transmission was not always so linear, and several examples from vernacular languages show the complex ways in which Jews interacted with Hebrew and the other languages around them.

The scholarly instinct has historically privileged oral transmission or dismissed textual connections when no evidence can prove any transmission without some degree of doubt. Jewish studies scholars have not yet embraced the idea that medieval Jews, although they spoke Hebraico-French, could read French. Joseph Dan, one of the earliest scholars to acknowledge the transmission of non-Jewish literary romance into Hebrew, summarizes three relevant texts as the products of external influence: the Hebrew translation of the popular sixteenth-century Spanish romance *Amadís de Gaula* (Amadís of Gaul), the Hebrew translation *Mishle Sendebar* (Tales of Sendebar), and the Hebrew Alexander romances.[4] He does not provide specific examples, however, to suggest

3. Time mediated through Christian construction was a common medieval trope. See Miriamne Ara Krummel, *The Medieval Postcolonial Jew, in and out of Time* (Ann Arbor: University of Michigan Press, 2022).

4. Joseph Dan, "Hebrew Versions of Medieval Prose Romances," *Hebrew University Studies in Literature* 6 (1978): 1–9.

textual transmission as an explanation for how the texts moved into Hebrew—an omission surely forgivable given the scope of his article and his groundbreaking studies of the relationship between Jewish and non-Jewish texts. He also draws a comparison between a story in the pietistic manual *Sefer Ḥasidim* (Book of the Pious) and an earlier version of the same story by the Latin author Caesarius of Heisterbach, but he denies the possibility of a written link. Because the two share only the facts of the legend, "this fact seems absolutely to rule out the possibility that Rabbi Judah and Caesarius shared any written source for such a source would have left a deeper similarity both in the anecdotes they related and the conclusion they derived from it."[5] Here, Dan rejects the possibility of a shared written source. In a similar comparison between a story told by Peter the Chanter in his *Verbum Abbreviatum* (Abridged Word) and a later version by R. Judah the Pious in *Sefer Ḥasidim*, a thoughtful study of the version and its oral characteristics leads the author to assume an oral source for the Jewish version.[6] Although he reaches a logical conclusion after considering the evidence, he does not consider methodically the alternative of a textual source.

Rella Kushelevsky succinctly states, in an article aptly titled "Jews Reading Arthurian Romance from the Middle Ages," that "[the Jews of France] heard these stories told and read them in texts, and then reworked them into stories of their own in Hebrew."[7] The mention of orality first denies that the act of reading is the original source of transmission from the non-Jewish tradition. Also, her mention of reading is halfhearted because she does not explain (because of manuscript length, assuredly) the access of French literature for French Jews. This tendency to see orality as the first step along the transmission path, or understate a possible textual connection, explains why no Jewish literary scholars have traced possible paths of manuscript transmission from non-Jewish to Jewish sources—until now. Rather than assuming an oral tradition, I treat the texts as a literary medium separate from their possible oral origins. In this, I follow the example of Simon Gaunt, who advocates reading Old French texts while cognizant of the

5. Joseph Dan, "Rabbi Judah the Pious and Caesarius of Heisterbach: Common Motifs in Their Stories," *Scripta Hierosolymitana* 22 (1971): 26–27.

6. Elisheva Baumgarten, "Shared Stories and Religious Rhetoric: R. Judah the Pious, Peter the Chanter and a Drought," *Medieval Encounters* 18, no. 1 (January 2012): 40–41.

7. Rella Kushelevsky, "Jews Reading Arthurian Romances from the Middle Ages: On the Reception of Chrétien de Troyes's *Yvain, the Knight of the Lion*, Based on Manuscript JTS Rab. 1164," *AJS Review* 42, no. 2 (November 2018): 381–82.

authorial intent to create a new cultural form distinct from the existing oral tradition.[8] Although we cannot definitively separate the oral channels from the textual channels, this chapter forges a new path by treating the medieval textual sources without privileging the oral tradition.[9]

A broad overview of oral culture appears in Walter Ong's *Orality and Literacy*, in which he establishes certain characteristics of oral literature, that is, literature that emerges from an oral tradition.[10] In an article focusing specifically on the medieval period, Ong presents medieval texts as maintaining features of oral culture, suggesting a linear progression from orality to literacy without ambiguity.[11] In response to some of his theories on divisions between orality and literacy, Ruth Finnegan argues against an analytical categorization of the two terms and for greater contextualization.[12] Consider the genre of slam poetry, a modern example of spoken word poetry that performs written expression, comparable to the paradigmatic example of Homer's *Odyssey* and its own often-changing and performative poetics.[13] Brian Stock writes, "The spoken and the written . . . provide us with insights into a system of mental representations in which 'orality' and 'literacy' play the roles of categories that classify a wide variety of social conventions having little or nothing to do with whether they are spoken or written."[14] For example, the medieval ability to recite texts from memory, a seeming feature of an oral society, stems ultimately from an intimate engagement with text.[15] Evelyn

---

8. Simon Gaunt, *Retelling the Tale: An Introduction to French Medieval Literature* (London: Duckworth, 2001), esp. 40–42.

9. See a similar model offered in Joshua Levinson, *Ha-Sipur She-Lo' Supar: Omanut Ha-Sipur Ha-Mikra'i Hamurhav Be-Midreshe Hazal* [The Twice-Told Tale: A Poetics of the Exegetical Narrative in Rabbinic Midrash] (Jerusalem: Magnes, 2005), esp. chap. 4.

10. Walter J. Ong, *Orality and Literacy: The Technologizing of the Word*, 3rd ed. (London: Routledge, 2012).

11. Walter J. Ong, "Orality, Literacy, and Medieval Textualization," *New Literary History* 16, no. 1 (1984): 1–12.

12. Ruth H. Finnegan, *Literacy and Orality: Studies in the Technology of Communication* (New York: Blackwell, 1988).

13. John Miles Foley, *How to Read an Oral Poem* (Urbana: University of Illinois Press, 2002).

14. Brian Stock, *Listening for the Text: On the Uses of the Past* (Philadelphia: University of Pennsylvania Press, 1990), 7. For an analysis of the problematic dichotomy of orality and literacy, see also Ward Parks, "The Textualization of Orality in Literary Criticism," in *Vox Intexta: Orality and Textuality in the Middle Ages*, ed. A. N. Doane and Carol Braun Pasternak (Madison: University of Wisconsin Press, 1991), 46–61.

15. Mary Carruthers, *The Book of Memory: A Study of Memory in Medieval Culture* (Cambridge: Cambridge University Press, 1992), esp. 9–11, 46–48, 106–12, 122–23, 161–72, 258–59. The interconnectedness between medieval text and performance is discussed in Evelyn Birge Vitz, Nancy Freeman Regalado, and Marilyn Lawrence, eds., *Performing Medieval Narrative* (Cambridge: Boydell and Brewer, 2005).

Birge Vitz's seemingly radical idea that the Old French author and father of medieval romance Chrétien de Troyes was a performative minstrel, not a clerk immersed in text, demonstrates this interconnectedness in a new light.[16] In other words, both oral and textual channels worked to transmit knowledge in the Middle Ages, without a clear scholarly consensus on the relationship between the two.[17]

Hebrew literature has a rich history of orality; to take one relevant example, rabbinic stories (midrash) were formed orally before they were transmitted to text in the late antique period and may have functioned as fodder for sermons.[18] The medieval Hebrew folktales, especially the ones crafted in the East, make use of oral versions, maintaining a linear relationship between orality and literacy.[19] Textuality and literacy were also closely linked among Jews of medieval northern Europe at a time when the medieval Talmudic commentators of France relied on a program of textual transmission combined with oral pedagogy.[20] A thirteenth-century Roman rabbi writes that it is still acceptable to read the Pentateuch in Aramaic if it is recited in Italian.[21] This implies that

16. Evelyn Birge Vitz, *Orality and Performance in Early French Romance* (Woodbridge, UK: D. S. Brewer, 1999), esp. chap. 4.

17. Mark C. Amodio, ed., *New Directions in Oral Theory: Essays on Ancient and Medieval Literatures* (Tempe: Arizona Center for Medieval and Renaissance Studies, 2005); A. N. Doane and Carol Braun Pasternak, eds., *Vox Intexta: Orality and Textuality in the Middle Ages* (Madison: University of Wisconsin Press, 1991).

18. At least the rabbis claim to have their stories handed down from oral authorities. See the discussion in chapter 7 of Alexander Samely, *Forms of Rabbinic Thought and Literature* (Oxford: Oxford University Press, 2007), 116–40; Galit Hasan-Rokem, *Web of Life: Folklore and Midrash in Rabbinic Literature* (Stanford, CA: Stanford University Press, 2000); Jeffrey L. Rubenstein, *Talmudic Stories: Narrative Art, Composition, and Culture* (Baltimore, MD: Johns Hopkins University Press, 1999). The relationship between orality and textuality appears in a range of Jewish literary epochs. Consider the studies in Yaakov Elman and I. Gershoni, eds., *Transmitting Jewish Traditions: Orality, Textuality, and Cultural Diffusion* (New Haven, CT: Yale University Press, 2000).

19. Dan Ben-Amos, "Jewish Folk Literature," *Oral Tradition* 14 (1999): 140–274. His definition of Jewish folk literature appears on page 140. Eli Yassif, "Oral Traditions in a Literate Society: The Hebrew Literature of the Middle Ages," in *Medieval Oral Literature*, ed. Karl Reichl (Berlin: de Gruyter, 2012), 499–519.

20. Gerard Nahon, "Orality and Literacy: The French Tosaphists," in *Studies in Medieval Jewish Intellectual and Social History: Festschrift in Honor of Robert Chazan*, ed. Elliot R. Wolfson, Lawrence H. Schiffman, and David Engel (Leiden: Brill, 2012), 145–68.

21. Judah ben Benjamin Anaw (ca. 1215–1280). See Hermann Vogelstein and Paul Rieger, *Geschichte Der Juden in Rom* (Berlin: Mayer, 1895), vol. 1, 339, 378–80; D. S. Blondheim, *Les Parlers Judéo-Romans et la Vetus Latina: Étude sur les rapports entre les traductions bibliques en langue Romane des Juifs au Moyen Âge et les anciennes versions* (Cambridge: Cambridge University Press, 1925), lxxii–lxxiii; Gad Freudenthal, "Arabic and Latin Cultures as Resources for the Hebrew Translation Movement," in *Science in Medieval Jewish Cultures*, ed. Gad Freudenthal (Cambridge: Cambridge University Press, 2012), 97.

an oral translation of the Bible was circulating, at least in thirteenth-century Italy, or that Torah readers translated on the spot. These developments explain the natural tendency to view northern European Hebrew narrative as a product of an oral tradition, with text always subordinated in the scholarly conversation.

The uncertainty about Jewish literacy of Old French and German persists by resting on the unavoidable facts that Jews of medieval Ashkenaz had a common Hebrew literary and oral tradition and they rarely—if ever—wrote in the Roman alphabet. It would be an easy assumption that medieval compilers of Hebrew folktales also drew on oral stories as their base. This instinct to assume an oral tradition first isolates the Jewish romance tradition from its source texts and therefore isolates it from the elite literary culture of Western Europe. Despite tepid suggestions made in scholarship for the past hundred years, this book is the first to present a supportable argument for Jewish knowledge of French stories through text. Most scholarship has used the existence of Hebraico-French glosses in Hebrew manuscripts to determine the French literacy of medieval French Jews. Here, however, I use the narratives themselves to confirm literacy.

In this chapter, I will analyze closely each author and his text to propose more accurate transmission patterns for his source material. Despite recent scholarship that compares the content of various Hebrew stories to their French antecedents, no one has looked for patterns of manuscript transmission of the original traditions to localize and contextualize the Hebrew version. While non-Jewish texts were not the only type of material that the Jewish authors used for the translated works presented here (many incorporated oral folktales or internally transmitted Aramaic or Hebrew stories from the past), non-Jewish written stories played an oversized role in the formation of those texts, even if they also had aspects of other Jewish and non-Jewish material contained within.

Mishle Shu'alim (Fox Fables)

Berechiah ha-Nakdan clearly owes a debt to the twelfth-century French author Marie de France. Most of his fables represent a translation from Marie's *Ysopet*, a collection of animal fables in Anglo-Norman French (with some manuscripts attesting to Old French versions) that she, in turn, translated from the Latin Aesopic tradition. Scholars have traced his usage of her stories on a manuscript level, a fact that challenges the prevailing scholarly theory that medieval northern European Jews heard

French stories only orally. In the Hebrew text of one of his fables featuring two deer, the source text from Marie features two servants instead, although the narrative remains unchanged. In the Marie version, two serfs are whispering together in a field, attempting to look clever by pretending they have something secretive to talk about, when a passerby speaks with them. In the Berechiah version, two *deer* are whispering together in a field when a passerby speaks to them. The French word for serfs, *serfs*, closely resembles the word for deer, *cerfs*, and Berechiah's change can be attributed to a scribal error in his source text.[22] If Berechiah or the other French authors who wrote *cerfs* relied on an oral version of the story, they would not change the content of the story; *serf* and *cerf* are homonyms, which means the story still makes sense if the words are heard rather than read.

Because the word "servants" appears to be the original meaning of the fable, the word "deer" is the more problematic version. If Berechiah only heard the fables orally, he would choose to write "servants" because it makes more sense. But he chooses "deer" for his translation because he is clearly using a textual translation.

Using this information, we can further localize the origin of Berechiah's text. All the manuscripts that contain the alternate reading have a continental origin rather than an English one, and they appear in Old French rather than Anglo-Norman. This questions the theory that Berechiah wrote his fables in England and places him firmly in a French textual context.[23] Let us also recall that Berechiah translated a Latin text into Hebrew, Adelard of Bath's *Quaestiones Naturales* (Natural Questions). Even if he used an intermediary of a French text, the closeness of the original text and his new creation suggests that he relied on text rather than oral sources.

Melekh Artus (King Arthur)

Melekh Artus (King Arthur) is a Hebrew translation of Arthurian stories with a completion date of 1279. The *Melekh Artus* text appears at the end

22. Marie de France, *Die Fabeln Der Marie de France*, ed. Karl Warnke (Halle: Niemeyer, 1898); Moses Hadas, "Introduction," in Berechiah ben Natronai Ha-Nakdan, *The Mishle Shu'alim (Fox Fables) of Rabbi Berechiah Ha-Nakdan*, trans. Haim Schwarzbaum (Jerusalem: Institute for Jewish and Arab Folklore Research, 1979).

23. Joseph Johnson, "Animal Speech and Human Handwriting in the *Ysopet* of Marie and the Roman de Renart" (PhD diss., New York University, 2017). I thank him for his analysis of the provenance of the *cerf* manuscripts, and his opinion that the change does not render the fables meaningless.

of Vatican Urbinati 48, a Hebrew manuscript that also contains calendrical treatises and a commentary on a Talmudic tractate. Consisting of only seven folios and written in two different hands from the rest of the manuscript, the *Melekh Artus* text (on folios 75r–77r) breaks off mid-folio, mid-sentence. Given the different appearance of the parchment of the *Melekh Artus* story compared to the text that precedes it in the manuscript and the different scribal hands, it is possible that the story was bound in the manuscript after it was already written. The text was first edited by A. Berliner in 1885 and translated by Moses Gaster in 1909.[24] Not until 1969 was a modernized, more accurate edition and translation available in English, and an updated version appeared in 2003.[25] A handful of articles and references have pointed to the uniqueness of the *Melekh Artus* text, with many referring to it as a romance or as a translation from the Christian world placed inside a Jewish context.[26]

Medieval Arthuriana has a rich history, with its earliest iterations in Latin, Welsh, English, and French.[27] The first Arthurian stories appeared in Latin texts, and King Arthur's story was notably told in depth by Geoffrey of Monmouth in his Latin *Historia regum Britanniae* (History of the Kings of England) around the year 1138. Translated and reframed into Anglo-Norman French by Wace shortly after, the stories were popularized among French speakers and readers. At the end of the twelfth century, Chrétien de Troyes created enduring stories based around King Arthur's court, and other contemporary poets, including Marie de France, Thomas of Britain, and Béroul, composed their own Arthurian adventures.[28] Subsequent authors translated Arthurian stories from

---

24. Moses Gaster, "The History of the Destruction of the Round Table as Told in Hebrew in the Year 1279," *Folk Lore* 20 (1909): 272–94.

25. Curt Leviant, *King Artus: A Hebrew Arthurian Romance of 1279* (Syracuse, NY: Syracuse University Press, 2003).

26. M. Schüler, "Die hebraische Version der Sage von Arthur und Lanzelot aus den Jahre 1279," *Archiv für das Studium der neueren Sprachen und Literaturen* 122 (1909): 51–63; Howard Needler, "Refiguring the Middle Ages: Reflections on Hebrew Romances," *New Literary History* 8, no. 2 (1977): 238–42; Giancarlo Lacerenza, "'Melek Artûs': I Temi Arturiani Ebraizzati Nel "«Sefer Ha-šmad»," in *Macrotesti Fra Oriente e Occidente: 4. Colloquio Internazionale, Vico Equense, 26–29 Ottobre 2000*, ed. Giovanna Carbonaro, Natalia L. Tornesello, and Eliana Creazzo (Soveria Mannelli (Catanzaro): Rubbettino, 2003), 101–18; Paul R. Rovang, "Hebraizing Arthurian Romance: The Originality of Melech Artus," *Arthuriana* 19, no. 2 (2009): 3–9; Tamar S. Drukker, "A Thirteenth-Century Arthurian Tale in Hebrew: A Unique Literary Exchange," *Medieval Encounters* 15, no. 1 (March 2009): 114–29.

27. Norris J. Lacy and James J. Wilhelm, eds., *The Romance of Arthur: An Anthology of Medieval Texts in Translation* (London: Routledge, 2012).

28. See, for example, R. Howard Bloch, *The Anonymous Marie de France* (Chicago: University of Chicago Press, 2011); Barbara N. Sargent-Baur, *The Romance of Tristran by Béroul and Béroul II:*

these and other sources into their own vernaculars, often significantly changing the characters, plots, and structure of the original tales.[29] The source text that the Jewish author of *Melekh Artus* (King Arthur) used is the anonymous Lancelot-Grail cycle, a five-part collection of stories featuring the Arthurian characters of King Arthur, Lancelot, Merlin, and more: the *Estoire del Saint Graal* (History of the Holy Grail), *Merlin*,[30] *Lancelot*,[31] *Queste del Saint Graal* (Quest of the Holy Grail),[32] and *Mort Artu* (Death of Arthur).[33]

The first Arthurian story translated by the Jewish author begins with Arthur's birth.[34] King Uter Pendragon falls in love with Izerna/Igerne, who is married to the Duke of Titormel or Til Tomeil. Uter brings his troops in battle against the duke, and in the midst of the fighting, Uter calls upon his magician Merlin. Merlin devises a magical disguise so that Uter can make his way into Izerna's bedroom and lie with her; she thinks that the man with her is her husband. She conceives a child, the future King Arthur. That night, the duke is killed in battle, and shortly after, Uter marries the pregnant Izerna. They agree that the child will be given to Merlin to raise. The Hebrew story then describes a separate episode featuring Lancelot de Lac and King Arthur's Knights of the Round Table. After the Quest for the Holy Grail, many of Arthur's knights have died. Arthur arranges a tournament for all the young knights to prove themselves worthy of joining the Round Table. One of these knights is Lancelot, who is embroiled in a love affair with Arthur's

---

A Diplomatic Edition and a Critical Edition (Toronto: University of Toronto Press, 2015); Chrétien de Troyes, *The Complete Romances of Chrétien de Troyes*, trans. David Staines (Bloomington: Indiana University Press, 1991).

29. Victoria Coldham-Fussell, Miriam Edlich-Muth, and Renée Ward, eds., *The Arthurian World* (London: Routledge, 2022); Elizabeth Sherr Sklar and Donald L. Hoffman, eds., *King Arthur in Popular Culture* (Jefferson, NC: McFarland, 2002); Regina Psaki and Gloria Allaire, eds., *The Arthur of the Italians: The Arthurian Legend in Medieval Italian Literature and Culture* (Cardiff: University of Wales Press, 2014); David Hook, *The Arthur of the Iberians: The Arthurian Legends in the Spanish and Portuguese Worlds* (Cardiff: University of Wales Press, 2015).

30. John Conlee, ed., *Prose Merlin* (Kalamazoo, MI: Medieval Institute Publications, 1998).

31. Corin Corley, trans., *Lancelot of the Lake* (Oxford: Oxford University Press, 2008).

32. Judith Shoaf, trans. and ed., *Quest of the Holy Grail* (Peterborough, Canada: Broadview, 2018); Norris J. Lacy, *Lancelot-Grail: The Quest for the Holy Grail* (Woodbridge, UK: Boydell & Brewer, 2010).

33. Jean Frappier, *La mort le roi Artu: roman du XIIIe siècle* (Paris: Librairie Droz, 1996).

34. New evidence has suggested that *Melekh Artus* is a manuscript copy of a previously made translation. See Leon Jacobowitz-Efron, "The Linguistic Provenance of the Hebrew *King Arthur* (1279) Reassessed," *Journal of the International Arthurian Society* 12, no. 1 (September 1, 2024): 62–86, https://doi.org/10.1515/jias-2024-0003. I am grateful to Christopher M. Berard and Leon Jacobowitz-Efron for sharing their thoughts on this topic.

queen Guinevere despite his efforts to extricate himself. Lancelot disguises himself as an independent knight for the tournament. In the middle of his courageous efforts on the field, the manuscript cuts off.

While early scholars associated *Melekh Artus* with Italian versions of the King Arthur stories,[35] I propose that the Hebrew author, even if he lived in northern Italy, was drawing exclusively on Old French versions.[36] The author clearly translates from two sections of the popular five-part medieval collection the Lancelot-Grail cycle, using the *Merlin* for his first part and the *Mort Artu* for the second.[37] At times, he engages in close literal translation; at others, he rewrites the episodes. *Melekh Artus* provides the best single indication of French to Hebrew translation in thirteenth-century northern Europe. But to make this argument, we must correct previous scholarship of *Melekh Artus* involving its provenance. The earliest scholar of *Melekh Artus* assumed an Italian origin for the text, insisting on a now-lost Italian exemplar.[38] Manuscript evidence reveals instead an Arthurian tradition in northern Italy that reflected a Francophone cultural sphere. The distinction between French and Italian in thirteenth-century northern Italy is not precise enough for us to confirm an Italian exemplar. Instead, scholars refer to a Francophone linguistic and literary tradition in which French culture permeated to Franco-Italian speakers in northern Italy.[39] As will be seen, the scribe of this copy of *Melekh Artus* (if not the original translator) emerged from this Franco-Italian linguistic tradition because of his orthographical decisions and the cultural circumstances around his writing.

---

35. Moritz Steinschneider, *Die hebraeischen Übersetzungen des Mittelalters und die Juden als Dolmetscher. Ein Beitrag zur Literaturgeschichte des Mittelalters, meist nach handschriftlichen Quellen* (Berlin: Kommissionsverlag des Bibliographischen bureaus, 1893), 968; Schüler, "Die hebraische Version der Sage von Arthur und Lanzelot aus den Jahre 1279," 51–63; Gaster, "The History of the Destruction of the Round Table," 274–76.

36. Keith Busby, "Arthuriana in the Italian Regions of Medieval Francophonia," in *The Arthur of the Italians*, ed. Gloria Allaire and F. Regina Psaki (Cardiff: University of Wales Press, 2014), 11–20; Caroline Gruenbaum, "The Quest for the 'Charity Dish': Interpretation in the Hebrew Arthurian Translation Melekh Artus (1279, Northern Italy)," *Medieval Encounters* 26, no. 6 (February 2021): 517–42.

37. The Lancelot-Grail Cycle, also known as the Vulgate Cycle, contains five major sections drawn from sources ranging between 1210 and the mid-1230s. These sections include (1) *The History of the Grail*, (2) *Merlin*, (3) *Lancelot*, (4) *The Quest for the Holy Grail*, and (5) *The Death of Arthur*. For an overview of the Lancelot-Grail Cycle and *Prose Merlin* French tradition, see the introduction in Conlee, *Prose Merlin*, 1–18.

38. Schüler, "Die hebraische Version der Sage von Arthur und Lanzelot aus den Jahre 1279."

39. Busby, "Arthuriana in the Italian Regions of Medieval Francophonia."

In accordance with the earlier scholarship, the modern editor of the *Melekh Artus* text categorizes the transliterated words in *Melekh Artus* as "Italian." The first one appears in the margin next to the first word on the folio: the Hebrew word שמד, here meaning "destruction" (but elsewhere can take the meaning of "persecution," as in a religious persecution). The author has spelled out the vernacular "l'distruzione" (לדשטרוציאון, destruction). We can also compare this heading to a slightly later Italian poem, the *Struzione della Tavola Ritonda* (The Destruction of the Round Table), which tells the story of *Mort Artu*.[40]

In the modern translation and edition, the editor has provided Italian spellings of the Romance words in a way that supports his theory of an Italian intermediary. The words can be read, however, not as Italian words but as French words. Curt Leviant reads, for example, "his face was covered by a helmet and his head was covered by a helmet," with a note that the word "helmet" is transliterated as *capperone* (והקפרון).[41] His Italian spelling of the word, however, does not acknowledge the possibility of a Hebraico-French origin. Elsewhere in examples of thirteenth-century Hebraico-French from northern France, a Hebrew *kuf* represents the French *ch* (/*k*/), as it does for the word *chatie* in the Hebrew-French wedding song.[42] There are similar examples in the Troyes elegy, with *kuf* as the first letter in the Hebraico-French words *chatain*, *checun*, *chanteient*, and *chatie*.[43]Reading with these orthographical suggestions, *capperone* becomes the Old French *chaperon*, for "hood, cowl."

Another of the supposed Italian words is the name of Uter Pendragon's wife, Igerne in the French sources, which appears as איזרנא (Izerna) in the Hebrew. Leviant notes that this spelling is "undoubtedly an Italian variant" and compares it to a similar spelling in a fourteenth-century Italian *Vita di Merlino* (Life of Merlin).[44] Rather than understanding the

40. Maria Bendinelli Predelli, ed., *La Struzione Della Tavola Ritonda* (Florence: Societa Editrice Fiorentina, 2015).

41. Leviant, *King Artus*, 45.

42. See the equivalence table of Hebraico-French, transliteration, and pronunciation in Marc Kiwitt, "The Problem of Judeo-French: Between Language and Cultural Dynamics," *International Journal of the Sociology of Language* 2014, no. 226 (March 2014): 34, https://doi.org/10.1515/ijsl-2013-0074; Marc Kiwitt and Stephen Dörr, "Judeo-French," in *Handbook of Jewish Languages*, ed. Lily Kahn and Aaron D. Rubin (Leiden: Brill, 2015), 148–50; D. S. Blondheim, *Poèmes judéo-français du moyen âge* (Paris: Champion, 1927), 36; Kirsten A. Fudeman, "'They Have Ears, but Do Not Hear': Gendered Access to Hebrew and the Medieval Hebrew-French Wedding Song," *Jewish Quarterly Review*, no. 4 (2006): 542–67.

43. Kirsten A. Fudeman, "Restoring a Vernacular Jewish Voice: The Old French Elegy of Troyes," *Jewish Studies Quarterly* 15, no. 3 (September 1, 2008): 190–221.

44. Leviant, *King Artus*, 15.

Hebrew *zayin* as representing an Italian "z," the letter can also stand for the French pronunciation of the letter "j" in the name "Jacques."[45] When Hebrew letters spelled Old French words, the letter *zayin* did take the place of that French sound, which is equivalent to the transliterated ğ, with the graphemic value of a voiced postalveolar affricate/dʒ/or fricative/ʒ/.[46] *Aleph* as the final letter in a Hebraico-French word can also represent the "a" sound in French words that end in *e*, such as "ele" (אלא) or "grosse" (גרושא).[47] Thus, Leviant's "Izerna" could be the French "Igerne." The same phenomenon is at play with the name for Guinevere, זנברא, read as the French "Ginevre," instead of Leviant's "Zinevra."[48] Leviant's "valvasour" could just as easily be the French *vavasur* because the author of *Melekh Artus* himself alternates between keeping and dropping the letter *l* as "vavasour" and "valvasour." The fact that orthography of the vernacular, whether Old French, Judeo-Italian, Franco-Italian, or Hebraico-French, was not standardized blurs the distinction in the Hebrew manuscript.[49]

Even Leviant's transliterated "Lanzelot" with a *tzadey* could be the French "Lancelot." That Hebrew letter represents a variety of letters and sounds in Hebraico-French including צ, ṣ, ç, ç, ž, and ç.[50] At times, the *Melekh Artus* author abbreviates Lancelot, as in the French versions, as Lanz or Lanç (לנץ). In a late thirteenth-century poem from Tuscany, the poet spells Lancelot's name as "Lancillotto," in a spelling that clearly varies from the French model, even if we allow for regional dialects.[51] This Italianate spelling does not appear in *Melekh Artus*.[52]

The final complication in the theory of an Italian exemplar involves evidence from medieval Arthurian literary history. No prior Italian-language

45. For two overviews of Old French grammar and linguistics, see Eduard Schwan and Dietrich Behrens, *Grammaire de l'ancien français*, trans. Oscar Bloch (Leipzig: O. R. Reisland, 1913); Frédéric Duval, *Le Français Médiéval* (Turnhout: Brepols, 2009).

46. Kiwitt, "The Problem of Judeo-French," 34; Kiwitt and Dörr, "Judeo-French," 148–50.

47. See the examples of Hebraico-French in the Troyes elegy, edited and translated in Fudeman, "Restoring a Vernacular Jewish Voice."

48. Kiwitt, "The Problem of Judeo-French," 34; Kiwitt and Dörr, "Judeo-French," 148–50.

49. The terminology of the medieval Jewish vernacular changes when we move from a textual to an oral sphere, providing a distinction between the function of each language. While "Hebraico-French" refers to French written in Hebrew characters, the term "Judeo-French" refers to the form of French spoken by Jews.

50. Kiwitt and Dörr, "Judeo-French," 149.

51. Busby, "Arthuriana in the Italian Regions of Medieval Francophonia."

52. For a comparison to words appearing in Judeo-Italian, see Aaron D. Rubin, "Judeo-Italian," in *Handbook of Jewish Languages*, ed. Lily Kahn and Aaron D. Rubin (Leiden: Brill, 2015), 297–364; Giuseppe Sermoneta, *Un Glossario Filosofico Ebraico-Italiano Del XIII Secolo* (Rome: Edizioni dell'Ateneo, 1969).

version of the stories contained in *Melekh Artus* exists, and scholars use the Hebrew text to propose knowledge of some of these Arthurian characters in Italy.[53] Therefore, no evidence suggests that *Melekh Artus* used any texts other than those written in French. Even in the later example of "The Ring," a fourteenth- or fifteenth-century Hebrew story from Italy, its source material is assumed to draw from Chrétien de Troyes' *Yvain*—not from an "Italian" exemplar, but from oral or written iterations based on a Franco-Venetian version.[54] The most widely circulated Arthurian legends in thirteenth-century Italy were the stories of Tristan, contained in several song poems (*cantari*) and romances.[55] If *Melekh Artus* drew on the Italian tradition of Arthurian stories, we would expect to see more references to Tristan and his popular story cycle.

Although it does not include Tristan, *Melekh Artus* recalls other episodes in the Arthurian canon besides the sections from which it is translated. The author writes that Galehaut (גאלוט) assisted in finagling Guinevere and Lancelot's first meeting. Galehaut, or Galahad in its French spelling, appears in the *Lancelot du Lac* and the *Vulgate Lancelot* or *Lancelot Propre*, as the third section of the five-section Lancelot-Grail cycle. In the modern edition, the Lancelot section is divided into six parts and features as a main source of action for the entire cycle. In this section, Galehaut arranges for Lancelot and Guinevere's first romantic encounter, and he appears briefly in the other sections of the cycle as well. The original passage corresponding to this section of *Melekh Artus* does not mention Galahad, and it could be an addition by the Hebrew author that was known to him from other Arthurian texts.[56]

The *Melekh Artus* author was familiar with the vast Francophone Arthurian corpus. He references the *Quest of the Holy Grail* in transliteration from French (or Franco-Italian) as *Libro de la Queste del Sangraal*. Elsewhere in the text, he refers to Mordred and alternative genealogies that do not appear in the *Mort Artu* source text from which the narrative originates.[57] The author writes in an intertextual reference, "And the reason why [Lancelot] is called 'del Lac', is it not written in the book

53. Daniela Delcorno Branca, "La tradizione della Mort Artu in Italia," *Critica del testo* 7, no. 1 (2004): 1000–1023.

54. Kushelevsky, "Jews Reading Arthurian Romances from the Middle Ages," 396.

55. Marie-José Heijkant, "From France to Italy: The Tristan Texts," in *The Arthur of the Italians*, ed. Gloria Allaire and F. Regina Psaki (Cardiff: University of Wales Press, 2014), 41–68.

56. Norris J. Lacy, *Lancelot-Grail: The Death of Arthur*, vol. 7 (Cambridge: D. S. Brewer, 2010), 4.

57. His versions likely come from the Robert de Boron tradition. Nigel Bryant, ed., *Merlin and the Grail: Joseph of Arimathea, Merlin, Perceval: The Trilogy of Prose Romances Attributed to Robert de Boron* (Woodbridge, UK: D. S. Brewer, 2003).

about him? And thus there you will find when he found out his name."[58] The reference to a "book" (ספר, *sefer*) about him distinguishes a physical textual object from a story transmitted orally (מעשה, *ma'aseh*). Broad knowledge of the Arthurian canon in *Melekh Artus* suggests that the author was well versed in the Francophone texts circulating in thirteenth-century northern Italy, not simply the scant Italian-language versions or oral retellings.

Nearly all passages from the second half of the Hebrew tale of *Melekh Artus* have a direct translation from its source text. In one section, the Hebrew reads, "At dawn the King rose to prepare himself for the journey and stood at the window of the castle where he had lodged. He looked out and saw Lanç's horse; he recognized it because he had given it to him as a present."[59] The French source from the Lancelot-Grail cycle reads, "King Arthur, who was still there, leaning on a window sill, saw Lancelot's horse and recognized it as one he himself had given him."[60] I purposefully compared two English translations because the similarity is more powerful when one realizes that the two English translators were unaware of each other's translations. The detail of the window and the recognition of the horse showcases the extremely close textual connection.

Sefer ha-Ma'asim (Book of Tales)

The influences on *Sefer ha-Ma'asim* spanned a wide range of Old French vernacular tradition, especially from the romance genre and from *lais*. Like his earlier coreligionist Berechiah, the anonymous author of *Sefer ha-Ma'asim* borrowed from Marie de France. Scholars have identified elements of tales in *Sefer ha-Ma'asim* to three of her *lais* in particular: *Chaitivel*, *Guigemar*, and *Yonec*.[61] I will especially emphasize the importance of *Yonec* for understanding Tale No. 67, "Solomon's Daughter." In "Solomon's Daughter," the second part of the tale tells how Solomon locked up the daughter of Joshua, the high priest, after learning she was going

58. והסיבה למה נקרקא דללק הלא היא כתובה בספרו. וגם כן שם תמצא מתי נודע אליו שמו. Leviant, *King Artus*, 12, 14.

59. Leviant, *King Artus*, 35.

60. Norris J. Lacy, ed., *Lancelot-Grail: The Old French Arthurian Vulgate and Post-Vulgate in Translation* (Cambridge: D. S. Brewer, 2010), 3.

61. Rella Kushelevsky, *Tales in Context: Sefer Ha-Ma'asim in Medieval Northern France* (Detroit, MI: Wayne State University Press, 2017), 39–82.

to marry a man born out of wedlock. An eagle flies the bastard-groom into the tower, and the girl conceives a child with him.[62]

Kushelevsky notes a preexisting vernacular tradition of a girl confined in a tower, such as in *Aucassin et Nicolette*, as part of the "horizon of expectations of the Jewish audience of *Sefer ha-Maʿasim*."[63] That particular French story, however, appears in only one manuscript and is considered to have the "highest claim to exclusivity in medieval French."[64] Another point of comparison, then, would be the similar story that appears in Marie de France's *Yonec*, a *lai* that comprised part of her *Lais* collection. The first reference to Marie de France and her *lais* appears in England in the late twelfth century; the first manuscript containing them dates to 1265 (London, British Library Harley 978) and is the only manuscript that has all twelve *lais* organized in a way that may reveal the original authorial intent.[65] The *lais* were popular in the thirteenth century, with versions appearing elsewhere in Europe throughout the medieval period. In her epilogue, Marie herself states that she translates her *lais* from English to French, but without her original sources, we cannot do a complete analysis of the transmission and interpretative processes that she takes.

There are more extant thirteenth-century copies of *Yonec* than any other of Marie's *lais*, and the parallels between the two stories imply a close connection between the Anglo-Norman French version and the later Hebrew iteration. In the French story, a rich man imprisons his beautiful wife in a tower to keep her contained for him alone. While the lord is away, she receives a surprise visitor in the form of a hawk, who transforms into a handsome knight. The maid and the knight become lovers, and eventually she conceives a child. When the husband learns

62. One scholar believes that Berechiah may have written a thirteenth-century version of this story contained in Oxford, Bodl. Or. 156 (the article mistakenly has a shelfmark of Oxford 183). In this version, the story plays an exegetical role in the form of *midrash*. Michael Chernick, "Marie de France in the Synagogue," *Exemplaria* 19, no. 1 (Spring 2007): 183–205. This tale is parallel to one that appears in a fourteenth-century Ashkenazi manuscript of Midrash Tanḥuma and the motif of the maiden in the tower possibly has earlier iterations in Jewish literature. See Kushelevsky, *Tales in Context*, 583.

63. Kushelevsky, *Tales in Context*, 62. The concept of a horizon of expectation emerges from Hans Robert Jauss, *Toward an Aesthetic of Reception* (Minneapolis: University of Minnesota Press, 1982). See also Rella Kushelevsky, "'King Artus' as a Jewish Romance: Horizons of Expectation and Genre Configurations," in *Medieval and Early Modern Romance*, ed. Caroline Gruenbaum and Annegret Oehme (Kalamazoo, MI: Arc Humanities, 2023), 107–28.

64. Ardis Butterfield, *Poetry and Music in Medieval France: From Jean Renart to Guillaume de Machaut* (Cambridge: Cambridge University Press, 2002), 191.

65. Keith Busby, "The Manuscripts of Marie de France," in *A Companion to Marie de France*, ed. Logan E. Whalen (Leiden: Brill, 2014), 304.

of her deceit, he kills the knight, but the lovers' son, the eponymous Yonec, becomes a strong and just lord.[66] The similarities of the stories' details, such as the knight in the form of a bird and the subsequent conception in the tower, speaks to a close literary tradition.

Despite these specific references, the content of the stories in *Sefer ha-Ma'asim* do not appear to be translated directly from their source; rather, they borrow certain literary elements while occasionally changing major characters and plot developments. Motifs common to courtly love literature, such as lovers' tests, animal companions, and otherworldly journeys, appear in the Hebrew story collection mixed with more traditional plot elements from Jewish sources.[67] Thus, *Sefer ha-Ma'asim* cannot prove textual engagement by itself, but taken in conjunction with nearly contemporaneous texts, its reliance on textual sources becomes more possible. In this way, it is not as convincing an example as the others mentioned here for textually based transmission; it is more likely that its author used oral and written sources from both Hebrew and French. It does, however, present paradigmatic examples of turning a non-Jewish story into a Jewish one: for example, the story in the tower has replaced its original French knights with the Jewish figures Solomon and the high priest.

Dukus Horant

The fragmentary romance written in early Yiddish or German in Hebrew characters uses language in a different way from nearly any other medieval Ashkenazi text. *Dukus Horant* tells a new version of themes from popular Germanic story cycles (such as the mid-thirteenth-century *Kudrun* and other epics) featuring a bridal quest. The eponymous Duke Horant undergoes a journey to Greece to bring back a bride, Hilde, for his king, the German King Itene.[68] Hilde's father, Hagen, has a history of killing his daughter's suitors. Horant arrives in Greece with riches and accompanied by three giants. He woos Hilde by singing, but the text cuts off before the ending is realized.

This is one of the earliest Yiddish narratives, written for a Jewish audience but consisting of a German story. The Jewish author of *Dukus Horant*

66. Busby, "The Manuscripts of Marie de France"; Marie de France, *Fables*, ed. Harriet Spiegel (Toronto: University of Toronto Press, 1987).

67. Douglas Kelly, *The Art of Medieval French Romance* (Madison: University of Wisconsin Press, 1992).

68. Jerold C. Frakes, ed., "Dukus Horant," in *Early Yiddish Texts 1100–1750: With Introduction and Commentary* (Oxford: Oxford University Press, 2004), 33–43; Frakes, "Dukus Horant," 2014.

relied on several German traditions to craft his new story. The character of Hilde appears in the Middle High German epic *Kudrun* (ca. 1250), where she is a minor figure. The giants, Annegret Oehme has argued, originate in the German text *King Rother* (late twelfth century).[69]

Rather than translate the material in Hebrew, the anonymous author "translated" it into a Jewish script, thereby transmitting it readily to a Jewish audience. Apart from a handful of Hebraisms, it avoids Jewish content and has more often been analyzed in the field of German studies than in Jewish studies. *Dukus Horant* and other early Yiddish texts exist in a liminal space between a language tentatively referred to as Judeo-German or German written in Hebrew characters, and the fully Jewish language of Yiddish.[70] The story uses themes from the medieval genre of romance: love, adventure, magical happenings, and a happy ending. By moving this popular narrative theme into a Jewish script (and arguably into the Jewish language of early Yiddish), the author translates the story cycle for his audience, even if the narrative of his text is ultimately an original production. Without known evidence for either an oral or a textual source, we can only speculate about the avenues through which its author attained the narrative context for his story.

In *Melekh Artus*, the opening lines of the text do not mention hearing, listening, or telling. The author begins the text with a reference to its textual origin specifically: "this is the book of the destruction of King Arthur's Round Table, and I have translated it in the year 1279 from the vernacular into Hebrew."[71] There is no reference to orality in the prologue at all; he uses the words "translation" or "translate" (from the root עתק) seven times and "book" (ספר) four times.

The quotation cited in the introduction to this book reveals another example of reliance on a physical book rather than orality. A thirteenth-century Hebrew romance based on non-Jewish Alexander the Great stories refers to its source text as a Latin "book": "Not because I see myself as wise, nor because of my skill with language, have I decided to translate this book from Latin into Hebrew, for I am most ignorant and unwise. Indeed, I wished to translate it after I saw it written in the

69. Annegret Oehme, "Angelic Giants and Monstrous Kings in the Old Yiddish Dukus Horant," *Euphorion* 116, no. 3 (2022): 345–66.

70. Gabriele L. Strauch, "Text and Context in the Reading of Medieval Literature—A Case in Point: Dukus Horant," *Exemplaria* 3, no. 1 (January 1991): 67–94.

71. זה ספר השמד הטבלה העגולה שלהמלך ארטוס ואני העתקתיו בשנת ט"ל לפרט מלשון לעז אל לשון עברי. Leviant, *King Artus*, 8.

book of the Christians."[72] The mention of a "book of the Christians" (בספר הנצרים) and of translation (בהעתקה) confirms the author's engagement with a physical object from which to translate. If we compare this to the prologue in Marie de France's *Ysopet*, we find a striking similarity to the emphasis on writing and reading:

> Those who are well-read
> Ought to pay close attention
> To the great books that were written,
> To the exemplary tales
> Which the philosophers found
> And wrote down and recalled.
> For morality's sake they wrote down
> The good sayings that they heard.[73]

The repetition of reading and writing again suggests an emphasis on textuality, as though the author consciously wants the reader to know that her story is text based. The last line references memory (*escristrent e remembrerent*), but it places the verb "to remember/recall" after the verb "to write," emphasizing memory as a result of writing, not its impetus. Marie de France emphasizes here the importance of a textual chain, from Aesop to her, which she relies on to imbue her translated stories with authority. This results from changing language systems; in Marie's world, French was still coming into its own compared to Latin as an authoritative language for original works. As one recent scholar noted, Marie's prologue shows that "the prestige of translation is used to transfer authority to her vernacular texts."[74]

For medieval Jews, translation did not imbue authority upon Hebrew texts, and for that reason, authors did not usually signal when they

---

72. This manuscript was destroyed in a fire, but its prologue was transcribed in Israel Lévi, ed., *Le roman d'Alexandre: texte hébreu anonyme* (Paris: Librairie A. Durlacher, 1887), xiii–xiv. It was translated in Shamma Boyarin, "Hebrew Alexander Romance and Astrological Questions: Alexander, Aristotle, and the Medieval Jewish Audience," in *Alexander the Great in the Middle Ages*, ed. Markus Stock (Toronto: University of Toronto Press, 2016), 100n5.

73. Marie de France, *Fables*, 28:

> Cil ki seivent de lettruüre / Devreient bien mettre cure
> Es bons livres e escriz / E as [es]samples e as diz
> Ke li philosophe troverent / E escristrent e remembrerent.
> Par moralité escriveient / Les bons proverbs qu'il oieient,
> Que cil amender se peüssent / Ki lur entente en bien eüssent.

74. Michael Lysander Angerer, "Translatio Studii as Literary Innovation: Marie de France's Fresne and the Cultural Authority of Translation," *Exemplaria* 34, no. 4 (October 2, 2022): 341–62, https://doi.org/10.1080/10412573.2022.2144489.

translated from non-Jewish texts. If we look at linguistic clues, though, we see more evidence that learned Jews relied on textual traditions from the vernacular rather than oral channels exclusively. For the most part, Hebraico-French represents a phonetic transliteration of Old French into Hebrew characters, often with commonly used Hebrew words mixed in without translation, usually words relating to Jewish life cycle events or specifically Jewish terms such as "bride," "groom," or "study hall." If the texts were transliterated into the Latin alphabet, any Old French scholar could read them without much difficulty (despite the strangeness of reading phonetically a decidedly nonphonetic language). Hebraico-French, however, incorporates several linguistic features that deviate from a purely phonetic purpose. In several cases, Hebraico-French adds an extra *he* to the ends of feminine words to represent a grammatical feature in Hebrew. But the added letter does not change the pronunciation of the word. In a thirteenth-century poem, we see, for example, a line transliterated into Old French as "troblee eit notre joie" (טרובלאה איט נוטראה גואייאה).[75] The pronunciation for *troblee* and *notre* has a single *e* sound at the end. The Hebraico-French, however, adds a second *e* sound in the form of the Hebrew *he*. The added letter seems to mark the adjectives *troblee* and *notre* as feminine for orthographical or etymological purposes. This graphemic distinction and similar ones present in Hebraico-French appear in other vernacular Jewish dialects as reflections of an older etymological tradition from Latin and Greek loanwords.[76]

For our purposes, these linguistic features warn us that a categorization of Hebraico-French as merely phonetic neglects the grammatical and etymological considerations of the scribes. Not only did they rely on their oral understanding of French, they also engaged in textual considerations. Similarly, the use of translation and transmission from non-Jewish to Jewish texts does not involve simple word-for-word equivalence or oral sources but stems from complex literary processes.

Despite a well-attested literary culture, only several hundred texts in Hebraico-French survive, and most of these consist of a few lines or phrases. Many of these medieval Hebraico-French lines or phrases appear as glosses to Hebrew texts, written above words or in the margins to translate and describe words in Hebrew. Based on this textual evidence, it becomes clear that Jews of medieval France relied on French for their

75. *Elégie de Troyes*, line 5, translated and cited in Fudeman, "Restoring a Vernacular Jewish Voice," 198.

76. Kiwitt, "The Problem of Judeo-French."

spoken language and on Hebrew for their written language.[77] Jews of northern Europe, like the Christians around them, lived in "cultural diglossia," a dual-language system in which one language was used for oral communication and the other for textuality.[78] For their Christian neighbors, Old French (or Franco-Italian for the region of *Melekh Artus*) was the spoken language, while Latin was used for most texts.

The European-wide shift to the vernacular to record stories and poems was a centuries-long process spanning many literary genres. It began partially as a response to a rise in lay piety, a movement in which nonclergy people became more spiritual.[79] This was achieved through the vernacularization of devotion, specifically the creation of religious poetry and prose in the vernacular that was easily accessible for non-Latin learners.[80] More reliance on the vernacular for recording stories and poems began during the eleventh and through the thirteenth century in France, sparking a cultural revolution that inspired other vernacular texts in Castilian, English, Italian, and German in the Late Middle Ages. A distinction between the types of texts produced in Latin and those in Old French continued despite the rise in popularity of the vernacular—Latin was still reserved for more scholarly pursuits in religion, medicine, and philosophy, and Old French was used for courtly love stories, poetry, historiography, satire, and fables.[81]

---

77. For a more detailed analysis of Hebraico-French iterations, see the introduction in Kirsten A. Fudeman, *Vernacular Voices: Language and Identity in Medieval French Jewish Communities* (Philadelphia: University of Pennsylvania Press, 2011), 1–25. Original scholarship on the topic includes Blondheim, *Les Parlers Judéo-Romans et la Vetus Latina*; Menachem Banitt, "Une Langue-Fantôme: Le Judéo-Français," *Revue de Linguistique Romane* 27 (1963): 245–94.

78. This concept was first developed in 1959 in Charles A. Ferguson, "Diglossia," *WORD* 15, no. 2 (January 1959): 325–40; Joshua A. Fishman, "Bilingualism with and without Diglossia; Diglossia with and without Bilingualism," *Journal of Social Issues* 23, no. 2 (April 1967): 29–38; Harold F. Schiffman, "Diglossia as a Sociolinguistic Situation," in *The Handbook of Sociolinguistics*, ed. Florian Coulmas (Oxford: Blackwell, 1997), 205–16, https://onlinelibrary-wiley-com.proxy.library.nyu.edu/doi/pdf/10.1002/9781405166256.ch12; Alan Hudson, "Outline of a Theory of Diglossia," *International Journal of the Sociology of Language* 2002, no. 157 (2006): 1–48.

79. Nicole R. Rice, *Lay Piety and Religious Discipline in Middle English Literature* (Cambridge: Cambridge University Press, 2009); Miri Rubin, ed., *Medieval Christianity in Practice* (Princeton, NJ: Princeton University Press, 2009).

80. Renate Blumenfeld-Kosinski, Duncan Robertson, and Nancy Bradley Warren, eds., *The Vernacular Spirit* (New York: Palgrave Macmillan, 2002); Jocelyn Wogan-Browne, Ruth Evans, Andrew Taylor, and Nicholas Watson, eds., *The Idea of the Vernacular* (University Park: Pennsylvania State University Press, 1999).

81. Gabrielle M. Spiegel, *Romancing the Past: The Rise of Vernacular Prose Historiography in Thirteenth-Century France* (Berkeley: University of California Press, 1995); Jennifer Saltzstein,

In the terms outlined by studies on diglossia, the subject matter of Latin texts deemed it a high-register or highly valued language, while vernaculars were low-register or less valued languages. High-register languages are typically reserved for education, religious practice, and public speaking, while low-register languages are used as the spoken word on the street and, in modern day, for cultural activities and entertainment not under the umbrella of the high register.[82] Though it might seem that the vernacular is never a textual language and the high-register language is never spoken, this is not a true dichotomy. As a highly valued language, Latin was not just written but also incorporated in performative church functions, with the clergy and laypeople alike memorizing prayers and reciting them in Latin. In the church, schools, universities, and courts, Latin was incorporated as oral pedagogy.[83] These oral iterations of Latin, however, had their origins in a text, whether the Bible or legal text, rendering Latin not merely a written language or a literary language but a "textualized language."[84] Just like Latin, we cannot generalize about Hebrew as a purely written language without oral functionality. This understanding of diglossia as not dichotomously textual or oral fits with what we know about Hebrew as a living language in the synagogue, where men and women performed it through recitation of prayers and reading the Torah, and in the rabbinic study halls, where students memorized and analyzed it.

But the opposite was almost always true: Jews of medieval northern Europe almost never wrote in their low-register language, French. Unlike in Christian Europe, where the low-register language of French flourished in the later Middle Ages as a language for both religious and secular writing, Jewish Europe never truly attempted widescale secular writing in French. As we will see, a privileging of Hebrew as a language for writing led to an imbalance in the number and type of texts produced in Hebrew as opposed to Hebraico-French. At the same time, however, the varied corpus of Hebraico-French texts attests to a Jewish engagement with the vernacular on a textual level.

The Refrain and the Rise of the Vernacular in Medieval French Music and Poetry (Rochester, NY: D. S. Brewer, 2013).

82. Schiffman gives an overview of recent theory on diglossia with modern distinctions for highly valued (H) and less valued (L) languages. Schiffman, "Diglossia as a Sociolinguistic Situation," 205–6.

83. Jan M. Ziolkowski, "Cultural Diglossia and the Nature of Medieval Latin Literature," in *The Ballad and Oral Literature*, ed. Joseph Harris (Cambridge, MA: Harvard University Press, 1991), 195.

84. Ong, "Orality, Literacy, and Medieval Textualization," 5.

Hebrew was always considered the primary written text, with the vernacular used only when necessary and almost always in relation to a Hebrew word or phrase.[85] The medieval French Jewish commentator Rabbi Solomon ben Isaac of Troyes (Rashi, 1040–1105) wrote his biblical and Talmudic commentaries in Hebrew and included Hebraico-French glosses and single-word translations when necessary.[86] Knowing that he translates difficult Hebrew words to Hebraico-French, and that he spoke Hebraico-French as his vernacular, his decision to write in Hebrew reflects a conscious privileging of that language. For Rashi and his contemporaries, Hebrew was the only acceptable choice for a biblical commentary. Because it was nearly always restricted to glosses and single-word translations alongside medieval Hebrew texts, Hebraico-French was, literally, marginal.

The variety of uses and functions of Hebraico-French attests to this subordinated status but presents more complex ways in which Jews navigated between their two languages. Bilingual glossaries, colophons, marginalia, and documentary evidence clarify the interconnected nature of the diglossic society. One thirteenth-century Hebrew-French glossary, Strasbourg Ms. 3.950, contains three columns. The first column has a word in biblical Hebrew, followed by the Hebraico-French equivalent, then finally the explanation of the term in a medieval type of Hebrew. BNF Hébreu 302, a biblical commentary with a colophon dating to 1241, contains the Hebraico-French terms in line with the Hebrew text rather than in a separate physical arrangement. Some biblical glossaries are written primarily in Hebraico-French, with Hebrew used only as a reference.[87] The thirteenth-century Hebrew-French Leipzig Glossary is a full biblical glossary that emerged from Rouen and traveled through Alsace, where annotations in Middle High German (or Yiddish) were added to the existing Hebraico-French words in the margins.[88]

Plentiful examples of loanwords appear both in stories translated from vernacular, non-Jewish texts and in stories without a discernible non-Jewish origin. One story from *Sefer Ḥasidim* tells of a vampiric

85. Fudeman, *Vernacular Voices*, 123.

86. Arsène Darmesteter and D. S. Blondheim, *Les Gloses Françaises Dans Les Commentaires Talmudiques de Raschi* (Paris: Champion, 1929).

87. Mayer Lambert and Louis Brandin, *Glossaire hébreu-français du XIIIe siècle: recueil de mots hébreux bibliques avec traduction française* (Paris: E. Leroux, 1905); Kiwitt and Dörr, "Judeo-French."

88. Menachem Banitt, ed., *Le Glossaire de Leipzig*, 4 vols. (Jerusalem: Académie nationale des sciences et des lettres d'Israël, 1995).

woman who subsists on blood from the living.[89] The story uses a non-Jewish term (stryx or striga, שטרייש) to describe the woman, and the content of the story lacks any references to Jewish life and behavior. Even this pietistic group felt a connection to the demonic features of contemporary German literature, believing that those figures were relevant for Jewish readers as well. Another story tells of a dragon (דרגון, transliterated as *dragon*).[90] The author begins, "There is a certain type of demon [*mazik*] called a dragon [*dragon*] in Greek."[91] The readers would expect to see the Greek version of the word in Hebrew, *drakon* (דרקון) because the author mentions that the word is in Greek despite its unusual spelling. It is also unusual not to refer to a dragon with a biblical or rabbinic Hebrew word (מזיק or תנין). It is possible that the change from the Greek spelling of the word (*drakon*) to a more Romance-sounding version (*dragon*) suggests influence from German or French.[92] Neither *stryx* nor *dragon* (unlike *drakon*) are words with a biblical or rabbinic Hebrew attestation. Other examples of language sharing from Yiddish or Middle High German, such as the use of vernacular prepositions, quotidian vocabulary, calques, and application of German meanings onto Hebrew words, in *Sefer Ḥasidim* may not have been conscious on the part of the author.[93]

The seamless use of code-switching and language equivalence is a sign of elision between the two cultures. When Rashi cannot find a suitable Hebrew explanation for obscure biblical words, he switches to Hebraico-French. In *Melekh Artus*, the translator's decision to keep words untranslated also attests to his desire to find a middle ground between Jewish and Christian literary culture. In the passage above, as elsewhere, he refers to the Knights of the Table (הפרשים שלהטבלא). Instead of translating the word "table," he transliterates it, recording phonetically the Romance word *table*. In this, he recognizes the object of the "table" as a non-Jewish figure, almost a character itself with a name.

89. Parma H 3280, paragraph 1465, available on the Princeton University *Sefer Ḥasidim* database, https://etc.princeton.edu/sefer_hasidim/index.php.

90. Parma H 3280, paragraph 379. Ivan G. Marcus, ed., *A Facsimile Edition of Sefer Ḥasidim, MS Parma H 3280* (Jerusalem: Hebrew University Dinur Center, 1985), 87.

91. David I. Shyovitz, *A Remembrance of His Wonders: Nature and the Supernatural in Medieval Ashkenaz* (Philadelphia: University of Pennsylvania Press, 2017), 156.

92. David Rotman, "At the Limits of Reality: The Marvelous in Medieval Ashkenazi Hebrew Folktales," *Jewish Studies Quarterly* 20, no. 2 (June 2013): 113–14. See also Shyovitz, *A Remembrance of His Wonders*, 42–43, 156–57, 240, 264.

93. Angel Sáenz-Badillos, *A History of the Hebrew Language* (Cambridge: Cambridge University Press, 2012), 265–66.

Elsewhere, he refers to a helmet as a *chaperon* (קפירון), again maintaining the original French or Franco-Italian word.[94]

Examples of full Hebraico-French texts from northern France are unusual, and they often alternate between Hebrew and the vernacular in Hebrew letters. We can consider the unusual case of a thirteenth-century Hebraico-French and Hebrew macaronic wedding poem that exemplifies Jewish oral and textual engagement with Hebrew. The poem alternates between Hebraico-French and Hebrew for a poem of six nine-line stanzas followed by a seventh stanza of eight lines. It appears alongside the *Maḥzor Vitry* (a popular northern European Jewish prayer book for the High Holidays) in a manuscript dating to the second half of the thirteenth century from Lorraine or Champagne (it is now located at the Jewish Theological Seminary).[95] In one of the Hebraico-French lines, the author writes, "Notre *ḥatan* eit ariveiz," our bridegroom has come.[96] The word "*ḥatan*" is a Hebrew word, while the rest of the line is French. Words that are specific to the Jewish community, in this case to designate a Jewish groom, or religious terms such as the word for "tabernacle" or "Jerusalem," occasionally appear as loanwords from the Hebrew language when they are included in a Hebraico-French text.[97]

This poem has been referred to as an example of code-switching,[98] in which a bilingual person switches between languages in the middle of a sentence or combines grammatical forms from one language to the other; we see this phenomenon elsewhere in medieval macaronic poetry.[99] The Arabic genre of *muwashshah* was popular in twelfth- and thirteenth-century communities. It consisted of a Hebrew or Arabic poem with a couplet in the vernacular at the end.[100] Code-switching, as expressed in the *muwashshah*, suggests a literary community comfortable in both their languages.[101]

94. Leviant, *King Artus*, 44.

95. Fudeman, "They Have Ears, but Do Not Hear."

96. Fudeman, "They Have Ears, but Do Not Hear," 560.

97. Kiwitt, "The Problem of Judeo-French," 41–47, has several examples from Hebraico-French texts, including *beṣim*, "testicles"; *təpīllin*, "phylacteries"; *maʿarab̲*, "west"; *mizraḥ*, "east"; *darom*, "south"; *ṣapōn*, "north"; and the toponym *Yərušalayim*, "Jerusalem."

98. Fudeman, *Vernacular Voices*, 45–46.

99. Ziolkowski, "Cultural Diglossia," 202.

100. Tova Rosen, "The *Muwashshah*," in *The Literature of Al-Andalus*, ed. Maria Rosa Menocal, Raymond P. Scheindlin, and Michael Sells (Cambridge: Cambridge University Press, 2000), 163–89.

101. Fudeman, *Vernacular Voices*, 45.

Another bilingual text is the *Elégie de Troyes* (Troyes Elegy), a pair of late thirteenth-century poems commemorating the hanging of thirteen Jewish residents after a murder accusation against one of them in 1288.[102] The poems consist of one Hebrew poem and one Hebraico-French poem, both describing the same events in slightly different ways. We also have extant a pair of verse narratives describing the story of Esther penned by Crescas Caslari in 1327 in Avignon. One of the narratives is in rhymed couplets in the Jewish French dialect of Judeo-Provençal, and the other is in Hebrew.[103] In these two cases, Hebraico-French and Judeo-Provençal always accompanies the Hebrew. A more unusual text, perhaps the only one of its kind, is a Hebraico-French medical description of fevers, *Fevres*, written in a French dialect from Champagne or Burgundy in the late thirteenth or early fourteenth century that does not accompany a Hebrew version.[104]

Beyond the vernacular, clearly demonstrated by macaronic, bilingual texts, and code-switching examples, what non-Jewish texts, in what languages, did our French and Italian Jews know? The textual evidence does not support widespread or systematic knowledge of Latin in northern Europe—there is no evidence to imply a communal knowledge of the language by the average, nonlearned Jew.[105] When available, documents such as charters and deeds of property or financial transactions between Jews and non-Jews from this period in northern Europe are always bilingual and in both the Roman alphabet and Hebrew script. The main document was written in Latin (or Anglo-Norman French) and a complete copy, or a shorter copy, was translated into Hebrew. Even a signature in the official language would suffice.[106]

We have examples of Jews who did read Latin, alerting us to the existence of multilingual cultural conversations occurring in northern Europe. Out of the eighteen translations from Latin to Hebrew in

102. Susan Einbinder, "The Troyes Laments: Jewish Martyrology in Hebrew and Old French," *Viator* 30 (January 1, 1999): 201–30; Fudeman, "Restoring a Vernacular Jewish Voice."

103. Susan L. Einbinder, "A Proper Diet: Medicine and History in Crescas Caslari's 'Esther,'" *Speculum* 80, no. 2 (2005): 437–63.

104. Julia Zwink, "Étude Lexicographique Du Traité Anonyme 'Fevres': Une Compilation Médicale En Ancien Français, Écrite En Caractères Hébraïques," *Panace@* 7, no. 24 (2006): 250–60. This is the only stand-alone medical text that I know from medieval northern France or Germany.

105. Fudeman, *Vernacular Voices*, 15–18.

106. Malachi Beit-Arié, *Hebrew Manuscripts from East to West: A Comparative Codicology* (London: British Library, 1992), 3. One should note, however, that a signature alone does not deny or confirm literacy, whether in Hebrew or the vernacular.

the twelfth century, seventeen were produced by a single translator, a convert with the pseudonym Doeg ha-Edomi.[107] Christian knowledge of Hebrew was closely tied to the activities of converts. In thirteenth-century Spain, converts to Christianity spurred missionizing movement of the Dominican and Franciscan friars because only they knew the Hebrew necessary to debate and discredit biblical and rabbinic texts.[108] Attaining Latin for polemical purposes occurred in the south as well. The Provençal writer Jacob ben Reuven, for example, translated portions of a Latin text and selections from the Latin New Testament in his polemical anti-Christian text, *Milḥamot ha-Shem* (Wars of the Lord) (ca. 1170).[109] The acquisition of Latin even in the southern Jewish communities was restricted to a learned scholarly elite consisting of philosophers and doctors.[110]

Joseph Bekhor Shor, a northern French scholar from the thirteenth-century Tosafist school, indicates a knowledge of Latin through his refutation of specific Christian biblical interpretations.[111] The famous twelfth-century scholar Rabbi Samuel ben Meir (Rashbam, 1085–1158) may have had access to Latin commentaries as well.[112] One Hebrew scholar posits (erroneously, in my view) that Rashbam is the *only* medieval Jewish figure with reading familiarity with Latin, concluding that other scholars learned about Christian exegesis only through oral communication.[113]

One of the only translations into Hebrew of a Latin text on northern French soil is a philosophical-scientific text, a Hebrew version of

107. Gad Freudenthal, "Arabic and Latin Cultures as Resources for the Hebrew Translation Movement," in *Science in Medieval Jewish Cultures*, ed. Gad Freudenthal (Cambridge: Cambridge University Press, 2012), 76.

108. Robert Chazan, *Daggers of Faith: Thirteenth-Century Christian Missionizing and Jewish Response* (Berkeley: University of California Press, 1989); Robert Chazan, "The Barcelona 'Disputation' of 1263: Christian Missionizing and Jewish Response," *Speculum* 52, no. 4 (October 1977): 824–42; Jeremy Cohen, *The Friars and the Jews: The Evolution of Medieval Anti-Judaism* (Ithaca, NY: Cornell University Press, 1984).

109. David Berger, "Gilbert Crispin, Alan of Lille, and Jacob Ben Reuben: A Study in the Transmission of Medieval Polemic," *Speculum* 49, no. 1 (1974): 34–47.

110. David Berger asserts that all Jewish authors of polemical texts read Latin. David Berger, "Mission to the Jews and Jewish-Christian Contacts in the Polemical Literature in the High Middle Ages," *American Historical Review* 91, no. 3 (1986): 590n68.

111. Avraham Grossman, "Bekhor Shor, Joseph Ben Isaac," in *Encyclopaedia Judaica*, ed. Michael Berenbaum and Fred Skolnik (Detroit, MI: Macmillian, 2007).

112. Sara Japhet, "Did Rashbam Know the Vulgate Latin Translation of the Song of Songs?," *Textus* 24 (2009): 263–85.

113. Ephraim Kanarfogel, *The Intellectual History and Rabbinic Culture of Medieval Ashkenaz* (Detroit, MI: Wayne State University Press, 2013), 85–87, 103–5.

Aristotle's *Liber de animalibus* (On Animals), British Library, MS Sloane 3029. The translation to Hebrew follows Michael Scot's Latin translation of 1220, from the Arabic version. Aristotle's text, then, underwent three translations: into Arabic, Latin, then Hebrew.[114] Other philosophical, astronomical, and medical translations from Latin to Hebrew in medieval northern Europe are beginning to be explored, with a more complete picture of Latin engagement to emerge in future scholarship.[115]

Our French-Jewish author Berechiah alludes to his own knowledge of Latin. In the beginning of a Hebrew adaptation of *Quaestiones naturales*, a twelfth-century work in Latin by Adelard of Bath, that is attributed to him, he writes an apology to his readers. He writes that he has found in the text "non-Jewish writings" translated by Arabic-speakers. He "cleansed it from the hand of the Gentile" through his translation, putting it into Hebrew.[116] This likely refers to a Latin or French translation of the Arabic that Berechiah then translated into Hebrew.[117] Only in recent years has Berechiah's knowledge of Latin become more plausible as more evidence about medieval Jewish engagement with Latin has emerged. Some of his fables, such as the one of the "Statue and Man," stem from a Latin source, because a French version is not extant.[118]

Hebrew translations of Arabic works also existed in northern Europe, including Moses ben Isaac ben Hanessiah's *Sefer haShoham* (The Onyx Book), based on Judeo-Arabic teachings by Judah ibn Hayyūj (ca. 945–ca. 1000 CE) and Jonah ibn Janāḥ (ca. 990–ca. 1055) and produced in late thirteenth-century England.[119] Medieval England also gave us Abraham Ibn Ezra's translation in 1160 of the Arabic author Ibn al-Muthannā's commentary on the astronomical tables of al-Khwārzinī, which now

114. Mauro Zonta, "The Zoological Writings in the Hebrew Tradition," in *Aristotle's Animals in the Middle Ages and Renaissance*, ed. Carlos G. Steel, Guy Guldentops, and Pieter Beullens (Leuven: Leuven University Press, 1999), 44–68.

115. Y. Tzvi Langermann, "Was There Science in Ashkenaz?," *Simon Dubnow Institute Yearbook* 8 (2009): 1–26.

116. Berechiah ben Natronai Ha-Nakdan, *Dodi Ve-Nechdi*, ed. and trans. Hermann Gollancz (Oxford: Oxford University Press, 1920), 16; Tamás Visi, "Berechiah Ben Naṭronai Ha-Naqdan's *Dodi ve-Neḵdi* and the Transfer of Scientific Knowledge from Latin to Hebrew in the Twelfth Century," *Aleph* 14, no. 2 (July 2014): 46–47.

117. Visi, "Berechiah Ben Naṭronai Ha-Naqdan's *Dodi ve-Neḵdi*"; Ha-Nakdan, *Dodi Ve-Nechdi*, i–ii.

118. Haim Schwarzbaum, *The Mishle Shu'alim (Fox Fables) of Rabbi Berechiah Ha-Nakdan* (Jerusalem: Institute for Jewish and Arab Folklore Research, 1979), 473.

119. Moses ben Isaac Hanessiah, *Sefer Ha-Shoham*, ed. Benjamin Klar (London: Jewish Historical Society of England, 1947).

only survives in Hebrew and Latin translations.[120] Another translation from Arabic to Hebrew appeared circa 1200 in northern Europe: Obadiah ben Samuel's Hebrew version of Jonah ibn Janāḥ's *Book of Criticism*.[121] Another text written originally in Judeo-Arabic, *Mivḥar ha-Peninim* (Choice of Pearls), attributed to Solomon ibn Gabirol with Judah ibn Tibbon's translation, was included in Parma 2295, alongside a thirteenth-century northern European Hebrew story collection.[122] We cannot know, however, if translators produced these Hebrew versions in northern Europe or, more probably, that they originated in the south and moved to Ashkenaz. Transmission of texts from the south to the north could happen quite easily, with several known intellectuals traveling that direction, including Berechiah.

The translations from Judeo-Arabic or Arabic into Hebrew expands the text's audience to include Hebrew readers in northern Christendom, where Arabic literacy was less common. The translations of texts from the vernacular, such as Marie de France's *Ysopet* written in French, into Hebrew, however, restrict its new audience. Translating into Hebrew then limits its readership to a male intellectual elite, leaving behind the women, children, and less-educated men who would have been more comfortable hearing the story in its original language of old French. This is a major difference between the pathways of translation in medieval Christian Europe, where expansion of vernacular texts made it possible for wider readership for those who did not read Latin. In this way, there is a reversal of the expected trend of translation from the high-register language to the low-register language in order to reach the masses.

Medieval northern European Jews often internalized the distinction between low and high languages, assigning different languages for different purposes. A striking example of one author's relationship to his languages appears in a thirteenth-century northern European colophon,

120. Bernard R. Goldstein, ed., *Ibn Al-Muthanna's Commentary on the Astronomical Tables of al-Khawarizmi* (New Haven, CT: Yale University Press, 1967); Shlomo Sela and Gad Freudenthal, "Abraham Ibn Ezra's Scholarly Writings: A Chronological Listing," *Aleph* 6 (2006): 22.

121. David Téné, ed., *Sefer Ha-Hassagah, Hu'Kitab al-Mustahlaq, Le-R. Yonah Ibn Janah, Be-Targumo Ha-'ivri Sel Ovadiyyah Ha-Sefaradi* (Jerusalem: Academy of the Hebrew Language and the Bialik Institute, 2006).

122. Malachi Beit-Arié, *Hebrew Manuscripts in the Biblioteca Palatina in Parma Catalogue: Palaeographical and Codiocological Descriptions*, ed. Benjamin Richler (Jerusalem: Jewish National and University Library, 2001); Rella Kushelevsky, *Sigufim U-Pituyim: Ha-Sippur Ha-'ivri Be-'ashkenaz. Ms. Parma 2295 [de-Rossi 563]* (Jerusalem: Magnes, 2010); Rella Kushelevsky, "The Image of Woman in Transition from East to West: The Tale of R. Meir and His Friend's Wife in the Book of Comfort and in Manuscript Parma 2295 de Rossi 563," *Aschkenas* 11, no. 1 (January 2001): 9–38.

dated to 1279. The author writes: "I, Yeḥiel ben Rabbi Eliezer, have written for my own use and completed these vernacular glosses [le'azim] on the 24 books [of the Bible] the 16 Av of the year 39 of the shorter reckoning [5039 Anno Mundi or 1279 CE] in the town of Delsberg."[123] On the previous folio, the same scribe wrote in Hebraico-French: "He who has written this manual is named Vivant de Belley, Who has [as a wife] the daughter of Sir [Don] Solomon, A right fair woman."[124] His identification with the French name "Vivant de Belley," attests to the vernacularity incorporated into the daily life of a medieval French Jew. Yeḥiel is essentially a translation of Vivant because both contain a root form for the word "living"; in Hebrew, the name is translated "may God live," and in French, it is "he who is living." Often, the French name Vivant has the Hebrew equivalent of Ḥayyim, "life."[125] The reference to God in the Hebrew name Yeḥiel elevates the name to a more holy version of the French Vivant, rather than the literal Ḥayyim. His choice of that Hebrew name instead of Ḥayyim might reflect a professional decision to emphasize the piety of the work he does as a copyist.

The scribe Yeḥiel/Vivant included vowel signs under the Hebraico-French letters to aid with ambiguous pronunciation, while the Hebrew colophon has no vowels. This discrepancy emerges from the lack of standard orthography in Old French written in Latin letters; no standardization of Hebraico-French existed.[126] The lack of standardization in Hebraico-French reflects its status as a spoken language, similar to contemporaneous, written Old French, which had a variety of spelling and grammatical discrepancies. The medieval spoken languages of northern Europe (English, Italian, French) did not undergo any academic process of standardization until the modern period.

It is noteworthy that Vivant uses Hebrew to describe the process of writing, and Hebraico-French to discuss the particulars of his personal life. For him, Hebrew was a literary language for the purposes of situating his opus in its historical context with date and location, while Hebraico-French was a true vernacular. We can assume that Yeḥiel used that name in his religious activities, as the name that appeared in prayers

123. Parma, Biblioteca Palatina, MS ebreo 2924, fol. 217r; Colette Sirat, *Hebrew Manuscripts of the Middle Ages*, ed. and trans. Nicholas de Lange (Cambridge: Cambridge University Press, 2002), 5.

124. Sirat, *Hebrew Manuscripts of the Middle Ages*, 6.

125. See the names recorded in both Hebrew and Hebraico-French in Fudeman, "Restoring a Vernacular Jewish Voice," 191.

126. Kiwitt and Dörr, "Judeo-French."

for his health, and the name that would appear on his Hebrew marriage document, the *ketubah*. But Vivant, his name in the low-register language, would be the name used in social situations, the one his wife and children called him at home.

In the thirteenth-century macaronic wedding song, the verses in each language attest to a textual, in addition to an oral, tradition. The Hebraico-French verses compare the bridegroom to a courtly conqueror who faces his enemies in battle and captures a castle (i.e., the bride), while the Hebrew verses contain bawd references to consummation through profane utilization of biblical Hebrew verses and vocabulary. Kirsten A. Fudeman explains the differences in tone between the languages as one of gender; while the men in the audience could understand both the vernacular and the Hebrew lines, the women did not possess enough knowledge of Hebrew to understand those sections. The innuendo apparent in the Hebrew would not have been heard by female ears.[127] Early modern books written in the vernacular of Yiddish were intended for the edification of women. As Moses Altschuler writes in the beginning of his 1596 ethical text *Brantshpigl* in Yiddish:

> The book was written in Yiddish for women and men who are like women in not being able to learn much. So that when the Sabbath comes, they may read this and they will be able to understand what they read. For our holy books are in the sacred tongue and often include complicated exegetical arguments from the Talmud, and they are not able to understand. . . . The great masters of the Kabbalah teach us, and write, that not every human being possesses equal understanding. Thus I write this book for women and for men who cannot fundamentally read or understand the holy books in the sacred tongue.[128]

This rationale did not yet exist in the earlier medieval period, when the vernacular, although seen as a language that women could understand, was not usually used as a written language. What, then, is the purpose of translating Old French texts into Hebrew? By translating

127. Fudeman, "They Have Ears, but Do Not Hear," 560. See also the Catalan wedding songs in Jaume Riera i Sans, ed., *Cants de noces dels jueus catalans* (Barcelona: Curial, 1974); David A. Wacks, *Double Diaspora in Sephardic Literature: Jewish Cultural Production before and after 1492* (Bloomington: Indiana University Press, 2015), 149.

128. Translated in Chava Weissler, "'For Women and for Men Who Are Like Women': The Construction of Gender in Yiddish Devotional Literature," *Journal of Feminist Studies in Religion* 5, no. 2 (1989): 9.

literary material into Hebrew, the audience becomes more restricted than it would be for a text in the vernacular, which would have been available to men, women, and children—in the words of the Yiddish text, "women and men who are like women in not being able to learn much." If narrative material written in Hebrew was recited out loud, it is possible that it was then translated back into the vernacular by the performer. If the stories were translated back into the vernacular on the fly during a reading, then they entered back into their source language. Scholarship has shown that sermons, although often written in Hebrew, were intoned for the congregation in the vernacular, at least by the early modern period.[129] Were medieval stories also recited in the vernacular, regardless of the language in which they were written? As the next chapters will demonstrate, the stories clearly had messages that were meant to resonate with an audience that was larger than the small, restricted class of the literate, suggesting that vernacularity was somehow omnipresent, even in texts written in Hebrew.

129. Marc Saperstein, "Italian Jewish Preaching: An Overview," in *Preachers of the Italian Ghetto*, ed. David B. Ruderman (Berkeley: University of California Press, 1992), 22–40; Israel Bettan, *Studies in Jewish Preaching: Middle Ages* (Lanham, MD: Hebrew Union College Press, 1987), 57; Marc Saperstein, "The Sermon as Oral Performance," in *Transmitting Jewish Traditions*, ed. David D. Gilmore (New Haven, CT: Yale University Press, 2000), 248–77.

Chapter 3

Translating Morality

Berechiah ha-Nakdan and His Animal Fables

In *Sefer Ḥasidim* (Book of the Pious), the late medieval pietistic text from Ashkenaz, its authors note, "If one hears a good explanation, a pertinent question, or a convincing answer from a Christian, an apostate, or from one who entices others to sin, do not name the source when you quote the saying."[1] This piece of advice from the insular pietists, even as it warns Jews about spreading the word of non-Jews, simultaneously acknowledges the wisdom that non-Jews possess. Christians and apostates can give a "good explanation, a pertinent question, or a convincing answer" that would then be repeated by a Jew in a discussion. These somewhat problematic non-Jews nonetheless provide intelligent kernels of wisdom for application in Jewish intellectual circles.

1. אדם ששמע טעם טוב או קושיא
טובה או תירוץ טוב ממין או
ממשומד או מאדם שמחטיא אתה הרבים
אל יאמר דבר משמו

Parma H 3280 paragraph 790. Ivan G. Marcus, ed., *A Facsimile Edition of Sefer Hasidim, MS Parma H 3280* (Jerusalem: Hebrew University Dinur Center, 1985). It also appears in the Bologna edition as paragraph 982. See the Princeton University *Sefer Hasidim* database for editions and transcriptions: https://etc.princeton.edu/sefer_hasidim. I thank Emilie Amar-Zifkin for bringing this paragraph to my attention.

In the nonrabbinic texts of medieval Ashkenaz, we see an appreciation for non-Jewish wisdom through the integration of non-Jewish sources into Hebrew texts. The seamless mélange of non-Jewish ethical and moral instruction into Hebrew fables and stories suggests an appreciation for and practicality to this instruction. This appreciation transcends religious identity and observance because the new Hebrew versions are often devoid of any Judaizing techniques to make the source texts more palatable. Jewish narrative has a long history of incorporating universalized folktale and wisdom literature; even some of its exegetical stories, meant to understand rabbinic or biblical texts better, can be described as falling under various well-established categories of folktale motifs.[2]

As a genre, folktales and fables have a universal appeal that makes them easily transportable across cultures. They lack localization and periodization, often featuring generic characters in vaguely described locales.[3] This is especially true for animal fables, which use animals to promote moral messages. Here, I speak about fables and folktales together because I feel that the narrative portion of these genres—although not necessarily their moral or prologue—similarly embody the idea of wisdom that transcends a specific place or peoplehood.

Both oral and textual versions of folktales and animal fables proliferated in medieval Europe from the twelfth century onward. Hebrew versions of moralistic Arabic folktales, including translations of *The Book of Sindibad*, *Kalila we-Dimna* (Kalila and Dimna), and *Barlaam and Josephat*, appealed to Jewish audiences, regardless of religion, place, or time.[4] Hebrew collections of Arabic and Christian proverbs also emerged in medieval Spain, including *Mivḥar ha-Peninim* (Choice of Pearls) and *Misre ha-Filosofim* (Morals of the Philosophers).[5] All these examples were

2. David Rotman, "At the Limits of Reality: The Marvelous in Medieval Ashkenazi Hebrew Folktales," *Jewish Studies Quarterly* 20, no. 2 (June 2013): 101–28; Tamar Alexander-Frizer, *The Heart Is a Mirror: The Sephardic Folktale* (Detroit, MI: Wayne State University Press, 2008); Emanuel Bin Gorion, ed., *Mimekor Yisrael: Selected Classical Jewish Folktales* (Bloomington: Indiana University Press, 1990).

3. For two comprehensive introductions to the genre and its relevance for medieval literature, see Stith Thompson, *The Folktale* (Berkeley: University of California Press, 1977); Bruce A. Rosenberg, "Folklore Methodology and Medieval Literature," *Journal of the Folklore Institute* 13, no. 3 (1976): 311–25.

4. Haim Schwarzbaum, *The Mishle Shu'alim (Fox Fables) of Rabbi Berechiah Ha-Nakdan* (Jerusalem: Institute for Jewish and Arab Folklore Research, 1979), xxi.

5. Marina L. Gorlach, Jeffrey H. Taylor, and Leslie A. Taylor, "The Hebrew Translations of Boethius's *De Consolatione Philosophiae*," in *Vernacular Traditions of Boethius's* De Consolatione Philosophiae, ed. Noel Harold Kaylor Jr. and Philip Edward Phillips (Kalamazoo, MI: Medieval Institute Publications, 2016), 125–42; Mauro Zonta, "Medieval Hebrew Translations of Philosophical

produced not in Ashkenaz but in the communities of southern France and Spain and across the Mediterranean in the Near East.

Medieval Jewish authors engaged in translation of secular materials in the south, especially in the realms of science and medicine, but they also participated in translating entertaining folktales and fables. In thirteenth-century Toledo, Jacob ben Eleazer translated *Kalila we-Dimna*, a widely attested collection of fables that appears in medieval Romance languages, Arabic, and Hebrew.[6] The story's titular characters are jackals in the role of courtiers, who tell stories to their king (a lion) to teach him proper kingly behavior.

Kalila we-Dimna was originally translated from Persian to Arabic, and thereafter transmitted to the entire Western European world, by a Zoroastrian convert to Islam, Abdallah ibn al-Muqaffa'.[7] John of Capua translated the popular Arabic collection of folktales *Kalila we-Dimna* from an early thirteenth-century Hebrew version. His Latin version, *Directorium humanae vitae, alias parabola antiquorum sapientum* (The Guide of Human Life, or the Proverbs of the Ancient Sages), became the exemplar for many subsequent vernacular translations.[8] Although we lack the medieval text that John of Capua used, the two parallel routes of Hebrew circulation (via John of Capua's version and via Jacob ben Eleazer) suggest a widespread popularity. The fourteenth-century Provençal-Hebrew author, Kalonymus ben Kalonymus, mentions it dismissively as a text lacking in seriousness.[9]

---

and Scientific Texts: A Chronological Table," in *Science in Medieval Jewish Cultures*, ed. Gad Freudenthal (Cambridge: Cambridge University Press, 2012), 17–73; Steven Harvey, "The Introductions of Thirteenth-Century Arabic-to-Hebrew Translators of Philosophic and Scientific Texts," in *Vehicles of Transmission, Translation, and Transformation in Medieval Textual Culture*, ed. Robert Wisnovsky, Faith Wallis, Jamie C. Fumo, and Carlos Fraenkel, vol. 4 (Turnhout: Brepols, 2011), 223–34; Abraham Solomon Halkin and Angel Saenz-Badillos, "Translation and Translators," in *Encyclopaedia Judaica*, ed. Michael Berenbaum and Fred Skolnik, vol. 20 (Detroit, MI: Macmillan Reference, 2007), 94–102; Jonathan Decter, "The Rendering of Qur'anic Quotations in Hebrew Translations of Islamic Texts," *Jewish Quarterly Review* 96, no. 3 (Summer 2006): 336–58.

6. J. Derenbourg, *Deux Versions Hebraique Du Livre de Kalilah et Dimnah* (Paris: Vieweg, 1881); Angeles Navarro Peiro, "La Versión Hebrea de 'Calila y Dimna' de Ya'aqob Ben El'azar," *Jewish Studies at the Turn of the Twentieth Century* 1 (1999): 468–75; Revital Refael-Vivante, "The Influence of 'Kalila and Dimna' on Medieval Hebrew Fable Literature," in *Énoncés Sapientiels et Littérature Exemplaire*, ed. Marie-Sol Ortolá (Lorraine, France: Presses Universitaires de Lorraine, 2013), 45–79.

7. David A. Wacks, "The Performativity of Ibn Al-Muqaffa's Kalīla Wa-Dimna and Al-Maqāmāt Al-Luzūmiyya of Al-Saraqustī," *Journal of Arabic Literature* 34, no. 1/2 (April 2003): 181–82.

8. John of Capua, *Directorium vitae humanae alias parabola antiquorum sapientum: version latine du livre de Kalilah et Dimnah, 1er fascicule*, ed. Joseph Derenbourg (Paris: Vieweg, 1887).

9. Kalonymus ben Kalonymus, *Iggeret Ba'alei Hayyim*, ed. Yisrael Toporovsky (Jerusalem: Mossad ha-Rav Kook, 1949); Morris Epstein, ed. and trans., *Tales of Sendebar* (Philadelphia: Jewish Publication Society, 1967), 117.

Kalonymus similarly casts judgment on another medieval Hebrew text, *Mishle Sendebar* (Tales of Sendebar). This folktale collection appears in Ashkenaz by the thirteenth century, when we find a copy of *Mishle Sendebar* in Oxford, Bodl. 135, which also contains *Mishle Shuʿalim* (Fox Fables) and *Sefer ha-Maʿasim* (Book of Tales). It was likely translated from Arabic in the early Middle Ages in the Near East.[10] In addition to Arabic, the premedieval Eastern versions appear in Syriac, Greek, and Persian.[11] By the late medieval period, a version of the story reached the wider European community as the *Seven Sages of Rome*, translated into French, Middle English, and German.[12] A Yiddish version also enjoyed popularity in the sixteenth century.[13]

The story of *Mishle Sendebar* tells of a king whose son studies under the mentorship of a sage (named Sindibad, or Sendebar in Hebrew). The sage warns the son that he is in grave danger unless he remains silent for one week, which he does. The unaware king, desperate to break his son's silence, sends one of his wives to persuade the prince to talk. The wife attempts to seduce the prince, however, although he rebuffs her advances. She claims that he raped her, an accusation that causes the prince to be sentenced to death. Each of the king's seven advisers then tells the king stories detailing the treacheries of women to persuade him of the wife's own treachery, although the wife has a counterstory about the treacheries of sons in return. At the end of the seven days, the prince breaks his silence, and the queen receives her punishment. In the Hebrew *Mishle Sendebar*, Sendebar and the king grant her a pardon.

In *Mishle Sendebar*, as well as in the *Kalila we-Dimna* tradition, the characters and plot are devoid of any religious features. Even after the translation process from Arabic to Hebrew, the characters do not themselves become Jewish; their names and plot features scarcely change. The story imparts its ambiguous moral lessons on its readers

10. Morris Epstein, "'Mishle Sendebar': New Light on the Transmission of Folklore from East to West," *Proceedings of the American Academy for Jewish Research* 27 (1958): 1–17, https://doi.org/10.2307/3622494.

11. Epstein, *Tales of Sendebar*, 1–11.

12. Killis Campbell, ed., *The Seven Sages of Rome* (Boston: Ginn, 1907); Hans R. Runte, J. Keith Wikeley, and Anthony J. Farrell, eds., *The Seven Sages of Rome and the Book of Sindbad: An Analytical Bibliography* (New York: Garland, 1984); Mary B. Speer, ed., *Le Roman Des Sept Sages de Rome : A Critical Edition of the Two Verse Redactions of a Twelfth-Century Romance* (Lexington, KY: French Forum, 1989); Ralf-Henning Steinmetz, ed., *Die Historia von Den Sieben Weisen Meistern Und Dem Kaiser Diocletianus* (Tübingen: Niemeyer, 2001).

13. Ruth von Bernuth, "A Friend in Need Is a Friend Indeed? Friendship, Love, and Loyalty in the Yiddish Seven Sages of Rome," in *Medieval and Early Modern Jewish Romance*, ed. Caroline Gruenbaum and Annegret Oehme (Kalamazoo, MI: Arc Humanities, 2023), 129–52.

about women's fickleness and the importance of familial bonds through the Hebrew language but not through any other aspects of Jewish culture.

As in the Hebrew versions of *Kalila* and *Sendebar*, Berechiah ha-Nakdan conveys his non-Jewish source material as moralistic Hebrew wisdom in the form of fables. Berechiah ha-Nakdan is unique among all the other translated fables, folktales, and wisdom collections mentioned earlier in this chapter for two reasons: (1) he produces his translation in Ashkenaz, and (2) he translates his material not from Arabic but from French.

Mishle Shu'alim (literally Fox Fables) contains over one hundred animal fables in rhymed Hebrew prose.[14] These fables follow the Aesopic tradition of animals whose disputes and comportment mirror those of humans. In rabbinic language, the term "fox fables" refers not only to fables featuring foxes but to animal fables in general. According to the Talmud, foxes are associated with fable-telling, as in b. Berakhot 61b, which features R. Akiva telling a fable about a fox and a fish. The ancient rabbi Meir apparently knew three hundred fox fables.[15] In post-Talmudic rabbinic narratives, Bar Kappara is said to have recited three hundred fables, and another parable tells of a fable-reciting fox.[16] The notable French exegete and commentator Rashi (Rabbi Solomon ben Isaac, 1040–1105) uses a fable about a fox in his commentary on BT Sanhedrin 38b.[17]

Each of Berechiah's fables ends with a short summary or epimythium that bridges the gap between the animal world and the human world, often completed by a biblical, philosophizing or Talmudic citation in verse, no more than a few lines long. Most of these fables are translated from Old French or Latin sources, but Berechiah modifies them to include biblical and rabbinic language, and contemporaneous adages. The author follows the exhortation of the pietistic authors of *Sefer Ḥasidim* in not citing his French source, but the influence from Marie de France is unmistakable, with some borrowing from Latinate

14. Berechiah ben Natronai Ha-Nakdan, *Mishlei Shualim*, ed. A. M. Habermann (Tel Aviv: Schocken, 1946); Berechiah ben Natronai Ha-Nakdan, *Fables of a Jewish Aesop: Translated from the Fox Fables of Berechiah Ha-Nakdan*, trans. Moses Hadas (New York: Columbia University Press, 1967). Occasionally, I refer to Hadas's translation and have made silent emendations as needed.

15. Babylonian Talmud Sanhedrin 38b–39b.

16. Vayikra Rabba 28.2; Bereshit Rabba 78.7; David Stern, *Parables in Midrash: Narrative and Exegesis in Rabbinic Literature* (Cambridge, MA: Harvard University Press, 1991), 4, 46–47.

17. Zipporah Shukry, "The Wolf and the Fox in the Well," *Laographia* 22 (1964): 491–97.

sources either directly or indirectly via Old French.[18] Many of his fables represent a reworking from Marie's *Ysopet*, a collection of animal fables that she, in turn, translated to Anglo-Norman French from the Aesopic tradition in the late twelfth century.[19]

In his prologue, Berechiah directs his text toward the wealthy in his community, those who are "longing for silver and lovers of gold" (כוספי כסף ואוהבי זהב) but "fear extending a hand for wealth" (היראים לשלוח יד בהונם).[20] It is these wealthy, unmotivated men who will learn from his didactic fables. He writes,

> In the island of the sea is a congregation bereft of intelligence,
> crowned with scorn, and its family debased.
> The ear of its many rich is uncircumcised,
> but to the one who asks, and to the one who gives, [it is] circumcised.[21]

The phrase "uncircumcised ears" does not refer to those people who were not circumcised physically but rather to the uneducated (as in Jeremiah 6:10: To whom shall I speak and give warning, that they may hear? Behold, their ear is dull [i.e., their ear is uncircumcised], and they cannot attend; behold, the word of the Lord is become unto them a reproach, they have no delight in it). His prologue attacks the wealthy communities who have, according to this biblical reference, lost sight of their covenant with God. Scholars have suggested that the "island of sea" refers to England, where Berechiah may have resided, but without any other concrete evidence.[22] His reference to the immoral wealthy could easily refer to his contemporaneous Jewish community of northern France, which boasted several wealthy members.[23]

Several of Berechiah's fables remind us that the wealthy may not always remain so, a reality for contemporaneous Jews of medieval northern Europe. Jewish communities in thirteenth-century England and northern France suffered through unpredictable waves of economic

18. Tovi Bibring, "Le chemin corrigé: Moralités inédites dans la fable 'La souris et la grenouille' de Marie de France et 'Rat avec Rainette et Aigle' de Berekiah Hanaqdan," in *Le récit exemplaire: 1200–1800*, ed. Véronique Duché-Gavet and Madeleine Jeay, Colloques, congrès et conférences sur la Renaissance européenne 67 (Paris: Classiques Garnier, 2011), 40–42.

19. Marie de France, *Fables*, ed. Harriet Spiegel (Toronto: University of Toronto Press, 1987).

20. Ha-Nakdan, *Mishlei Shualim*, 4–5.

21. Ha-Nakdan, *Mishlei Shualim*, 5.

22. Ha-Nakdan, *Mishlei Shualim*, 3.

23. Ruth Nisse, *Jacob's Shipwreck: Diaspora, Translation, and Jewish-Christian Relations in Medieval England* (Ithaca, NY: Cornell University Press, 2017), 91–93.

persecution and periodic exile.[24] He writes of the wheel of fortune in his prologue, which makes the wealthy poor. In his first fable, a powerful lion becomes sickly, and the inferior creatures take their revenge by attacking him in his weakness. When he recovers his strength, he despondently recalls how his counselors had become his enemies, and his slaves had turned against him. Berechiah summarizes the fable: "This is a parable about a man who is filled with wealth and honor, and whose neighbors serve him. But when a day of misfortune comes that he becomes impoverished and down-trodden (מטה ידו), they will stand away from his affliction, separate from him and remove his righteousness from him. They will be fed up with him whom they had chosen."[25] His fable reminds his readers of the fickleness of wealth—all the more reason to treat the lowly with respect.

Every fable in *Mishle Shuʿalim* addresses social issues stemming from power, wealth, or vices that affect the wealthy. These specific concerns about wealth and authority in a didactic text designate it clearly and unequivocally as part of the literary subgenre of mirrors for princes. These manuals exist in the eastern and the western medieval world in disparate languages and religious cultures.[26] They propose to teach moral behavior to rulers through stories, often with political undertones. The ultimate aim is to teach princes and members of the upper echelon of society about how to administer justice and treat their subjects equitably.[27]

A traditional mirror-for-princes subgenre is exemplified by the Arabic text by al-Ghazālī (d.1111), *Nasīhat al-Mulūk* (Counsel for Kings), which gives birth to the scholarly tendency to call this advice literature when it appears in Middle Eastern texts. The paradigmatic Latin example appears in John of Salisbury's twelfth-century *Policraticus*, which teaches leadership strategies and is considered the first political science treatise in medieval Europe.[28] We see another example of advice litera-

24. Robin R. Mundill, *The King's Jews: Money, Massacre and Exodus in Medieval England* (London: Continuum, 2010), 21–42, 145–66.

25. Ha-Nakdan, *Mishlei Shualim*, 7.

26. Linda T. Darling, "Mirrors for Princes in Europe and the Middle East: A Case of Historiographical Incommensurability," in *East Meets West in the Middle Ages and Early Modern Times: Transcultural Experiences in the Premodern World*, ed. Albrecht Classen (Berlin: de Gruyter, 2013), 223–42, https://www.academia.edu/4117152/Mirrors_for_Princes_in_Europe_and_the_Middle_East_A_Case_of_Historiographical_Incommensurability.

27. Charles Brucker, "The Fables of Marie de France and the Mirror of Princes," in *A Companion to Marie de France*, ed. Logan E. Whalen (Leiden: Brill, 2014), 226.

28. Karen K. Jambeck, "The 'Fables' of Marie de France: A Mirror of Princes," in *In Quest of Marie de France: A Twelfth-Century Poet*, ed. Chantal Anne-Marie Maréchal (Lewiston, NY: Mellen, 1992), 65.

ture, or mirror for princes, in *Kalila we-Dimna*. The jackals' stories often address a political issue relevant to the king's rule. Although we do not have definitive dates for the text's translation into Hebrew, the itinerant writer Abraham Ibn Ezra refers to the work in the twelfth century.[29] Berechiah was certainly familiar with the text in either written or oral form because he crossed paths with Ibn Ezra and other Arabic-reading writers in northern Europe and on his own travels south.[30] A Hebrew version of *Kalila we-Dimna* was also bound with the same thirteenth-century manuscript that contains one of the earliest copies of Berechiah's fables, Bodl. Or. 135.[31]

Marie de France continually refers to the same didactic tenets in her text and directs her advice to the wealthy. The similarities to the *Policraticus* have led scholars to consider the *Ysopet* as a mirror for princes as well.[32] In her prologue, she compares her text to the correspondence by the emperor Romulus, who writes to his son with advice on how to govern properly. She writes, "Romulus, who was emperor / Wrote to his son, handing out to him / And showing him through examples / How he should be guarded himself / Against the deceitful ways of human beings."[33]

Marie's own examples, stories, and their accompanying morals reflect a conscious engagement with this literary subgenre. Marie promotes ideals in accordance with the behavior specified in the *Policraticus*, including warnings against vices and promotion of virtues.[34] She uses vocabulary of

29. Dan Ben-Amos, "Jewish Folk Literature," *Oral Tradition* 14 (1999): 180.

30. Gad Freudenthal and Jean-Marc Mandosio, "Old French into Hebrew in Twelfth-Century Tsarfat: Medieval Hebrew Versions of Marbode's Lapidary," *Aleph* 14, no. 1 (January 2014): 11–187; Gad Freudenthal, "Abraham Ibn Ezra and Judah Ibn Tibbon as Cultural Intermediaries: Early Stages in the Introduction of Non-Rabbinic Learning into Provence in the Mid-Twelfth Century," in *Exchange and Transmission across Cultural Boundaries: Philosophy, Mysticism and Science in the Mediterranean World = Yeda' Ḥotseh Gevulot Tarbut: Filosofyah, Misṭiḳah u-Mada' Be-Agan Ha-Yam Ha-Tikhon*, ed. Haggai Ben-Shammai, Shaul Shaked, Sarah Stroumsa, and Shlomo Pines (Jerusalem: Israel Academy of Sciences and Humanities, 2013), 52–81.

31. Rella Kushelevsky, "R. Berechiah's Imprint on *Sefer Ha-Ma'asim*: The Reception of *Mishlei Shu'alim*," in *Berechiah Ben Natronai Ha-Naqdan's Works and Their Reception*, ed. Tamás Visi, Tovi Bibring, and Daniel Soukup (Turnhout: Brepols, 2019), 141–61.

32. Brucker, "The Fables of Marie de France and the Mirror of Princes," 223; Jambeck, "The 'Fables' of Marie de France."

33. Marie de France, *Fables*, 28:
Romulus, ki fu emperere
A sun fiz escrit, si manda
E par essample li mustra
Cum il se deüst cuntreguater
Que hum nel p[e]üst enginner.

34. Jambeck, "The 'Fables' of Marie de France," 66.

feudalism, such as *leialté* and *felunie* (loyalty and villainy), and *honur* and *deshonur* (honor and dishonor), which places her text firmly in a courtly sphere, another feature of the mirror-for-princes genre.[35] Rather than generalize about applying virtues to improve one's moral character, she aims for her readers to be rich or *Seigneurs*. Her ideal characters are wise and knowledgeable about philosophy, as the *Policraticus* demands for successful rulers.[36] Marie and her exemplar John of Salisbury urge their readers to be watchful and prudent. John of Salisbury writes that a prudent man often succeeds "because he is not forestalled by the snares of schemers, but advancing as it were along an invisible path, and not publishing what he purposes, he thus attains to the goal of his intention."[37]

Like Marie and John of Salisbury, Berechiah continually warns against greed, impudence, vanity, and envy and advocates loyalty, honor, courtesy, prudence, and respect. His fable "Viper and Man" contains a motif that is strikingly similar to John of Salisbury's insistence on prudence. In this story, a man and a viper become friends, but the viper is cautious of the man's love for him. As a test, the viper tells his friend that he will bring the man a treasure that the man cannot touch. The viper brings him an egg and leaves. The man consults with his wife and the two of them decide to open the egg to reveal the treasure—an egg yolk. When the viper returns to see the egg broken, his friend insists it was an accident. Not a gullible type, the viper terminates their friendship. Berechiah writes in the epimythium, "the moral is to keep your distance from a man who approaches for the sake of his silver and his gold. For when he is entrusted with his wealth, he will mislead him with his guile and deprive him of his soul for the sake of his silver and his wealth."[38] This fable argues for prudence when the rich befriend the poor.

He often intends his epimythia to apply to rich men in need of temperance. In "Dog, Cheese, and Water," a greedy dog has a chunk of cheese in his mouth. Upon spotting his reflection in the water, he wants to snatch up the second piece of cheese that he sees before him. When he opens his mouth to grab it, he loses his original piece of cheese to the water. Berechiah writes, "I have seen this characteristic in the man whose heart is full of desire. He is laden with silver and gold, and desiring all, loses all."[39] He adds on a verse adapted from Proverbs, and an explana-

35. Jambeck, "The 'Fables' of Marie de France," 66.
36. Jambeck, "The 'Fables' of Marie de France," 66–67.
37. Translated in Jambeck, "The 'Fables' of Marie de France," 68.
38. Ha-Nakdan, *Mishlei Shualim*, 86; Ha-Nakdan, *Fables of a Jewish Aesop*, 141.
39. Fable 5, כלב, גבינה ומים. Ha-Nakdan, *Mishlei Shualim*, 12.

tory poem that ends, "He thought to add to what was enough / And lost two days' worth of food."[40] The advice for the greedy rich man acts as a warning for those in positions of wealth who always crave more. Marie directs her wrath to the rich as well, as she does in "The Lion, the Sheep, and the Goat." She offers, "the rich man wishes to have honor / and doesn't care if he loses love. / If there is any gain to be shared / The rich will keep it all."[41] Berechiah scorns the rich in several fables, telling the poor to band together and subdue the rich ("Spider, King, Slave," no. 111)[42] and criticizing rich who speak ill of the poor ("Ant and Mouse," no. 110).[43] These less-than-complimentary tales reinforce the dangers of tyranny, both for those already in power and for those ascending.

In Berechiah's "The Rich Man and the Serpent," the author criticizes misuse of power and authority among the Jewish community.[44] In this fable, a rich man has the custom of providing milk and food for a serpent. One day, the man's anger leads him to berate and punish his community, including the serpent. The serpent ceases visiting the man's house. Meanwhile, the man loses his fortune and becomes troubled. He comes to the serpent to make amends, weeping before him, but the serpent refuses to reconcile with the man, citing the traumatic violence he experienced. Rather than consider the serpent as the cause of the rich man's wealth and his subsequent downfall, as his sources do, Berechiah instead blames the rich man's fall from grace on his own actions. Through this connection, Berechiah's story relates immediately to his—or any—community with men in positions of power who abuse their subjects.[45] Comparable themes appear in his fables featuring lions and foxes, animals who often represent authoritative figures in medieval Hebrew literature.[46]

In "Sun and Moon," Berechiah appears to direct his tale to the nonwealthy. The sun, "whose rule is at night," begs to have the moon as a companion, but the universe (היקום) denies the sun's request, insisting that the sun is already too powerful. Berechiah summarizes in his epimythium, "this parable is for a man who has wealth, riches, honor, and

---

40. חשב להוסיף ספקו ויגרע אכל להשיב נפשו יומים. Ha-Nakdan, *Mishlei Shualim*, 12.

41. Marie de France, *Fables*, 58.

42. Ha-Nakdan, *Mishlei Shualim*, 123.

43. Ha-Nakdan, *Mishlei Shualim*, 122.

44. Tovi Bibring, "Vengeance, Justice et Repentir dans la Fable 'Le Riche et le Serpent' de Berrechia Ben Natronaï Hankdan," in *La Fable Avant La Fontaine*, ed. Jeanne-Marie Boivin, Jacqueline Toulet-Cerquiglini, and Laurence Harf-Lancner (Paris: Droz, 2011), 247–58.

45. Bibring, "Vengeance, Justice et Repentir," 248–49.

46. Revital Refael-Vivante, "Of Lions and Foxes: Power and Rule in Hebrew Medieval Fables," *Revista de Paz y Conflictos*, no. 2 (2009): 24–43.

livestock, and seeks to add to what he already has . . . do not listen to him and add strength to his strength. We listen to the words of wise Solomon [Prov.22:16]: 'one may give to the rich, yet will want come.'"[47] Berechiah really aims the tale at other wealthy figures, comparable to the other components of the universe who reject the sun's plea. Berechiah urges his readers not to give more money to those who already have; to head this advice, his readers must be in a stable financial position where they can afford financial exchanges. The genre of mirror for princes does not direct itself literally at kings but more generally to those in positions of power or wealth.

The status of the Christian nobility and the Jewish elites are strikingly similar. While the Christian nobility usually gained their wealth through positions of power in relation to the ruling authority, Jewish elites were also wealthy members of the community in authoritative positions. Mostly wealthy, educated merchants, these Jewish men established their authority as leaders in the internal community, the *kehillah*. The autonomous *kehillah* made legal decisions on behalf of the Jewish community.[48] In larger communities, the *kehillot* included rabbinic academies and educational institutions. The hierarchical divisions between the merchants or community leaders and their associates replicated the Christian feudal system.[49] Just like the wealthy princes who benefitted from the instructional manuals, the literate, educated Jewish body would have been wealthy as well.[50]

Berechiah directs his tales toward the Jewish elite, who were roughly equivalent to the feudal elite, through emulation of Marie's courtly language, as in "Dog, Ewe, Lion, Wolf, Bear." In this fable, a dog, a lion, and an eagle conspire to discredit a sheep and testify falsely against her; the poor sheep then dies bereft. Having waited for her demise, the eagle and lion eagerly tear into the sheep's body. Berechiah advises his readers against making false testimony, and writes, "they that wreak evil lord it over him / His efforts win him no profit; / Though armed with helmet and coat of mail, they avail him not. / They that measure wealth by

47. Ha-Nakdan, *Mishlei Shualim*, 85.

48. Louis Finkelstein, *Jewish Self-Government in the Middle Ages* (New York: Jewish Theological Seminary of America, 1924).

49. Jeffrey Woolf, "Communal and Religious Organization," in *The Cambridge History of Judaism*, ed. Robert Chazan (Cambridge: Cambridge University Press, 2018), 382.

50. Woolf, "Communal and Religious Organization," 382; Ephraim Kanarfogel, *Jewish Education and Society in the High Middle Ages* (Detroit, MI: Wayne State University Press, 2007), 20–23, 92, 94, 97.

handfuls / See him descend never to rise."[51] The term "coat of mail" (שריון) refers to heavy, expensive body armor worn by knights. Although he borrows from Marie's "The Dog and the Ewe," the reference to battle armor is original. The pseudo-knightly figures in Berechiah's epimythium give this fable a courtly air, referencing a popular French literary genre about which he was certainly aware. As we learn in this book (see, especially, chapters 2 and 4), medieval northern European Jews enjoyed hearing stories about knights and decorated their manuscripts with courtly images.[52]

In his "A Terrible and Formidable Knight," Berechiah includes an entire fable about a knight (פרש) who despondently throws all his weapons into the flames after he becomes unsuccessful on the battlefield. When he begins to throw his clarion (שופר) into the flames, his wife asks him what he is doing. He responds that the clarion, as the horn that begins a battle, is the instigator of bloodshed and throws it in the fire. Berechiah's source for this story is unknown.[53] The clarion is a shofar, a ram's horn used in the Bible, and in Jewish tradition, for ceremonies and holidays, and in battle (i.e., Joshua 6:1–5, Jeremiah 4:5, 19, 21). Berechiah's knight subverts the sanctity of the shofar by burning it, treating the shofar as a feudal weapon inciting violence rather than the biblical weapon that ushers in a holy battle of Israelites against their enemies. Berechiah firmly situates the story in a secularized, courtly environment of knights in battle, not one connected to the divinely sanctioned pursuits of the ancient Israelites.

Through the influence of Marie's secular tales, as well as the Arabic story collections he knew, Berechiah repurposes the genre of Hebrew folktales as a universal guide to ethical behavior for the wealthy. His text becomes a didactic mirror for princes with an emphasis on the personal relationship between the subject and his ruler. Marie's influence on Berechiah can be seen through his deemphasis on Jewish piety throughout his collection.

---

51. Ha-Nakdan, *Fables of a Jewish Aesop*, 20; Ha-Nakdan, *Mishlei Shualim*, 15.

52. See, for example, the Hebrew Ivan G. Marcus, "Why Is This Knight Different? A Jewish Self-Representation in Medieval Europe," in *Tov Elem—Memory, Community and Gender in Medieval and Early Jewish Societies: Essays in Honor of Robert Bonfil*, ed. Elisheva Baumgarten, Amnon Raz-Krakotzkin, and Roni Weinstein (Jerusalem: Bialik Institute, 2011), 139–52; Sara Offenberg, "Jacob the Knight in Ezekiel's Chariot: Imagined Identity in a Micrography Decoration of an Ashkenazic Bible," *AJS Review* 40, no. 1 (April 2016): 1–16.

53. Schwarzbaum, *The Mishle Shu'alim (Fox Fables)*, 444–46.

Through a reading of the *Ysopet* as a mirror for princes, we understand why there is a lack of divine role in most of Marie's fables—rulers, not God, take responsibility for their actions. Although *Ysopet* still contains Christian themes, God appears as a major feature in only four of Marie's fables: "The Hermit and the Peasant," "The Peasant Who Prayed for a Horse," "The Peasant Who Prayed for His Wife and Children," and "The Rich Man Who Wished to Cross the Sea."[54] In three of these, "The Hermit," "The Peasant Who Prayed for a Horse," and "The Rich Man Who Crossed the Sea," Marie tells her readers through the fables that one ought to trust God's will.[55] At the end of "The Peasant Who Prayed for a Horse," the epilogue teaches:

> No one should pray, then
> To have more than what he needs
> Rather, keep what God has given
> Which will suffice with full confidence.[56]

In "The Rich Man Who Wished to Cross the Sea," the man prays to God for his ship to come back to shore, but he continues to drift farther out. Eventually he prays for God to do his own will (*dist Deus fetes vostre pleisir*). After those words, he came to land exactly where he had wanted. Marie concludes:

> A wise man should be reasonable
> In praying to the omnipotent God
> Who does his will for him
> From this something great can come.
> God knows better what we need,
> Than hearts, which ebb and flow.[57]

Marie urges her readers to act morally when praying and to respect God's authority as a decision maker. The epilogue also relates to greed,

---

54. At a later age, Marie appears to have become more religious in her writing and in her personal life. She wrote *L'Espurgatoire Seint Patriz* (The Legend of the Purgatory of Saint Patrick) and, allegedly, *La Vie Seinte Audree* (The Life of Saint Audrey), two hagiographical texts. See chapter 5 in Logan E. Whalen, *Marie de France and the Poetics of Memory* (Washington, DC: Catholic University of America Press, 2008), 137–74.

55. Sahar Amer reads one of Marie's stories, "The Hermit and the Peasant," with a feminist lens, based on Marie's theological interpretation of the story of Adam and Eve. Sahar Amer, "Marie de France Rewrites Genesis: The Image of Woman in Marie de France's Fables," *Neophilologus* 81, no. 4 (October 1997): 489–99.

56. Marie de France, *Fables*, 160.

57. Marie de France, *Fables*, 252.

as with many of her fables, admonishing those who crave for more than they are allotted by God.

The moral of "The Peasant Who Prayed for His Wife and Children" emphasizes instead the interpersonal relationships associated with prayer rather than the godly relationship. In this story, a peasant is angry at the way that another peasant is praying too loudly for his family. The peasant curses the other's family. The epilogue reads, "This example wishes to say / That everyone should pray in such a way / That is agreeable to the people / And that is acceptable to God."[58]

Marie does not fault the peasant who curses the other's (innocent) family; rather, she blames the loud peasant for disturbing the other. Both peasants' interactions with God are inappropriate, with one peasant speaking too loudly and the other peasant cursing unnecessarily. Only the peasant speaking loudly receives a punishment. While cursing an innocent family should be a punishable offense and would seem to disturb God, the true sin is praying too loudly and disturbing *others*. In this story, the interpersonal relationship between people at prayer takes precedence over the divine relationship.

Because of Berechiah's adoption of the mirror-for-princes subgenre and influence from the non-Jewish source *Ysopet*, he too downplays God's presence, giving his text a secularized tone that is highly unusual in the Jewish literary spheres of northern Europe. The epilogues of *Sefer ha-Ma'asim* emphasize God's presence as the ultimate reward giver. But Berechiah departs from the expectations of medieval Hebrew folktale collections in the style of *Sefer ha-Ma'asim*: most notably, Berechiah's folktales do not reward piety. In fact, God as a central component to the idea of reward in the traditional Hebrew didactic genre does not figure for Berechiah in any meaningful way. Even a parable about a graven image does not engage with the biblical commandment not to make statutes but rather focuses on the relationship between the principal characters. In this fable, "Image and Man," a carver fashions a beautiful colored statue. Another man wishes to buy the statue to use as a gravestone, but the statue implores its creator not to sell it for that purpose: "I am yours, and you are my restrainer, I am clay, and you are my creator. And in your hands is all my spirit and my glory, to exchange my shame for my honor. Your hands have molded me and made me."[59]

58. Marie de France, *Fables*, 161.

59. Ha-Nakdan, *Mishlei Shualim*, 103.

The verses without a doubt refer to God's creation of man, as in the comparable biblical verses in which God has the role of physical maker of man: "The Lord God formed man of the dust of the ground" (Genesis 2:7); "we are clay, and you are the potter" (Isaiah 64:8); and "your hands have made me and fashioned me" (Psalms 116:73). One might assume that the fable refers to one's devotion to his creator, that is, God. Instead, Berechiah writes in his epimythium, "the moral is this: to flatter everyone whose hand gains power against you, and to whisper secrets to him to draw his heart toward you."[60] The moral does not refer to God but to the relationship between those in lower positions of power and their overseers. He continues, quoting the Talmud, "it is permitted to flatter wicked people in this world."[61] Despite a simple connection between that story and the Jewish tradition of banning idolatry, Berechiah chooses not to engage with piety. His authorial decision to avoid a biblical or pious moral parallels similar omissions in *Melekh Artus* (King Arthur), as will be seen in chapter 4.

The moral to "Viper and Man" ends with Berechiah's summary of advice specifically aimed at the wealthy. Several themes in the story relate to the story of the immoral serpent in Genesis—and yet, in Berechiah's version, the serpent is the *exemplary* character. In Genesis 3, the serpent cajoles the woman into eating the forbidden fruit, and the wife persuades her husband to follow suit; in "Viper and Man," the husband and wife conspire together to open the forbidden treasure. The description of the man as acting "with his guile" (בערמתו) recalls the description of the serpent in Genesis 3:1 as cunning or sly (ערום). Berechiah writes in his explanatory poem at the end, relating his own personal experience to the deceit of the man, "I found evil in him I thought a friend / On a good day, and at an evil time, I tried him."[62] He mirrors the language of the snake's appeal to Eve, "for God knows that in the day you eat thereof, then your eyes shall be opened, and you shall be as God, knowing good and evil" (Genesis 3:5), and God's rebuke to Adam, "Behold, the man is become as one of us, to know good and evil" (Genesis 3:22). Within the context of "Viper and Man," the reference to good and evil makes little sense. Using Genesis as a guide, however, we see a new distinction between good and evil based on human action. Eating the fruit directly

60. Ha-Nakdan, *Mishlei Shualim*, 103.
61. Babylonian Talmud Sotah 41b. Ha-Nakdan, *Mishlei Shualim*, 103.
62. Ha-Nakdan, *Mishlei Shualim*, 86.

contradicts God's prohibition; Adam and Eve act with the human impulses of curiosity, desire, and gullibility, impulses shared by the characters in the fable.

In "Viper and Man," the man and woman are ashamed of their decision (יבשו ממועצותיהם), but in Genesis 2:25, they are not ashamed of their nakedness (לא יתבששו) until they eat the fruit. The figures in "Viper and Man" are already exposed to the good and evil circumstances in which they live, allowing them to act with evil intent. Their regret stems not from a place of genuine remorse because the man subsequently dissimulates to the viper about the broken egg. Instead, their regret simply reflects the reality of living in a world in which they must make immoral decisions. It is not regret that leads them to repent.

Despite some attempts to read Berechiah's fables as anti-Christian polemic, the text does not overtly refer to Christians, Christianity, or spiritual chaos within the Jewish community. Ruth Nisse has firmly placed Berechiah in England and emphasizes his scathing attack on his community's decline into corruption in the entire text of the fables.[63] But Nisse overstates the references to England in *Mishle Shu'alim*, such as when she adds the word "England" to two references where it does not appear in the original text.[64] In her reading, Berechiah blames the corrupt English Jews for the attacks on their community in York in 1189 and 1190. By the middle of the thirteenth century, English Jewry suffered from family upheavals, prison sentences for coin clipping, and high rates of conversions.[65] Another reading sees Berechiah attacking the Jews of England for a personal issue; perhaps they were critical of his work.[66]

But read within the literary and social context of Berechiah's work, these analyses are unconvincing. His claims to reform the English community must be tempered by a realization that actions tied to their individual Jewish identity is not an issue he addresses in the fables. In the late twelfth century or early thirteenth century when Berechiah wrote,

---

63. Nisse, *Jacob's Shipwreck*, chap. 3, 75–101.

64. Nisse, *Jacob's Shipwreck*, 91.

65. Robert C. Stacey, "The Conversion of Jews to Christianity in Thirteenth-Century England," *Speculum* 67, no. 2 (April 1992): 263–83. See also the masterful study about medieval English Jewry: Adrienne Williams Boyarin, *The Christian Jew and the Unmarked Jewess: The Polemics of Sameness in Medieval English Anti-Judaism* (Philadelphia: University of Pennsylvania Press, 2020).

66. Norman Golb, *The Jews in Medieval Normandy: A Social and Intellectual History* (Cambridge: Cambridge University Press, 1998), 171.

conversion to Christianity was not worrisome in England, although it occurred in small measure. It was not until 1232, when royal and ecclesiastical authorities began conversionary tactics, that English Jewry underwent large-scale conversions.[67] A late thirteenth-century English writer, Meir of Norwich, addressed these concerns in his liturgical poem, "Put a Curse on My Enemy," which tells of the persecutions he and his community experienced.[68] Instead of concerns about his community's spiritual health, the issues Berechiah sees with the Jewish community are the same that plagued Marie de France, the entire reason for her writing, and must be understood within a literary context of dramatization and hyperbole. These sins include greed, immodesty, lack of empathy, and witlessness.

Although his Jewish contemporaries may have been more susceptible than most to these sins, we have no way of knowing. He does not refer specifically to conversion or piety as a motivating factor in his writing. In other words, there appears to be nothing specifically aimed at English Jews in his text that could not be applied to any well-off medieval community that struggled with maintaining ethical behavior. Eli Yassif reads against a recent analysis of the "Elephant and the Man in the Field" as anti-Christian polemic, seeing instead a representation of universal wisdom rather than a specific attack against unmentioned Christian enemies.[69] Another article explores fables of lions and their subordinates not in terms of polemical power struggles but in terms of universal fables on authority.[70]

Unlike the ethical prescriptions offered by *Sefer ha-Ma'asim* and *Sefer Ḥasidim*, two near-contemporaneous Hebrew texts that offer ethical teachings, Berechiah's fables do not overtly advocate for Jewish observance. Biblical references are extraneous to the moral, and references to Talmud or rabbinic law are rare. He uses only one fable drawn from the Talmud, a story about Rabbi Akiva and "The Fox and the Fish,"

---

67. Stacey, "The Conversion of Jews to Christianity in Thirteenth-Century England," 267.

68. There is a translation and edition in Susan L. Einbinder, "Meir b. Elijah of Norwich: Persecution and Poetry among Medieval English Jews," *Journal of Medieval History* 26, no. 2 (2000): 153–55. See also Meir's entire collection of poetry translated in Meir of Norwich, *Into the Light: The Medieval Hebrew Poetry of Meir of Norwich*, ed. Ellman Crasnow and Bente Elsworth, trans. Keiron Pim (Norwich: East Publishing, 2013).

69. Eli Yassif, "Storytelling and Meaning: Theory and Practice of Narrative Variants in Religious Texts," in *Religious Stories in Transformation: Conflict, Revision and Reception*, ed. Alberdina Houtman, Tamar Kadari, Marcel Poorthuis, and Vered Tohar (Leiden: Brill, 2016), 17.

70. Refael-Vivante, "Of Lions and Foxes."

which he universalizes by removing it from its Jewish context.[71] As Yassif argues, in the "The Fox and the Fish," despite its clear Talmudic origins, Berechiah's version excises the rabbinic phraseology and original anti-Roman polemical moral.[72] Yassif's analysis is supported when we examine the entire *Mishle Shu'alim* text, in which Berechiah never references Jewish observance (such as Shabbat, keeping kosher, or keeping purity laws) as a moral necessity. However, Berechiah's use of a Jewish language (Hebrew) and his use of common medieval Jewish adages and precepts nonetheless establish his text as one designated exclusively for a Jewish community.

In this way, Berechiah's fables are more comparable to the universal folktale collections *Mishle Sendebar*, or *Kalila we-Dimna*, which reached audiences from the Middle East to Western Europe in the medieval period.[73] The stories in those texts do not refer to religion or faith; rather, they describe animals or stock characters in relatable, timeless situations. Rather than rely on religious obligations as the source of ethical behavior for the wealthy, Berechiah inserts universal wisdom as his ethical authority, bypassing the Jewish God and Jewish scripture entirely. God does not determine ethical behavior—humans and human relationships do.

The moral messages of *Mishle Shu'alim* direct it toward a wealthy readership in need of guidance. We are again struck by his process of translating from French into Hebrew. To reach a wider audience, either the wealthy elite read his fables in Hebrew, or the fables were read out loud in French. In any case, the decision to write for this demographic underscores the existence of a receptive middle class, literate enough to appreciate the stories, whether read out loud or read at home, but not part of a rabbinic circle.

Reception of his fables had changed by the sixteenth century, when *Mishle Shu'alim* was translated into the popular vernacular of Yiddish and printed. In the 1583 printing of this Yiddish version, the title page describes the book as: "*Sefer Mishlei Shu'alim*, one hundred thirty-six fables, 'full of all good things' [Deuteronomy 6:11, Nehemiah 9:25], ethical values

71. Yassif, "Storytelling and Meaning."

72. Yassif, "Storytelling and Meaning," 15–16.

73. Refael-Vivante, "The Influence of 'Kalila and Dimna'"; Marianne Marroum, "'Kalila Wa Dimna': Inception, Appropriation, and Transmimesis," *Comparative Literature Studies* 48, no. 4 (December 2011): 512–40; Sharon Kinoshita, "Translatio/n, Empire, and the Worlding of Medieval Literature: The Travels of Kalila Wa Dimna," *Postcolonial Studies* 11, no. 4 (December 2008): 371–85; Epstein, *Tales of Sendebar*.

and morals, to give prudence to the simple and knowledge and discretion to young men [ref. Prov. 1:4]. Translated from Hebrew to Ashkenaz [Yiddish] by Koppelman from Brisk. Printed in Breisgau in the year [5]343 [1583]."[74]

In its Yiddish form, *Mishle Shu'alim* can easily impart "prudence to the simple" and "discretion to young men." In Hebrew, however, Berechiah cannot so easily reach that demographic audience. Instead, he straddles a middle ground between the French-speaking masses and the Hebrew-reading elite. As a final example of Berechiah's widespread appeal, a bilingual Latin-Hebrew version of *Mishle Shu'alim* was published in 1661 in Prague by Melchior Hanel, a Jesuit intellectual with various linguistic interests.[75] By the seventeenth century, then, the fables of *Mishle Shu'alim* had come full circle. From the Latin and Greek Aesopic tradition to Marie de France's French *Ysopet*, written in the language spoken by the medieval Jews of northern French; to Berechiah's Hebrew text for a wealthy, literate Jewish readership; to Yiddish, the spoken language of the early modern Jews of Ashkenaz; and finally, to Latin for a Christian audience, this singular collection of secular fables seamlessly suits several distinct medieval audiences.

74. Marvin J. Heller, *Studies in the Making of the Early Hebrew Book* (Leiden: Brill, 2007), 143.

75. Daniel Soukup, "Melchior Hanel (1627–1689) and His Latin Translation of Mishlei Shu'alim in the Context of the Respublica Litteraria," in *Berechiah Ben Natronai Ha-Naqdan's Works and Their Reception*, ed. Tamás Visi, Tovi Bibring, and Daniel Soukup (Turnhout: Brepols, 2019), 205–19, https://doi.org/10.1484/M.BEHE-EB.5.117470.

Chapter 4

“Of Foolish Passion”

Chivalric Romance in Medieval Jewish Culture

Despite consisting of only seven incomplete folios, the thirteenth-century manuscript Vatican Urbinati Ebraici 48 is one of the most significant medieval literary texts of its kind. It tells the well-known medieval French story of King Arthur’s miraculous birth and relates Lancelot and Guinevere’s love affair as a reason for the destruction of King Arthur’s Round Table. But in this version, the characters speak Hebrew.[1] Translating from at least two Old French sources or perhaps from a copy of an existing Hebrew translation from Old French, this Hebrew narrative, referred to by scholars as *Melekh Artus* (King Arthur), proves definitively that medieval Jews engaged with the French stories of King Arthur and his knights and purposefully planted seeds from medieval romance into Hebrew soil.

In the thirteenth century, a small corpus of Hebrew romance emerged in Ashkenaz or from Ashkenazi emigration, including *Melekh Artus*. These texts adapt and translate the vernacular French romance genre, which is difficult to define considering its many forms in prose, poetry,

1. For the only two modern editions or translations, see the translation by Moses Gaster, “The History of the Destruction of the Round Table as Told in Hebrew in the Year 1279,” *Folk Lore* 20 (1909): 272–94; Curt Leviant, *King Artus: A Hebrew Arthurian Romance of 1279* (Syracuse, NY: Syracuse University Press, 2003).

and narrative.[2] In general, romance is defined by its literary elements, usually including a main character who seeks adventure, encounters various excitements, and engages in consummated or unconsummated (courtly) love affairs with women. One author refers to the content of medieval English romance as "love, ladies, adventure and the happy ending," although for some characters, the endings are happier than for others.[3]

The twelfth-century author Chrétien de Troyes is considered the father of chivalric romance. He combines courtly love themes with chansons de geste, an older genre of rhymed prose narratives focused on martial exploits.[4] Written in his vernacular of Old French, Chrétien de Troyes's five known texts were composed in the last quarter of the twelfth century. They follow singular characters on their journeys for honor. These characters often attempt quests rather than the platitude of domestic life in a castle with a wife. Chrétien's episodes are influenced heavily by the late antique and early medieval Latin stories by Wace and Geoffrey of Monmouth that first introduced readers to the figures of King Arthur and his knights of the Round Table, as well as by Celtic symbols and legends.

Versions of Chrétien's narratives appear in their Old French form across medieval Europe, as well as in various European languages, including Old Norse-Icelandic and Greek, as early as the thirteenth century.[5] While some of these are translations, others adapt Chrétien's content by elaborating on the story of one of his characters, such as King Arthur, Tristan, or Perceval, and adding elements not present in

---

2. Keith Busby, "Romance, French," in *The Oxford Dictionary of the Middle Ages* (Oxford: Oxford University Press, 2010), http://www.oxfordreference.com/view/10.1093/acref/9780198662624.001.0001/acref-9780198662624-e-5062; Joseph J. Duggan, *The Romances of Chrétien de Troyes* (New Haven, CT: Yale University Press, 2001); Roberta L. Krueger, ed., *The Cambridge Companion to Medieval Romance* (Cambridge: Cambridge University Press, 2000); Douglas Kelly, *The Art of Medieval French Romance* (Madison: University of Wisconsin Press, 1992).

3. K. S. Whetter, *Understanding Genre and Medieval Romance* (Aldershot, UK: Ashgate, 2008), 50–51, 95–97.

4. Duggan, *The Romances of Chrétien de Troyes*; Chrétien de Troyes, *The Complete Romances of Chrétien de Troyes*, trans. David Staines (Bloomington: Indiana University Press, 1991); Douglas Kelly, *Chrétien de Troyes: An Analytic Bibliography* (London: Grant & Cutler, 1976).

5. Regina Psaki and Gloria Allaire, eds., *The Arthur of the Italians: The Arthurian Legend in Medieval Italian Literature and Culture* (Cardiff: University of Wales Press, 2014); Adam J. Goldwyn, "Arthur in the East: Cross-Cultural Translations of Arthurian Romance in Greek and Hebrew, Including a New Translation of 'O Presbus Ippotes' (The Old Knight)," *Latch* 5 (January 2012): 75–105; Marianne E. Kalinke, ed., *The Arthur of the North: The Arthurian Legend in the Norse and Rus' Realms* (Cardiff: University of Wales Press, 2011).

the original versions.[6] Thus, medieval romance often diverges widely from Chrétien's five extant narratives, but the themes of courtly love, honor, and loyalty remain and commonly feature Arthurian characters.

By the thirteenth century, an eight-volume collection of Arthurian legends appeared in Old French, dubbed by scholars as the Lancelot-Grail Cycle. This cycle, more than Chrétien directly, influenced the medieval Hebrew translators of romance. Yet the genre of romance cannot always be traced to a singular medieval source, and examples from Hebrew romance will display the extent to which romance as a genre embedded itself in the medieval Hebrew cultural imagination.

One aspect of romance especially embedded itself: the relationship between courtly love and marriage. The twelfth-century courtier Andreas Capellanus was the best-known medieval author to explore concepts (whether seriously or tongue in cheek) of passionate and flirtatious, but nonphysical, love as part of courtly behavior.[7] Gaston Paris, a nineteenth-century philologist, traced this behavior of courtly love through the medieval romances, such as the *Lancelot du Lac* section of the Lancelot-Grail Cycle.[8] The term "courtly love" has solidified itself as a major aspect of medieval romance, although it often loses some of its courtliness when characters engage in extramarital affairs. Courtly love often appears in opposition to marriage, as in the story of King Arthur, whose wife Guinevere cuckolds him with Lancelot.

This chapter explores how Hebrew translations of the non-Jewish literary genre of romance use that genre to promote certain ideals of marriage. In *Melekh Artus* and other thirteenth-century Hebrew romance from Ashkenaz, the Hebrew translators continue the motifs of their source texts about the importance of stable marriages amid the threat of courtly love. This view on marriage, as we will see, is not endemic to a particular religious affiliation. Despite relying on non-Jewish source texts, the Hebrew texts do not change their source material significantly.

---

6. Marie-José Heijkant, "From France to Italy: The Tristan Texts," in *The Arthur of the Italians*, ed. Gloria Allaire and F. Regina Psaki (Cardiff: University of Wales Press, 2014), 41–68; Arthur Groos and Norris J. Lacy, *Perceval/Parzival: A Casebook* (London: Routledge, 2012).

7. Andreas Capellanus, *The Art of Courtly Love*, trans. John Jay Perry (New York: Columbia University Press, 1941); Michael D. Cherniss, "The Literary Comedy of Andreas Capellanus," *Modern Philology* 72, no. 3 (1975): 223–37; David Carlson, "Religion and Romance: The Languages of Love in the Treatises of Gerard of Liege and the Case of Andreas Capellanus," in *Poetics of Love in the Middle Ages: Texts and Contexts*, ed. Moshe Lazar and Norris J. Lacy (Fairfax: University of Virginia Press, 1989), 81–92.

8. Gaston Paris, "Études Sur Les Romans de La Table Ronde: *Lancelot du Lac*," *Romania* 12 (1883): 459–534; Capellanus, *The Art of Courtly Love*.

Instead, their authors use medieval romance as a springboard for stories aimed at Jewish audiences about promoting marital success without denigrating the source texts whence romance came.[9]

Part of the uniqueness of the argument presented here is that it argues for the existence of Hebrew romance in or from Ashkenaz, distinct from the belletristic Hebrew literature produced in southern Spain and France. It has already been established that non-Jewish romance influenced Hebrew texts in the southern Mediterranean Jewish communities. Hebrew rhymed prose narratives such as Jacob ben Eleazer's *Sefer ha-Meshalim* (Book of Tales) incorporate themes of courtly love from the Romance languages and Arabic in the multilingual literary community of thirteenth-century Toledo.[10] Written in Spain, the twelfth-century narrative *Asher in the Harem* is the earliest known example of a fusion of Hebrew narrative with courtly love motifs and describes the pull of an unconsummated love from afar.[11] Given the tendency of southern Hebrew writers to engage with Arabic literary genres, such as the frametale narrative known as *maqama* and poetry, it is not surprising that they similarly borrowed romance from their Christian neighbors.

It may be surprising, however, that medieval Jews in Ashkenaz turned to non-Jewish texts of knights and romance to promote marital values. Texts written purely for entertainment were generally avoided in medieval northern European Jewish communities (as evidenced by the lack of belletristic poetry, for example). Several contemporary references to narrative texts imply that the narratives-qua-narratives do not carry the same importance as more pious or weighty texts. In *Sefer Ḥasidim* (Book of the Pious), the author prohibits covering (binding?) sacred books with romances (רומנץ), which were "worthless matters concerning the conflicts of kings."[12] In a thirteenth-century legal gloss from northern

9. Caroline Gruenbaum and Annegret Oehme, eds., *Medieval and Early Modern Jewish Romance* (Kalamazoo, MI: Arc Humanities, 2023).

10. Tovi Bibring, "A Medieval Hebrew French Kiss: Courtly Ideals and the Love Story of Sahar and Kima by Ya'akov Ben El'azar," *Jewish Quarterly Review* 109, no. 1 (Winter 2019): 24–37; Tovi Bibring, "Fairies, Lovers, and Glass Palaces: French Influences on Thirteenth-Century Hebrew Poetry in Spain—the Case of Ya'akov Ben El'azar's Ninth Mahberet," *Jewish Quarterly Review* 107, no. 3 (Summer 2017): 297–322; David A. Wacks, *Double Diaspora in Sephardic Literature: Jewish Cultural Production before and after 1492* (Bloomington: Indiana University Press, 2015), 35, 54–63.

11. Solomon Ibn Saqbel, "Asher in the Harem," in *Rabbinic Fantasies: Imaginative Narratives from Classical Hebrew Literature*, ed. Mark Jay Mirsky and David Stern, trans. Raymond P. Scheindlin (New Haven, CT: Yale University Press, 1990), 253–67.

12. *Sefer Hasidim*, Bologna edition, para. 142. Available at https://etc.princeton.edu/sefer_hasidim/index.php?a=manuscripts.

France, the writer notes that a certain Rabbi Judah believes one should not read from "war stories" written in the vernacular on the Sabbath.[13] His contemporary R. Isaac b. Samuel of Dampierre added that he thought this kind of reading should be forbidden on the weekdays too because it comes under the category of prohibited recreation from M. Avot 3:3 and rabbinic commentary on Psalms 1:1.[14] The essential content of the religious law prohibits any activities that promote unacceptable idleness or evil gossip. In Eleazer of Worms' *Darkhei Teshuvah* (Paths to Repentance), a woman listens to gossip and repeats it to her husband. As punishment, her ear becomes a hinge when she arrives in hell.[15] In a later medieval ethical will, R. Eleazer of Mayence (d. 1357) urges his sons not to play games of chance and to avoid frivolous conversation and dancing with the opposite sex. He advises his daughters to seek work continually because "idleness leads first to boredom, then to sin."[16]

Certain rabbis also seemed uncomfortable with nonrabbinic writing. The comprehensive law code *Shulḥan Arukh* (Set Table) forbade the reading of Immanuel ha-Romi's books on Shabbat as well as nonholidays, two centuries after the author's lifetime.[17] The *Shulḥan Arukh* compares his works to "romance" (דברי חשק), in a response to R. Judah's commentary about acceptable reading material. The late twelfth- to thirteenth-century rabbi Abraham b. Nathan ha-Yarhi disdains two types of entertainment: (1) literary compositions about unseemly matters, and (2) the use of scriptural language for amusement. He writes that this frivolity is not acceptable "when there is no festive meal honoring the groom and bride, and [i.e., or another] festive meal which fulfills a commandment, but merely at an optional meal."[18]

13. Tosafot on Shabbat, 116b:5. Translated in Kirsten A. Fudeman, *Vernacular Voices: Language and Identity in Medieval French Jewish Communities* (Philadelphia: University of Pennsylvania Press, 2011), 205n115.

14. Ivan G. Marcus, "Why Is This Knight Different? A Jewish Self-Representation in Medieval Europe," in *Tov Elem—Memory, Community and Gender in Medieval and Early Jewish Societies: Essays in Honor of Robert Bonfil*, ed. Elisheva Baumgarten, Amnon Raz-Krakotzkin, and Roni Weinstein (Jerusalem: Bialik Institute, 2011), 139.

15. Elisheva Baumgarten, *Practicing Piety in Medieval Ashkenaz: Men, Women, and Everyday Religious Observance*, Jewish Culture and Contexts (Philadelphia: University of Pennsylvania Press, 2014), 205.

16. Israel Abrahams, ed., *Hebrew Ethical Wills* (Philadelphia: Jewish Publication Society, 2006), 207–18.

17. Joseph Karo, *Shulchan Arukh Orach Chayim* (Maginei Eretz: Lemberg, 1893), 307:16–17.

18. Abraham b. Nathan HaYarhi, *Perush 'al massekhet kallah rabbati* (Tiberias, 1906), 20, cited in Talya Fishman, "A Medieval Parody of Misogyny: Judah Ibn Shabbetai's 'Minhat Yehudah Sone Hanashim,'" *Prooftexts* 8, no. 1 (1988): 101.

The contemporaneous rabbinic strictures, however, lack a certain gravitas. R. Isaac of Dampierre, as mentioned, forbids reading romance because it has the same recreational purpose as frivolities like gambling or gossip. These activities do not appear to have any particular punishments if transgressed. The prohibition on reading war stories on Shabbat is tied to the prohibition to read any literature on Shabbat.

In addition, there are mentions of the non-Jewish genre of romance even in rabbinic commentaries. In a thirteenth-century rabbinic commentary on *Song of Songs* erroneously attributed to Rashbam, the author writes, "and even today it is the way of the *trouvères* [troubadours who sang in Old French] to perform a song that tells about the love affair (מעשה אהבה) of two people in the love songs (שירי אהבה), as customary in the non-Jewish world (במנהג העולם)."[19] Even for a rabbi, vernacular love songs are appropriate comparisons for the canonical *Song of Songs* text, and an appropriate reference for his erudite readership. Hanna Liss argues that this commentary reads the *Song of Songs* as a secular literary text, with an emphasis on the love relationship between the two main characters.[20] This was an unusual emphasis among medieval Jewish interpretations of the *Song of Songs*, which generally allegorized the relationship as between God and Israel or the Jewish people.[21] The rabbinic commentary here considers troubadour poetry in conjunction with exegesis of a biblical book. Thus, the status of romance carries a negative reputation only among certain rabbis. In short, the extant disapproval of non-Jewish literature is tepid at best.

The evidence does not support that courtly texts in Hebrew were created for the purpose of pushing back against the minority status of the Jews who were reading and writing them. One reading of the Hebrew romances supposes that the Hebrew authors and audience portrayed knights as Jewish to fulfill a fantasy. To escape the world where Jews are exempt from certain social strata, including the feudal system, they created a fictional one in which knights speak Hebrew and recite biblical phrases. In this ludicrous world, Jews hold chivalric roles themselves.[22]

19. Hanna Liss, "The Commentary on the *Song of Songs* Attributed to R. Samuel Ben Meir (Rashbam)," *Medieval Jewish Studies* 1 (August 2007): 25.

20. Liss, "The Commentary on the *Song of Songs*," 1–27.

21. For a different perspective on the commentary's authorship, see Sara Japhet, "Did Rashbam Know the Vulgate Latin Translation of the Song of Songs?," *Textus* 24 (2009): 263–85.

22. For similar portrayals in texts from Spain, see Wacks, *Double Diaspora in Sephardic Literature*, 54–59, 72–77, 85–92.

By placing Jewish identities on these male characters who cannot "in real life" ever be Jewish, the Jewish male writer may be acting out a form of fantasy that is tied to expectations of medieval masculinity. In the traditional Jewish literary corpus, such as the rabbinic stories from the Talmud, Jewish heroes do not carry swords or march into battle like Chrétien's knights. They are sages, renowned for their ability to escape difficult situations through wise machinations, to outwit their enemies, and to pass fair and just legislation.[23] In the medieval chronicles depicting violent persecutions against their communities, Jews did take up swords, but they were often forced by their circumstances to turn them on themselves and their families in acts of martyrdom.[24] As knights, Jews could explore these alternative forms of masculine activities.

But this reading hinges on a fallacy, the misconception that Jews did not have any place in feudalism. In parts of Western and Central Europe, Jews were allowed to carry weapons (although probably revoked in the thirteenth century, Jews were not punished for transgressions of this type).[25] Medieval Ashkenazi scholars debated whether Jews could bear arms on the Sabbath, with the implication that they were allowed to carry weapons during the week. Eleazar of Worms wrote that contemporary historical circumstances forced Jews to wield weapons in their defense, "It happened once that great armies besieged Worms [in 1201]; then we allowed all Jews to carry arms on the Sabbath."[26] In thirteenth-century Bohemia, Jewish youth strolled around wearing swords and shields on Shabbat.[27] A German legal text from about 1325 illustrates one of its pages with a drawing of a man marked as Jewish by his hat but in all other ways identical to the images of non-Jews throughout the

23. See Rubenstein's tripartite exploration of rabbinic stories: Jeffrey L. Rubenstein, *Talmudic Stories: Narrative Art, Composition, and Culture* (Baltimore, MD: Johns Hopkins University Press, 1999); Jeffrey L. Rubenstein, *The Culture of the Babylonian Talmud* (Baltimore, MD: Johns Hopkins University Press, 2005); Jeffrey L. Rubenstein, *Stories of the Babylonian Talmud* (Baltimore, MD: Johns Hopkins University Press, 2010).

24. Ivan G. Marcus, "From Politics to Martyrdom: Shifting Paradigms in the Hebrew Narratives of the 1096 Crusade Riots," *Prooftexts* 2, no. 1 (1982): 40–52; Robert Chazan, *God, Humanity and History: The Hebrew First Crusade Narratives* (Berkeley: University of California Press, 2000); Susan L. Einbinder, *Beautiful Death: Jewish Poetry and Martyrdom in Medieval France* (Princeton, NJ: Princeton University Press, 2002).

25. David Biale, *Power and Powerlessness in Jewish History* (New York: Schocken, 1986), 72; Christine Magin, "Armed Jews in Legal Sources from the High and Late Middle Ages," *Jewish Studies* 41 (2002): 67–81.

26. Biale, *Power and Powerlessness in Jewish History*, 73.

27. Eyal Levinson, "Adolescence and Masculinities in Jewish Society in Medieval Ashkenaz [Heb.]" (PhD diss., Hebrew University of Jerusalem, 2017), 87. See also Eyal Levinson, *Gender and Sexuality in Ashkenaz in the Middle Ages* (Jerusalem: Shazar, 2022).

manuscript: he sits atop a horse and carries a sword, with the mention by the author that "'here take note of a special distinction: Weapons are forbidden to priests and scholars to do them honour, [but] forbidden to Jews to contribute to their shame."[28] Regardless of the legality of and reasons for bearing weapons, some medieval Jews looked a lot like knights.

Several rabbinic commentaries and stories feature knights or mention chivalric endeavors.[29] In a northern French rabbinic (Tosafist) gloss on a Talmudic section about the holiday of Sukkot, the rabbi suggests that chivalric tournaments happened at weddings, we can read: "they ride on horses in the direction of the groom and joust [lit. fight] with one another."[30] Even if this did not occur at Jewish weddings (the subject of that phrase is unclear), the familiarity with the tournament implies that Jews certainly witnessed such events.[31] Chivalric tournaments served as examples in biblical commentaries. In his commentary *Pa'aneah Raza*, R. Isaac ben Judah ha-Levi (active in Sens in the second half of the thirteenth century) quotes an explanation that compares Jacob's wrestling with the angel to a chivalric tournament, with the angel representing a defeated knight: "*Why are you asking about my name?* (Genesis 32:29) Since this is the way combatants and fighters behave, that the victor asks for the name of his defeated opponent, and boasts in the city of his exploits, but the defeated [knight] keeps his name secret [from him] for this very reason."[32] The pietistic manual *Sefer Ḥasidim* also uses knights as examples for Jewish behavior—mostly to showcase what *not* to do—showing familiarity with knightly behavior while the author criticizes it: "If a man confronts misfortune, he should think of how knights go to war to demonstrate their valor (גבורתם). They do not run away from the sword since it is shameful if they do so. As a result, they are killed or wounded just on account of shame, even though they will receive no reward from their lords when they die in battle. But Scripture says,

28. Recorded in the Sachenspiegel, UB Bibliotheca Palatina (UB Heidelberg), Cod. Pal. germ. 164 (unpaginated), available at https://heidicon.ub.uni-heidelberg.de/#/detail/573146, translated in Magin, "Armed Jews in Legal Sources," 74.

29. Emily Taitz, *The Jews of Medieval France: The Community of Champagne* (Westport, CT: Greenwood, 1994), 117–18; David Malkiel, *Reconstructing Ashkenaz: The Human Face of Franco-German Jewry, 1000–1250* (Stanford, CA: Stanford University Press, 2009), 213–14.

30. Marcus, "Why Is This Knight Different?," 142.

31. Tosafot to b. Sukkot 45a, quoted in Hanna Liss, *Creating Fictional Worlds: Peshaṭ-Exegesis and Narrativity in Rashbam's Commentary on the Torah* (Leiden: Brill, 2011), 192.

32. R. Isaac ben-Judah ben-Levi, *Pa'aneah Raza* (Warsaw, 1867), 37a, cited in Liss, *Creating Fictional Worlds*, 192–93.

Though He slay me, yet will I trust in Him (Job 13:15), which means I will serve Him despite not receiving a material reward."[33]

Let us recall, however, that characters in any story can be negative examples without an underlying polemical intent—imperfect characters make a story interesting and instructive. Jews read and illuminated Hebrew manuscripts decorated with knights, and the wealthiest families lived in houses decorated with images of heraldic arms and courtly processions, similar to a fresco on walls that survived from a Jewish home in fourteenth-century Zurich (see figures 3 and 4).[34] Medieval Jews of Germany consciously imitated the courtly traditions of illuminated manuscripts when producing their own illustrated manuscripts.[35]

In the translations, however, the authors depict Jewish figures not as knights but the opposite: they make Christian knights into Hebrew speakers. In the fables, Berechiah ha-Nakdan uses the animals to promote universal values with an emphasis on Jewish wisdom, and *Melekh Artus* portrays knights whose religious identity is irrelevant to the plot and moral. This process simply involves translating the story into Hebrew, embedding it with Talmudic or biblical phrases, and adding a veneer of Jewish morality in the translator's prologue. But the texts fall short of turning the entire narrative into a Jewish one; the stories and characters still exist in a foreign, non-Jewish world, although it is a hybrid one in which its actors speak in Jewish language (or through a Jewish script).[36]

---

33. *Sefer Hasidim*, Parma 359, Princeton University *Sefer Hasidim* database, https://etc.princeton.edu/sefer_hasidim/index.php, accessed August 2018, translated in Marcus, "Why Is This Knight Different?," 151.

34. Sara Offenberg, "A Jewish Knight in Shining Armour: Messianic Narrative and Imagination in Ashkenazic Illuminated Manuscripts," *University of Toronto Journal of Jewish Thought* 4 (2014): 1-14; Sara Offenberg, "Jacob the Knight in Ezekiel's Chariot: Imagined Identity in a Micrography Decoration of an Ashkenazic Bible," *AJS Review* 40, no. 1 (April 2016): 1-16; Joseph Shatzmiller, *Cultural Exchange: Jews, Christians, and Art in the Medieval Marketplace* (Princeton, NJ: Princeton University Press, 2013), 61-72. Scenes from the Arthurian corpus even appeared on the walls of the Alhambra during the late medieval Islamic Nasrid court with modifications designed to associate the episodes with specific ideological aim. See Cynthia Robinson, "Arthur in the Alhambra? Narrative and Nasrid Courtly Self-Fashioning in the Hall of Justice Ceiling Paintings," *Medieval Encounters* 14, no. 2-3 (January 1, 2008): 164-98.

35. Eva Frojmovic, "Jewish Scribes and Christian Illuminators: Interstitial Encounters and Cultural Negotiation," in *Between Judaism and Christianity: Art Historical Essays in Honor of Elisheva (Elisabeth) Revel-Neher*, ed. Elisabeth Revel-Neher, Katrin Kogman-Appel, and Mati Meyer (Leiden: Brill, 2009), 281-306.

36. Tamar S. Drukker, "A Thirteenth-Century Arthurian Tale in Hebrew: A Unique Literary Exchange," *Medieval Encounters* 15, no. 1 (March 2009): 128; Wacks, *Double Diaspora in Sephardic Literature*, 202-5.

FIGURE 3. Fresco on the wall of a house. Brungasse 8, Zurich, fourteenth century. Courtesy of Schauplatz Brunngasse. Copyright by Amt für Städtebau, Stadtarchäologie Zürich.

This is especially true in the German-Jewish epic *Dukus Horant* (Duke Horant), which even more exceptionally portrays knights who do not speak Hebrew. They mostly do not relinquish their Christian identities, even as they are translated into a Jewish script for a Jewish audience. A single passage exemplifies this:

> Now when Pentecost had come, and the queen was to go to prayers, the streets were spread with many a rich silk cloth, worked so beautifully with praiseworthy gold. Both men and women packed the street, when the king was to go to church. Loud music was heard from many minstrels. One could hear the music for more than a mile. The wide streets became crowded with such great throngs. The queen was dressed in rich velvet. It was green in color, with gold and worthy jewels. The very beautiful queen wore a golden crown. Then the townsman said: "Horant, dear my lord, do you not wish to see the noble queen? You will never see a maiden so marvelous. She is like the radiant sun." "Yes, I would very much like to see the beautiful maiden."[37]

37. Jerold C. Frakes, trans., "Dukus Horant," in *Early Yiddish Epic* (Syracuse, NY: Syracuse University Press, 2014), 172.

FIGURE 4. Close-up of the fresco from figure 3 (reproduction). Brungasse 8, Zurich, fourteenth century. By Beat Scheffold. Courtesy of Schauplatz Brunngasse. Copyright by Amt für Städtebau, Stadtarchäologie Zürich.

Here, the queen and king go to church and their prayers during Pentecost, using the Christian term to denote the time of year. The characters behave in traditional ways expected within the pages of a romance: they wear ornate clothes; participate in raucous entertainment; and speak to one another in flattering, courtly ways. However, the word for "prayer" here and elsewhere in the text is a rare example of a Hebraism in the work, *tefilah* (variously spelled תפלה and תיפלה), alluding to the idea of Jewish prayer. Even *Dukus Horant*, the most German of medieval German-Jewish works, nods to the Jewish experience not only in its choice of script but also, although rarely, in its depiction of Jewish religious life.

This mélange of knight and Jew, and German and Hebrew, although ostensibly contradictory, fits with our understanding of northern European Jewish literature. Despite the non-Jewish content of the story, the authors could not produce a Jewish text in the Middle Ages without considering the Jewish or Hebrew literary tradition. The literary tradition in the north did not allow for Jewish writers to produce original secular works in the vernacular. When a literary language rests on the biblical canon and religious literature, then it inherently contains religious material. The "Jewishness" and the "literariness" are so connected that one cannot be extracted from the other.

Barbara Newman describes this phenomenon in the greater medieval world as the "crossover": rather than placing the secular and the sacred as two opposing ideals, medieval Christian authors crossed between them.[38] The texts can be read as secular, as sacred, or as texts that contain both readings simultaneously. Two of our texts, *Melekh Artus* and *Sefer ha-Ma'asim* (Book of Tales), reflect this sense where the biblical, canonical text is used only as a vehicle for expressing certain universal ideas. We recall the idea of the neutral *shibbutz* introduced in chapter 1, which describes Hebrew that uses biblical language for neutral purposes, not necessarily as intertextual references.

Although this book generally avoids functional poetry like *piyyut* (liturgical poetry), wedding songs provide a blend of poetry and narrative that can be useful for this discussion of literary themes. The thirteenth-century wedding song from Champagne incorporates courtly love through a unique mélange of Hebrew and French. Intended to be sung at a wedding ceremony or the celebration afterward, the song begins with "*El givat ha-levonah / notre hatan eit ariveiz*" ("to the hill of frankincense / our groom has come"). The macaronic song, with verses alternating in Hebrew and Hebraico-French, uses different imagery depending on the language expressing it. In the *Elégie de Troyes* (Troyes Elegy), a pair of late thirteenth-century laments in Hebrew and Hebraico-French depicting the killing of Jews in Troyes in 1288, Susan Einbinder has shown that the poems "preserve the traces of a highly acculturated Jewish minority responsive to the norms of beauty and sanctity expressed in the Christian world, and creating from them a new vehicle for its particular cultural ideals."[39] The French text relies on courtly language and convention to address more immediately the events that took place, while the Hebrew version uses biblical language to focus on its theological concerns in a conventional way.[40]

In the wedding song, the distinction between the French and Hebrew sections also speak to distinct differences in the literary tradition of the two languages. The Hebraico-French verses reflect aspects from the courtly love stories of Chrétien de Troyes. In his French tales, knights prize honor and virtue, and strive for honor through conquests while eschewing a domestic life. In Chrétien's *Yvain, ou Le Chevalier au lion* (Yvain, or the Knight with the Lion), for example, Yvain settles down

38. Barbara Newman, *Medieval Crossover: Reading the Secular against the Sacred* (Notre Dame, IN: University of Notre Dame Press, 2013).

39. Susan Einbinder, "The Troyes Laments: Jewish Martyrology in Hebrew and Old French," *Viator* 30 (January 1, 1999): 208.

40. Kirsten A. Fudeman, "Restoring a Vernacular Jewish Voice: The Old French Elegy of Troyes," *Jewish Studies Quarterly* 15, no. 3 (September 1, 2008): 190–221.

with his beloved but soon becomes antsy in the castle. He bids adieu to his new wife and sets out on a series of adventures. The wedding song also uses similar tropes of conquest (in the following, the Hebrew lines appear in italic, and the Hebraico-French in roman):

Surrender your castle!
For in his hand is a wine-red sword
If you are not going to turn it over to him,
No one could save you from him;
It will not go back in its sheath.
You stand to lose everything here.
On the other hand, he could fail completely.
Let my beloved (m.) come fight!
He does not refuse the battle
In a walled and gated city.
High river, sluice gate, lock (v. 4–13).
. . . .
May you be faint-hearted in folly (*or*: in the heat of the battle);
To the city anointed for war
You will come to give up your independence (v. 16–18).[41]

The references to castles, swords, and battles in "*El givat ha-levonah*" evoke the French vernacular heroes performing courtly exploits. Like Yvain, the bridegroom seems to be willing to abandon his beloved to wage war. While other Hebrew poetry, especially the poems from al-Andalus, features martial themes, those poems take on a religious dimension through praise of God and Israel.[42] The *Elégie de Troyes* also has theological themes dominating the text, although they exist alongside courtly imagery in the Hebraico-French version, and the function of the poem is not liturgical.

Although the wedding song contains biblical language, it does not reference God, Israel, or overtly pious tropes. A closer reading reveals that the language of conquest in fact hints at the wedding ceremony for which the song was composed rather than any theological themes. When read, or heard, in the context of a newlywed couple, the bridegroom's

41. Kirsten A. Fudeman, "'They Have Ears, but Do Not Hear': Gendered Access to Hebrew and the Medieval Hebrew-French Wedding Song," *Jewish Quarterly Review*, no. 4 (2006): 560–67.

42. Joseph Ṭobi, "The Religious Element in the War Poems of Samuel Ha-Nagid and in the Arabic Panegyrics in Andalusia," in *Between Hebrew and Arabic Poetry: Studies in Spanish Medieval Hebrew Poetry* (Leiden: Brill, 2010), 93–114.

desire to conquer a castle and plunder a new land takes on a sexual tone. The language of conquest appears in conjunction with sexual references—a fitting tone for a song used at a wedding. In the selection above, the "wine-red sword" out of its sheath that may fail has a phallic insinuation of the sexual act that will take place after the wedding, and a joke about the groom's possible impotence.[43] The city itself is the bride, with the sluice gate and lock as her genitalia.[44]

Through the use of innuendo and allusions, the Hebrew author stresses the importance of sexual compatibility for a newly wedded couple. This emphasis contradicts the themes of courtly love literature, in which the goal of marital wedding bliss is secondary to the importance of the conquest. The theme of consummation and marriage directly challenges the *fin'amor*, or courtly love of the romance genre—in which two lovers, one of whom might be married, suffer trials of an unrequited or unconsummated relationship. In general, medieval Jewish authorities on marriage in northern Europe emphasized consummation and procreation more than Christian thinkers.[45] The Torah and Talmud both mention sexual satisfaction as a conjugal right guaranteed by a husband.[46] To that end, we find in Hebrew secular literature themes of family cohesion, the importance of children and family tradition, and the concept of *shalom bayit* ("peace in the home") more than in the contemporary non-Jewish texts.

Melekh Artus also challenges the vernacular courtly love motif. Although we lack the concluding section in *Melekh Artus,* we can still understand

43. See a similar example in a Judeo-Catalan wedding song, in Wacks, *Double Diaspora in Sephardic Literature*, 241n90; Jaume Riera i Sans, ed., *Cants de noces dels jueus catalans* (Barcelona: Curial, 1974), 17.

44. Some early modern epigrammatic poems contain similarly veiled allusions and double entendres. Dan Pagis, *Al Sod Hatum: Le-Toldot Ha-Hidah Ha-'Ivrit Be-Italyah Uve-Holand* (Jerusalem: Magnes, 1986).

45. In general, medieval Jewry strove for sexual compatibility of a married couple, even when it did not lead to conception. See Avraham Grossman, *Pious and Rebellious: Jewish Women in Medieval Europe* (Waltham, MA: Brandeis University Press, 2004); Elisheva Baumgarten, *Mothers and Children: Jewish Family Life in Medieval Europe* (Princeton, NJ: Princeton University Press, 2004). In the Christian world, the quintessential mother was the Virgin Mary, a woman who did not engage in intercourse to conceive a child. Sexual compatibility was rarely a factor in medieval marriage. See Caroline Walker Bynum, *Holy Feast and Holy Fast: The Religious Significance of Food to Medieval Women* (Berkeley: University of California Press, 1987); James Brundage, *Law, Sex, and Christian Society in Medieval Europe* (Chicago: University of Chicago Press, 1987).

46. Wacks, *Double Diaspora in Sephardic Literature*, 164; David Biale, *Eros and the Jews: From Biblical Israel to Contemporary America* (Berkeley: University of California Press, 1997), 92–96; Tova Rosen, *Unveiling Eve: Reading Gender in Medieval Hebrew Literature* (Philadelphia: University of Pennsylvania Press, 2003), 122.

the author's motivations in writing a Jewish text using non-Jewish characters. He tells us in his prologue that he has edited the stories and left out a few folios, thus acknowledging that he consciously makes editorial decisions. He also informs us that he is telling this story in order to show sinners the proper path to repentance, which he will clarify in his conclusion. The story breaks off in the middle of its seventh folio, so we do not know what his conclusion was supposed to say.

The author gives us certain indications of his conclusion. His inclusion of *only* these two scenes from the Lancelot-Grail Cycle, the birth of Arthur and the tale of the tournament at Winchester, speak to an overall agenda because both these episodes revolve around inappropriate sexual relationships. In the Merlin portion, Arthur's father Uter connives with Merlin to find his way into Igerne's bed, although she is married. In the second section, Lancelot and Guinevere's adulterous relationship threatens King Arthur's relationship with his wife Guinevere. The Hebrew scribe has chosen these two sections of the text deliberately because they are both paradigmatic examples of negative love affairs. Lancelot and Uter/Merlin challenge the traditional framework of marriage through these affairs.[47] In a fourteenth-century manuscript with various Arthurian stories revolving around Tristan called the *Tristano Panciatichiano*, the compiler selectively chooses sections from the *Quest del Saint Graal* and *Mort Artu* (Death of Arthur) that discuss Lancelot's love for Guinevere to compare it with depictions of the story of Tristan and Iseult.[48] Lancelot acts as a model for the new hero Tristan, who confronts his own illicit love affair. In *Melekh Artus*, Lancelot and Uter are parallel figures, both grappling with their own affairs. The emphasis on the affairs of the two main characters proves that the theme of adultery is a key didactic message in the text.

The Hebrew author expresses his distaste for extramarital affairs through changes he makes from the French source texts and through carefully chosen biblical references. In the birth of Arthur section, he alters a section from the *Merlin* material to fit his own narrative. When

---

47. For more exhaustive gender studies in the Arthurian canon, see Carolyne Larrington, "Gender/Queer Studies," in *Handbook of Arthurian Romance: King Arthur's Court in Medieval European Literature*, ed. Leah Tether, Johnny McFadyen, Keith Busby, and Ad Putter (Berlin: De Gruyter, 2017), 259–72; Dorsey Armstrong, *Gender and the Chivalric Community of Malory's Morte d'Arthur* (Gainesville: University Press of Florida, 2003); Friedrich Wolfzettel, ed., *Arthurian Romance and Gender: Selected Proceedings of the XVIIth International Arthurian Congress* (Amsterdam: Rodopi, 1995).

48. Lori J. Walters, ed., *Lancelot and Guinevere: A Casebook* (London: Routledge, 2015), xxxvii.

Uter learns that the Duke, Igerne's husband, has been killed in battle because of Merlin's machinations, the French version states that Uter was very upset and wishes to make amends: "And the king responded to them and said he was very sorry about the death of the duke. And so the duke died, and his castle taken. The king spoke to his barons and told them that he was very sorry about the duke's misfortune. He asked them for advice on how he could make amends—he did not want men to blame him for this, because he did not hate the duke nor wish him any harm. He was very sorry about the misfortune, and said, 'I will make amends in any way I can.'"[49]

The king asks for advice from his counselors for two reasons. He does not wish to be blamed for the death of the duke, but he also mentions he did not have ill feelings toward the duke and did not want harm to come to him. He repeats his regret three times, and the passage completely removes him from the action of Merlin's ill-fated mission. The Hebrew text, on the other hand, writes explicitly that Uter wished for the duke's death: "When the king returned to his camp, he rejoiced to find the Duke lying dead and the castle taken by his army."[50] The Hebrew text thus emphasizes the unsettling circumstances of Uter's actions caused by lust, painting him as an unsympathetic murderer.

Elsewhere, the Hebrew author uses negatively charged language to refer to Guinevere and Lancelot's relationship through the use of biblical verses. This technique appears often in medieval Hebrew, to the point where biblical verses become an intrinsic part of the new textual creation, in the process of *shibbutz*. *Melekh Artus* uses intertextual biblical references to emphasize certain conclusions about its narrative. In a passage in *Melekh Artus*, the text takes on a definitively negative tone with an intertextual reading. The author writes that Uter falls in love with Igerne and "became quite ill" (לחתחלות) with love for her. This echoes the same biblical language used in the description of Amnon's incestuous love for his sister Tamar in 2 Samuel. He becomes ill with love for her: "And Amnon was so distressed that he fell sick because of his sister Tamar; for she was a virgin, and it seemed hard for Amnon to

49. "Et li rois respond & lor dist que moult li poise de la mort al duc. Ensi fu li dus mors & ses chastiaus perdues & li rois parla a ses hommes & lor dist que moult li pesa de la mescheance au duc & lor demanda conseil comment il porroit ceste chose amender que si homme ne len blamassent car il ne haoit pas le duc de mortel haine & moult li poise de le mesauenture que auenue li est si lamenderai a men pooir." Heinrich Oskar Sommer, *L'estoire de Merlin*, vol. II (Washington: Carnegie Institution of Washington, 1909), 68–69.

50. ובשוב המלך אל החיל מצא הדוכוס מת מושכב והקריה נלכדה וישמח. Leviant, *King Artus*, 18.

do any thing unto her" (2 Samuel 13:2). But his illness is not "lovesickness." The definition of the verb "to fall ill" in this case means specifically to fall ill because of his grief that he cannot have her. Through that intertextual comparison to an incestuous relationship, the *Melekh Artus* author emphasizes the unnaturalness of Uter's love. He also emphasizes a feeling of grief or tragedy, rather than lovesickness, that Uter ought to be feeling, comparing him directly with the detestable Amnon. This is not a neutral use of biblical language (*shibbutz*), but rather an intertextual use of biblical language for a purposeful comparison.[51]

A deliberate omission of biblical language complicates the depiction of Uter in *Melekh Artus*.[52] The story of Uter and Izerna directly parallels the biblical story of David and Bathsheba, not only in its medieval iterations but as early as its first appearance in book VIII of Geoffrey of Monmouth's *Historia regum britanniae* (History of the Kings of Britain). As depicted in 2 Samuel 11, the powerful King David sees Bathsheba, wife of Uriah, bathing on the roof, and he falls in love with her. David assigns Uriah to a dangerous position in battle and the fighter is killed. After Bathsheba mourns her husband, David takes her to his house and marries her. The story ends with an explicit cautionary tone, "but the thing that David did was displeasing in the eyes of the Lord" (2 Samuel 11:27). David, despite his heroic kingly deeds and propensity for poetry, was fallible in affairs of the heart.[53] If the author of *Melekh Artus* was writing in the style of a traditional medieval Hebrew author, he would undoubtedly refer to this story or a midrash of the incident. Instead, *Melekh Artus* provides no biblical allusions to 2 Samuel 11 nor any mention of the biblical figures, even in phrases that parallel the biblical story. When Bathsheba finds out about her husband's death, the biblical story reads, "and when Uriah's wife heard that her husband Uriah had died, she mourned her husband." The word "mourned" comes from the verb ס.פ.ד, a common verb with plentiful attestation throughout the Bible (i.e., Gen. 23:2; 1 Kings 13:30; Isaiah 32:12; Zech. 12:12). The *Melekh Artus* author writes similarly, "the Duchess grieved her husband and her

51. See chapter 1, notes 6 and 7 for more on neutral *shibbutz*.

52. It is also possible that these omissions were not deliberate but occurred only because the author was relying on memory for biblical quotations without the direct source nearby to consult. However, medieval Jewish authors normally have excellent recall of exact biblical citations.

53. See the many explanations for David's act in the Talmud, for example, Sanhedrin 107a, Avodah Zarah 4b, Shabbat 56a, Megillah 14a–b. Many Talmudic references and midrash promote the overwhelming power of God's forgiveness of David, acknowledging his crime while also reconciling the importance of his kingship.

heart was troubled by the wondrous event" because she realizes that her husband had died in battle nearly at the same time that she thought she was lying with him in bed.[54] This phrase does not appear in the Old French antecedents. Rather than use the biblical verb ספד, *Melekh Artus* uses the homonymous verb התאבל. Not an uncommon verb, its verbal forms appear often. If the two verbs have the same meaning, why does the author not use the verb with an obvious reference to the Uriah/Bathsheba episode? Elsewhere, he avoids the use of a commonly used rabbinic phrase "evil inclination" (יצר הרע) in favor of the expression "evil desire" (חשק הרע) to describe the impetus for Lancelot succumbing to his urges, with the word "desire" evoking the literary themes of vernacular romance.[55]

A few explanations are possible. The author may have translated word for word without thinking of the wider indications of his choices. However, we have proven in this chapter that is not the case, and his translator's decisions are meaningful. Maybe he did not want to draw a parallel between the biblical King David and Uter. The translator maintains the secularity of his vernacular source texts, which are also devoid of references to biblical episodes. At the same time, he does not want to glorify his vernacular characters through a comparison to King David or even the pious Bathsheba, who is an important figure as the mother of Solomon. But this explanation lacks weight because *Melekh Artus* already draws a comparison between King David and Lancelot when the author refers to Lancelot as a descendant of King David. The simplest explanation is that *Melekh Artus* adheres firmly to its nonbiblical stance by avoiding nonessential biblical references. This puts emphasis on the biblical references the author does use, suggesting that any comparison to a canonical Hebrew text is purposeful.

The uses of *shibbutz* in *Melekh Artus* cast aspersions on the status of love and passion in the story. Elsewhere, the Hebrew author speaks of Lancelot's love pejoratively, emphasizing the magnitude of his sinful ways:

> And as for Sir Lanç, he too began to feel his lust again and desired her [the Queen] as before and a thousand-fold more. And if before he lusted after her shrewdly and hid his sins, now he began to publicly demonstrate his lust in an exaggerated and unbecoming

54. Leviant, *King Artus*, 18.
55. Leviant, *King Artus*, 29.

> way. And she too, in her turn, until all the members of the court in general, and Agravain in particular, were aware of it, when she adorned and beautified herself with all her might out of her love for him, until she put all those who saw her at risk with her excessive beauty. And the people began to gossip about them both, saying that they were tied to one another in the bonds of love and of foolish passion. And it is this wicked passion which was the cause of the destruction of the Table, and of King Artus's death and the loss of the entire kingdom, as you shall see below.[56]

Although we do not have the conclusion with the author's intended moral to the stories he includes, he connects the passion between Guinevere and Lancelot to the main devastations of the King Arthur story cycle: the destruction of the Round Table, King Arthur's death, and the loss of Camelot. The author casts judgment on Lancelot's actions, referring to his "sins" (פשעיו). He also distinguishes between a more proper way of conducting a relationship and the openness with which Lancelot flaunts his affair. When he hides his relationship, he acts "shrewdly" (בחכמה); he begins to express his lust in an "exaggerated and unbecoming way" (לפרסם את חשקו יותר מידאי בעניין רע). Not only does he engage in an affair, he does not act covertly but rather with excessive publicizing "of love and of foolish passion."

This passage does not appear exactly in the source text. What we find instead is a similar reference to Guinevere's beauty, without the mention that the affair is the cause of the destruction of the kingdom. Instead of everyone being aware of their relationship, only Agravain "watched so intently that soon he knew beyond any doubt that Lancelot and the queen shared an illicit love . . . when Agravain was certain about the queen and Lancelot, he was very happy, more for the harm that might befall Lancelot than for the possibility of avenging the offense to the king."[57] Agravain then tells King Arthur about the affair. Rather than a communal offense, their sin is the means for personal

56. Leviant, *King Artus*, 28–29:
ומסיר לנץ גם הוא החל לשוב אל חשקו ולחשוק בה כמלפנים ויותר אלף פעמים. ואם מאז היה חושק בה בחכמה ומכסה פשעיו עתה החל לפרסם את חשקו יותר מידאי בעניין רע והיא גם כן מצידה עד שכל בני החצר בכלל ואגרבן בפרט היו מרגישים בדבר כשהיא היתה מהדרת ומקשטת עצמה בכל עוז מרוב חיבתו עד שהיתה מסכנת כל רואיה מרוב הפלגת יופיה. והתחילו העם להרנין על שניהם לאמר כי היו נאחזים לז בלז בחבלי אהבה וחשק סכלי. וזה החשק הרע היה סיבת השמד הטבלא ומיתת מלך ארטוש ואבדן כל המלכות כאשר תראה לפנים.

57. Norris J. Lacy, *Lancelot-Grail: The Death of Arthur*, vol. 7 (Cambridge: D. S. Brewer, 2010), 5.

retribution from Agravain, who despises Lancelot. This reading removes the blame from Lancelot and Guinevere, and places it on Agravain. *Melekh Artus* suggests, however, that the destruction of the Round Table is comparable to a persecution of an entire community of Jews because the first line of the text is: "This is the book of the destruction of the King Arthur's Round Table" (זה ספר השמד הטבלה העגולה שלהמלך ארטוס). The word "destruction" (שמד) could be a play on words, with the similar word for a persecution of the Jewish religion, usually involving forced conversion.[58] The destruction of the Round Table has no bearing on Jewish circumstances, so one could see the homonymic allusion either as a polemical attack on Christians or as a parody of the importance given the Round Table in vernacular culture. For the Jewish audience, the wordplay equates the destruction of the Round Table with a religious persecution, creating such an unlikely comparison as to be unexpected. This unexpectedness makes it humorous.

Humor, specifically in the form of parody and satire, can serve its own didactic function in a narrative. In the medieval period, authors occasionally used biblical quotations out of context for ironic or satirical purposes. Judah al-Ḥarizi's *Takhemoni* relies on biblical verse for satirical and unexpected results, usually for the effect of parodying social classes or individuals.[59] In the *Alphabet of Ben Sira*, the author parodies Talmud and midrash to the point of vulgarity. The beginning portion of the alphabetized tales describes the birth of Ben Sira, whose mother was accidentally impregnated by her father's sperm in a bathhouse.[60] Rather than scorning this body of literature, at least one rabbi seemed to take it as precedent for a legal code. One thirteenth-century Tosafist rabbi, R. Peretz of Corbeil, based a legal response on this portion of the *Alphabet of Ben Sira*, arguing for the possibility of a woman artificially

58. See, for example, its usage in the Talmudic passage Hullin101b, "it was a time of persecution."

59. Israel Davidson, "Parody in Jewish Literature" (PhD diss., Columbia University, 1907), 5–7; Ayelet Oettinger, "Criticism of the Estates in Judah Al-Ḥarizi's Book of Taḥkemoni and in European-Christian Literature of the Thirteenth Century: Affinity and Distinction," in *Studies in Medieval Jewish Poetry: A Message upon the Garden*, ed. Alessandro Guetta and Masha Itzhaki (Leiden: Brill, 2009), 85–115; Ayelet Oettinger, "Parody as a Satirical Weapon in Yehudah Al-Ḥarizi's *Book of the Tahkhemoni* [Heb.]," in *Mittuv Yosef: Yosef Tobi Jubilee Volume*, ed. Ayelet Oettinger and Danny Bar-Maoz (Jerusalem: A. Stern, 2011), 299–322.

60. Eli Yassif, *Sippurei Ben Sira Be-Yemei Ha-Benayim* (Jerusalem: Magnes, 1985), 197–99; David Stern and Mark Jay Mirsky, eds., "The Alphabet of Ben Sira," in *Rabbinic Fantasies: Imaginative Narratives from Classical Hebrew Literature*, trans. Norman Bronznick (New Haven, CT: Yale University Press, 1990), 167–202.

impregnating herself with her father's sperm.[61] Medieval Hebrew anti-Christian polemic also used parody. Profiat Duran exemplifies this approach in his letter "*Al tehi ka-avotekha*" (Be Not Like Your Fathers), which appeared at the end of the fourteenth century. In this satirical letter to a new convert to Christianity, Profiat Duran uses biblical quotations to polemicize his former friend's new religion.[62] Satire and parody are relatively unknown genres in northern European Hebrew literature, so one might be surprised to see it in *Melekh Artus* or in any other contemporary text.

We find, however, two examples of satire among our texts. The author of *Melekh Artus* and the composer of the wedding song "*El givat ha-levonah*" skillfully use parody and humor as an expression of the uniqueness of their own texts. In both texts, many of the satirical references involve sexual innuendo, while others poke fun at the characters or their activities.

In his prologue, where *Melekh Artus* explains the purpose of his translation, he also writes, "This apology should be enough for each intelligent man who acknowledges the truth, not one who makes it hard for himself to understand."[63] His readership, then, ought to be receptive to the text's truths while reading. While the prologue generally discusses the reasons for his reader to be accepting of his text's wisdom, the last phrase "one who makes it hard for himself to understand" (מקשה עצמו לדעת) has a striking double entendre. The phrase comes directly from a Talmudic reference in BT Niddah 13b to forbidden sexual activities: "Rav stated, 'a man who willfully causes erection (המקשה עצמו לדעת) should be placed under a ban.' But why does he not say, 'This is forbidden?' Because the man merely incites his evil inclination against himself."[64] Given the lighthearted content of the *Melekh Artus* story and its lack of engagement with Talmudic legalese in general, this reference appears quite out of place and therefore humorous.

A similar play on words with an allusion to sex appears when Lancelot arrives at court after his time in a monastery, doing penance for his sins:

---

61. Stern and Mirsky, "The Alphabet of Ben Sira," 168.

62. Maud Kozodoy, "The Hebrew Bible as Weapon of Faith in Late Medieval Iberia: Irony, Satire, and Scriptural Allusion in Profiat Duran's *Al Tehi Ka-Avotekha*," *Jewish Studies Quarterly* 18, no. 2 (June 2011): 185–201; Maud Kozodoy, *The Secret Faith of Maestre Honoratus, Profayt Duran and Jewish Identity in Late Medieval Iberia* (Philadelphia: University of Pennsylvania Press, 2015), 115–28.

63. Leviant, *King Artus*, 12: הסיבה השנית אל העתקתי והיא הנכבדת היתה כי בתכלית שלזה הספר ילמדו החוטאים דרכי התשובות ויזכרו אחריתם וישובו אל חשם כמו שתראה בסופו. ודיי בהתנצלותי זה אצל כל חכם מודה על האמת בלתי מקשה עצמו לדעת

64. Babylonian Talmud Niddah 13b.

"But Queen Guinevere was a thousand times happier than everyone else at his arrival. For all the days that he was alone at the retreat were days of mourning, of crying in secret, and of sickness. It is no wonder, for love is as strong as death—the love that Guinevere had for him since the day that she was united with him due to Galehaut's temptations, as is told in another story."[65] This important passage showcases the many literary abilities of our Hebrew author, one of which is a sexual allusion on the phrase "at his arrival" (בביאתו), which can refer to sex.[66] Because we soon find out that Guinevere and Lancelot quickly rekindle their sexual relationship, the phrase foreshadows the return of their passion for one another. While the author plays with sexual overtones, he also references his biblical canon: the line "love is as strong as death" directly quotes *Song of Songs* 8:6.

In the macaronic wedding song "*El givat ha-levonah*," the author also finds humor in the language of medieval literary conquest. Kirsten Fudeman has argued that the song has two readings, one that emerges from an audience familiar with the Hebrew and one for the audience members who know only French.[67] If we read the alternating Hebrew lines as an independent production, we find a repetition of sexualized allusions based on biblical verses such as "bread eaten in secret" (v. 41), a sexual allusion from Prov. 9:17, and "there is in this muscle something that gives taste" (v. 44.). The word "muscle" has a phallic intent and refers to the Talmudic passage in b. Hullin 100b.[68] The sexual references humorously anticipate the consummation of the marriage later that night and play with the idea of "conquest" of the bride as mentioned above.

The Hebrew lines of the poem and the references in *Melekh Artus* may present the only example of profane biblical references seen in a Jewish text of medieval northern Europe. In opposition to the symbiotic relationship of the Bible and text in rabbinic texts, such as midrash, in which the Torah provides intertextual authority, the macaronic thirteenth-century wedding song plays on the status of Hebrew by putting a new secular tone on the biblical language.[69] This is a hallmark

---

65. Leviant, *King Artus*, 27–28.

66. See Babylonian Talmud Yoma 86b and Mishna Kedushin 1:1. Leviant, *King Artus*, 27.

67. Fudeman, "They Have Ears, but Do Not Hear." See also the discussion about gendered language in chapter 2 of this book.

68. Samuel N. Rosenberg, "The Medieval Hebrew-French Wedding Song," *Shofar* 11 (1992): 22–37.

69. Daniel Boyarin, *Intertextuality and the Reading of Midrash* (Bloomington: Indiana University Press, 1990); Michael S. Berger, *Rabbinic Authority* (Oxford: Oxford University Press, 1998).

of much of the secular literature from Al-Andalus.[70] By turning biblical language into heavily sexualized material, the wedding song profanes the sacredness of the text. A similar use of satire appears in wedding songs from fourteenth- and fifteenth-century Catalonia written in the Jewish language of Judeo-Catalan, with emphasis on sexual prowess and compatibility through biblical language.[71]

The inclusion of this sexual wordplay adds a note of levity to *Melekh Artus*—a text that can be read as subverting certain biblical references. When he introduces Lancelot, for example, the author writes, "These are the generations of Sir Lancelot. Know that the king Bano of Benoic and the king Borz of Gaunes were brothers who married two sisters born of the House of David. King Bano had a son named Lancelot del Lac. The reason that he is named del Lac, is it not written in the story about him?"[72]

This passage, which marks the beginning of the Arthurian stories, contains a few allusions to biblical language, such as the phrase "these are the generations" (אלה תולדות), which appears in Genesis as a formula that precedes genealogies (i.e., "these are the generations of Adam in Genesis 2:4, or "these are the generations of Jacob" in Genesis 37:2). The Bible uses the same phrase "is it not written" (הלא היא כתובה) to denote an intertextual reference. Here, however, the phrase refers to a text from the Arthurian canon rather than the biblical reference we would expect. This opening passage introduces *Melekh Artus* as an alternative to a biblical text. By incorporating biblical genealogies into a secular text about non-Jewish characters and referencing the Arthurian canon rather than the Torah, the text appears to challenge the textual norms of the medieval Jewish literary sphere. At the very least, even if the author is not "challenging" those norms, he equates the Jewish literary sphere with the Arthurian canon.

The simple translation of the "Holy Grail" reveals the author's subversive take on the mission of the Knights of the Round Table. He has translated the "grail" as "charity dish" (תמחוי). In the Talmud, the section Bava Batra 8a proclaims that if one lives in a city for thirty days, he must contribute to the *tamchuy* (תמחוי)—the charity platter from which food is distributed to the poor—and if he lives there for three months,

70. See, for one example, the poem "Caress the Breasts of a Beautiful Woman at Night," by Moses ibn Ezra, in Raymond P. Scheindlin, *Wine, Women, and Death: Medieval Hebrew Poems on the Good Life* (Oxford: Oxford University Press, 1986), 90. This poem compares the female body to the limbs of sacrificial offerings.

71. Ilil Baum, "Hebrew-Catalan Medieval Wedding Songs: Satirical Functions of the Hebrew Component and Other Linguistic Aspects," *Journal of Jewish Languages* 4, no. 2 (August 16, 2016): 166–202.

72. Leviant, *King Artus*, 14.

he must contribute to the charity box, with the obligations of a resident increasing the longer he has lived there.[73] Because the Jewish audience was familiar with the story of the grail, the translator's decision would strike them as one that departs from the accepted understanding of the grail as a venerated object.[74]

It is possible that this subversion is a reproach of knightly culture. The very existence of a story of knights in Hebrew suggests that knights can be Jewish. The idea that masculine, idealized knights of the Arthurian cycle can speak Hebrew appears to undermine those knightly attributes: in the medieval period, Judaism was seen by the majority culture as antithetical to masculinity. Christian polemic against Jews often referred to Jews as feminine—one trope advanced the myth of Jewish male menstruation, while Jews in response viewed Christians as violent and licentious.[75] With Hebrew-speaking, quasi-Jewish identities, the Christian knights no longer have quintessentially Christian qualities. By extension, they are no longer masculine.

If Jews can subvert knightly culture, we might expect to see a pushback against the courtly love motif in Hebrew literature more generally. As mentioned, courtly love usually describes an unconsummated love between two unmarried partners that would appear to be untenable as a genre for Jewish consumption given the emphasis on consummation, procreation, and marital satisfaction in rabbinic law. But if the Hebrew authors genuinely rejected courtly love and romance completely, they

73. Talmudic passage, Bava Batra 8a: ולכל מילי מי בעינן י"ב חדש והתניא שלשים יום לתמחוי. It must be noted that the word תמחוי also referred to a specific type of bowl in the Talmud outside the context of charity; I assume here that the translator of *Melekh Artus* and his audience knew multiple meanings of the word and were aware of the wordplay here.

74. It was only in the later medieval versions of the grail legend that it took on a Christian meaning as the chalice from which Jesus drank. It is not clear if the Jewish audiences would have viewed it as a specifically Christian object, although they likely knew it was an important part of the plot in the Arthurian stories. Roger Sherman Loomis, *The Grail: From Celtic Myth to Christian Symbol* (New York: Columbia University Press, 1963). See chapter 2 of this book for references within *Melekh Artus* to other Arthurian legends that imply Jewish familiarity.

75. For the trope of male menses, see Noga Roguin Maor, Ariel Roguin, and Nathan Roguin, "Medieval Roots of the Myth of Jewish Male Menstruation," *Rambam Maimonides Medical Journal* 12, no. 4 (October 25, 2021): e0033, https://doi.org/10.5041/RMMJ.10454; C. Philipp E. Nothaft, "The Meaning of Judaeus and the Myth of Jewish Male Menses in a Late Medieval Astronomical School Text," *European Journal of Jewish Studies* 7, no. 1 (2013): 73–93. On the Jewish view of Christians, examples appear in Joseph Kimhi, *The Book of the Covenant of Joseph Kimhi*, trans. Frank Talmage (Toronto: Pontifical Institute of Mediaeval Studies, 1972); Robert Chazan, *Fashioning Jewish Identity in Medieval Western Christendom* (Cambridge: Cambridge University Press, 2004), 298–359; Alexandra Cuffel, *Gendering Disgust in Medieval Religious Polemic* (Notre Dame, IN: University of Notre Dame Press, 2007), pt. II.

would not have translated it. What we do find are examples like *Melekh Artus* that bring chivalry and courtly love into the Hebrew fold.

It is apparent, however, that *Melekh Artus* and the wedding songs do not subvert Christian literary themes for any anti-Christian polemical purpose. These subversions are more humorous than they are reproachful, with only a hint of satire, and the knights who speak Hebrew are no different from Chrétien's French knights, given how similar the translation is to the original. *Melekh Artus* does not condemn Christians for the chivalric themes that appear in their literature, such as tournaments or adulterous relationships, any more than contemporary Christian authors did. The emphasis on marriage as the ultimate goal in a medieval story was not limited to the Jewish iterations of romance. Even Chrétien, the great medieval French romance author, challenged the concept of the roving, unmarried, or unfaithful knight.[76] In his *Yvain*, Yvain leaves the domestic life of his castle for more adventures with his lion companion. His desire for glory in the tournament causes him to abandon his wife, Lunette. Rather than an idealized version of glory seeking, Chrétien may intend his story as a warning against abandoning one's domestic obligations.[77]

Chrétien's earliest romance, *Érec et Énide*, presents a version of an ideal marriage in which the pair marries at the beginning of the text and domestic life does not impede the action that Érec seeks because Énide accompanies her husband on his adventures.[78] In this romance, Chrétien explores the ideal of courtly love *within* an aristocratic marriage, perhaps in response to the popular genre of troubadour poetry with themes of extramarital love.[79] His *Cligès* is also a "denunciation" of the affair between Tristan and Isolde contained in an earlier *Tristan* romance.[80] Even stories that glorify passionate affairs often end with tragedy for the lovers, such as for Guinevere and Lancelot, or Tristan and Yseult in Béroul's version, thus seeming to denigrate the characters for their decisions to act upon their passions through extramarital affairs. In a unique fourteenth- or fifteenth-century Hebrew story from

76. Peter S. Noble, *Love and Marriage in Chrétien de Troyes* (Cardiff: University of Wales Press, 1982).

77. Chrétien de Troyes, *Le chevalier au lion ou le roman d'Yvain*, ed. and trans. David F. Hult (Paris: Librairie Générale Française, 2009).

78. Chrétien de Troyes, *Erec and Enide*, trans. Ruth Harwood Cline (Athens: University of Georgia Press, 2000).

79. Chrétien de Troyes, *Erec and Enide*, xxi–xxiii.

80. See the translator's introduction to Chrétien de Troyes, *Erec and Enide*, xvi.

Italy, the author has drawn on Chrétien's *Yvain* to form the basis of his tale. Like its French counterpart, the happy ending of the Hebrew story involves the reconciliation of the main character to his wife rather than the successful pursuit of virtue.[81] Guinevere and Lancelot's "illicit love" in the French version and "foolish passion" in the Hebrew are equally condemning. *Dukus Horant* treats its romantic love in the same way as a non-Jewish romance text would: Horant seduces the princess through his singing, and although the two "embrace," it is all performed "in a courtly manner." The seduction, we recall, is done under oath for his king, who has sent Horant to fetch the princess for him.[82]

A different type of romance appears in the thirteenth-century Hebrew folktale collection *Sefer ha-Ma'asim*, most of whose tales contain rabbinic or pious themes that would seem incongruous with non-Jewish genres. In the Hebrew tale "The Poor Bachelor and His Rich Maiden Cousin," a poor bachelor named Isaac and his wealthy cousin fall in love and go through a series of trials before they can marry. In this story, the cousin's parents realize the two have fallen in love. Because of Isaac's lack of wealth, the cousin's parents offer him and another suitor a deal: they give each of the bachelors a sum of money, and whoever returns in a year with more money will win the hand of their daughter. Isaac ventures off and becomes wealthy when he discovers a magical plant that cures the king's leprosy. In gratitude, the king rewards Isaac with a kingdom and material wealth. Isaac victoriously returns home and marries his cousin.

At the beginning of the story, Isaac and his cousin fall in love and initiate a relationship rather unconventionally. Isaac's rabbi tells him to lie in bed with his cousin. Isaac agrees, but puts a sword between him and his cousin to prevent them from engaging in sexual acts.[83] This sword undoubtedly originates in Béroul's Old French romance *Tristan et Iseult*,

81. Rella Kushelevsky, "Jews Reading Arthurian Romances from the Middle Ages: On the Reception of Chrétien de Troyes's *Yvain, the Knight of the Lion*, Based on Manuscript JTS Rab. 1164," *AJS Review* 42, no. 2 (November 2018): 391.

82. Frakes, "Dukus Horant," 174.

83. There is a fascinating illustration in a sixteenth-century Spanish Haggadah from Greece of a man and woman separated by a sword. In the context of the Haggadah, it portrays the punishment of the Jews in Egypt of *perishut derech eretz*, representing a break in sexual relations, and its depiction follows typical Italian-Jewish iconography. I do not know what the connection might be, if any, between this iconography, the Passover story, and the story here. Library of the castle of Chantilly, Bibliothèque du château Chantilly, 0732 (1352) f. 014v. The image appears also in Yosef Kaplan, ed., *The Early Modern Era, 1500–1750*, vol. 5 (New Haven, CT: Yale University Press, 2023), 556.

which features a sword serving the same purpose between the two eponymous lovers.[84] The manuscript tradition of Béroul situates the story in northern France, with the original text dating to the latter half of the twelfth century.[85] The dating and the location of *Tristan* makes it probable that the author of *Sefer ha-Ma'asim* knew it. *Tristan* tells the story of Tristan and Iseult's ill-fated love affair that they attempt to hide from Iseult's husband, King Marc.

In "The Poor Bachelor," the maiden's father sees the two in bed but realizes that they are sleeping together innocently with the sword as a barrier. He places his *tallit* ("prayer shawl" or "prayer robe") on them and leaves. In the French version, Iseult's husband Marc also sees the lovers and deems their relationship chaste, placing his glove atop his sleeping wife.[86] When the lovers awake and see the tokens left, they know that they have been caught. The editorial change from a glove to a *tallit* places the text within a Jewish framework because the *tallit* is worn while praying in a Jewish setting. Rella Kushelevsky has also identified rabbinic antecedents for this story that contribute to its Jewishness.[87] "The Poor Bachelor" is thus a combination of traditional rabbinic stories and specifically Jewish objects with contemporaneous secular motifs.

And yet the addition of the *tallit* does not make the story pious or any more acceptable to a Jewish audience. In other words, the addition of the *tallit* provides a Hebrew equivalent for the knightly glove of the source text, a linguistic exchanging of words rather than a change based on religious motivations. This is supportable by looking elsewhere in "The Poor Bachelor," which generally avoids piety as a motivation for

84. Rella Kushelevsky, "Chastity versus Courtly Love in 'The Poor Bachelor and His Rich Maiden Cousin,'" *Jewish Studies Quarterly* 20 (2013): 72; Stith Thompson, *Motif-Index of Folk-Literature: A Classification of Narrative Elements in Folktales, Ballads, Myths, Fables, Medieval Romances, Exempla, Fabliaux, Jest-Books and Local Legends* (Bloomington: Indiana University Press, 1955), para. T351; Anita Guerreau-Jalabert, *Index des motifs narratifs dans les romans arthuriens français en vers: XIIe–XIIIe siècles* (Geneva: Droz, 1992), 201. As Kushelevsky points out, this was a motif that appears in contemporaneous Old French and rabbinic Hebrew texts. It is described as "the sword of chastity" in the index of folktale motifs and appears in international folktales. See Thompson, *Motif-Index of Folk-Literature*, par. T351. In the Arthurian corpus, its only attestation is in the *Tristan* manuscripts. Guerreau-Jalabert, *Index des motifs narratifs*, 201.

85. Barbara N. Sargent-Baur, *The Romance of Tristran by Béroul and Béroul II: A Diplomatic Edition and a Critical Edition* (Toronto: University of Toronto Press, 2015).

86. Sargent-Baur, *The Romance of Tristran by Béroul and Béroul* II, v. 1996–2000.

87. Kushelevsky, "Chastity versus Courtly Love," 66–69.

its characters' actions. For example, after Isaac's teacher notices that he and his cousin have fallen in love, he offers the bachelor his advice:

> One day, the rabbi summoned Isaac and told him: "Listen, my son, to what I am instructing you, and God will be with you tonight. As soon as you arrive at your uncle's house, and you see your cousin there, take her, and embrace her, and kiss her." Isaac said to him, "Rabbi, how could I do such a terrible thing, to give into my evil inclination, while I am still able to escape it?" The rabbi said to him, "I swear that I will not let you go until you swear to me that you will do this thing." The young man took the oath before him.[88]

The rabbi's suggestion to embrace his cousin contradicts the traditional depiction of rabbis as upholders of piety and righteousness, especially as they appear elsewhere in the *Sefer ha-Ma'asim* collection. But Isaac's rabbi makes him swear to commit an impious act, of embracing his unmarried female relative. Isaac recognizes this, knowing that the deed will submit to his "evil inclination" (יצר הרע). The figure of the rabbi may be based on a similar story from the Talmud, in which a rabbi breaks the laws of family purity.[89] Kushelevsky refers to the rabbi's advice as "a gambit" that succeeds because the uncle learns about the relationship and allows the two to marry—eventually.[90] Regardless of the ultimate outcome of the story, the rabbi's behavior here challenges and possibly satirizes the authoritative figure. The next day, the rabbi then advises Isaac and his cousin to sleep in the same bed: "And after nine nights, his rabbi said: 'Go now and sleep in her bed.' He said, 'How can I do that? If my uncle hears this, he will kill me.' 'Do what I command you,' said the rabbi, 'and don't desist.' The boy went home, slept with her in her bed, and took a sword and placed it between them. And they lay side by side and slept until morning."[91] By using a rabbi to deliver the message that the lovers can engage in this nonpious, courtly

88. Rella Kushelevsky, *Tales in Context: Sefer Ha-Ma'asim in Medieval Northern France* (Detroit, MI: Wayne State University Press, 2017), 292–93. יום אחד קרא חרב לאותו יצחק וא"ל: לך בני שמע בקולי לאשר אני מצה אותך, ויהי א-להים עמך בלילה הזה. מיד כשתבא לבית דודך ותמצא שם קרובתך, קחנה ותחבקנה ונשוק אותה. א"ל: ר' איך אעשה חרעה הזאת להשיא יצר הרע עלי כל זמן שיכולתי להמלט ממנו? א"ל: בשבועה לא אניחך עד שתישבע לי שתעשה זאת. עמד הבחור ושבע לו.

89. Kushelevsky, "Chastity versus Courtly Love," 68.

90. Kushelevsky, "Chastity versus Courtly Love," 69.

91. Kushelevsky, *Tales in Context*, 294–95. ולאחר תשע לילות א"ל רבו: לך שכוב הלילה במטה. א"ל:איך אני אעשה זאת ושמע דודי והרגני? א"ל רבו: עשה כאשר אני מצוה אותך, ואל תניח. הלך הבחור ושכב עמה במיטה, ונטל חרב ושם ביניהם וישכבו יחד וישנו עד הבקר.

love behavior, the author ironically puts the rabbi in the position of mediator between Jewish tradition and courtly tradition. Through the device of the sword, Isaac himself unites these two seemingly opposite values: Jewish tradition and courtly tradition.

When Isaac receives his reward of marrying his cousin at the end of the tale, any religious observances or piety that Isaac possessed are not used as evidence for his deservedness. The tale ends: "And he had great wealth and was the ruler over all the land. He lived a long life and was greatly righteous all the days of his life, and sons and daughters were born to him. And that which happened to him, may it happen to us too. Amen."[92] In the first French translation of the text published in 1897, Israel Lévi translated the last sentence, "puissions-nous avoir le même sort!"[93] The word "sort" in French implies fate or destiny. To translate from the French, we would read "may we have the same fate!" The Hebrew text, however, contains no mention of the word "fate" and in fact no mention of divine intervention in any form. Only once does the narrative mention God's intervention in the story, as discussed below. Isaac becomes the maiden's husband not through his piety, which he has already at the beginning of the story as a Torah scholar, but through his ability to earn money after one year. Both Isaac's business acumen (although his money comes through a great deal of luck) and his status as a modest scholarly young man contribute to his ability to attain a successful marriage.

The deemphasis on success as solely divinely mediated reinforces the idea that the narrative itself, including the plot and characters, are the crucial aspects for understanding the story's message. God and pious references are not necessary to convey the didactic message. This is in stark contrast to other stories in *Sefer ha-Ma'asim*, which connect daily observances to a divine reward in heaven. The epilogue to another story in *Sefer ha-Ma'asim*, "Haninah, Mishael, and Azaria," describes the three Israelites who are spared from burning in a fire and condemns those who are not as honorable: "God uproots anyone who worships idols both from this world and the next, and he will see all the good that God will do for the righteous ones, and they will be ashamed and say: Woe unto us that we did not merit this honor, because we abandoned

92. Kushelevsky, *Tales in Context*, 303. והוא היה עשיר גדול ושר שליט בכל הארץ, ויחי האיש ימים רבים וצדיק וחסיד היה כל ימיו ויולד בנים ובנות וכשאר היה לו יהיה לנו אמן.

93. Israel Lévi, "Un recueil de contes juives inédits," *Revue des études juives* 34–35 (1897): 458–76.

a living God to worship a dead one. And then fire will emerge and consume all the apostates who abandoned God and did not repent."[94]

Despite many previous versions of this tale, this particular epilogue appears for the first time in the manuscript Oxford, Bodl. Or. 135, both in *Sefer ha-Ma'asim* and in a slightly different version in the same manuscript as part of a story collection called *Midrash aseret hadibrot* (Midrash of the Ten Commandments).[95] Not only does this epilogue promote a specifically Jewish commandment to worship one god and refrain from any idol worship, it also mentions apostates (המשומדים) who do not merit a reward in the world to come.

Some of the folktales in the collection focus on the importance of observing the Sabbath, such as "The Sabbath Observer and the Bear." In this story, three merchants are traveling when the time of the Sabbath approaches. Two of the men continue to travel, breaking the Sabbath rules in the process, while the third man rests for the night. The desecrators of the Sabbath encounter robbers, but the third man meets a bear who protects him from the thieves. The story concludes, "And now see how great is the reward of the righteous, those who carry out the commandments and observe the Sabbath. God performs a miracle for he who observes the Sabbath, and he who observes the Sabbath all the days of his life, all the more so. And now, come see how great is the reward of the righteous who perform the commandments and observe the Sabbath!"[96]

The epilogue reiterates, quite repetitively, the emphasis on Sabbath observance already contained in the narrative. This is the first known version of the story, although it is transmitted to later Ashkenazic story collections, including the *Mayse Bukh* (Book of Stories), in Hebrew and Yiddish.[97] While the content of the story shares some aspects with non-Jewish tales, the emphasis on the Sabbath marks it definitively as a story with Jewish importance.[98]

---

94. Kushelevsky, *Tales in Context*, 122–23. וכל העובד ע"ז הקב"ה עוקרו מן העולם הזה והעולם הבא ויראה הטובות שיעשה הק"בה לצדיקים ויבושו ויאמרו: אוי לנו שלא זכינו לכבוד זה על שהנחנו אל חי ועבדנו לאל מת. ואז תצא אש ותאכל כל המשומדים שעזבו הק"ה ולא חזרו בתשובה.

95. Kushelevsky, *Tales in Context*, 403.

96. Kushelevsky, *Tales in Context*, 140–41. ועתה בא וראה כמה שכרן של צדיקים, עושי מצות ושמורי שבת. ומה זה ששמר שבת עשה לו הק"ה נס, השמור שבת כלי ימיו על אחת כמה וכמה.

97. Kushelevsky, *Tales in Context*, 415.

98. See, for example, tale types B251.6. Animals keep religious precepts; B251.7. Animal makes religious oath; B251.9. Animals make religious responses; B435.4. Helpful bear; B580. Animal helps men to wealth and greatness; Thompson, *Motif-Index of Folk-Literature*.

In the story titled "The Commandment of *Tzitzit* (Fringes)," through his adherence to the commandment to wear *tzitzit* (fringes), a man persuades a harlot to repent and convert. The two enjoy a happy life together: "This was their reward in this world, and in the next, they will bask in the radiant light of the Divine presence. And always make sure that your sons are born in purity. And marry a pure woman who will not betray you. For this you will be rewarded with righteous sons, who will respect and honor you."[99] The characters not only receive worldly success but are assured of a place in the heavenly world to come. In the epilogue, the woman's repentance becomes linked to the obligation to marry and bear children. This folktale challenges the adulterous themes of contemporaneous courtly love literature by presenting marriage as the means to a reward.[100] Its focus on the Jewish custom of wearing *tzitzit* marks it as significantly different from the narrative content of "The Poor Bachelor," *Melekh Artus*, and *Mishle Shu'alim*, which do not contain specifically Jewish rituals. But "The Commandment of *Tzitzit*" similarly deemphasizes the traditional emphasis of courtly love in favor of marriage bonds.

In "The Poor Bachelor," the use of non-Jewish literary devices and plots ultimately create a humorous story that defends the importance of an appropriate marriage: Isaac cannot marry his cousin until he proves himself to be financially stable. The crucial moment of Isaac's story happens when he is stranded on a desert island, where he encounters a magical plant: "He raised his eyes and saw a plant. God inspired him to eat from it, and he stretched out his hand to the plant to eat it."[101] The plant, Isaac finds out, has magical healing properties. After his rescue, Isaac finds himself at the court of a king with leprosy, whom he heals with the plant. This results in grateful largesse—the king grants Isaac an entire city to command.

God's rationale for inspiring the bachelor is never stated. Although his status as a Torah scholar (תלמיד חכם) at the beginning of the text suggests his piety, he does not perform any particularly Jewish observances that would merit any divine rewards, such as wearing *tzitzit* or observing the Sabbath in the stories above. When God inspires him to reach for

99. Kushelevsky, *Tales in Context*, 156–57. וזה היה מתן שכרן בעולם הזה, לעולם הבא יהנו מזיר שכינה. ולעולם {הזהר שיהיו}בניך נולדים בנקיות. ושא אשה נקייה שלא יבגוד בך, כדי שיהו בניך זריזים במצות כבודך.

100 Kushelevsky, "Chastity versus Courtly Love," 432.

101. Kushelevsky, *Tales in Context*, 299. שם הק"בה בלבו לאכול ממנו, והושיט ידו ולקח מאותו עשב ואכל

the plant, there is no indication that Isaac has earned that inspiration through Jewish observance. However, Shamma Boyarin has argued that the label of Torah scholar, called a "son of Torah," in comparable medieval Hebrew folktales replaces the expected stock character of a knight in medieval non-Jewish tales. This son of Torah retains many of the characteristics of a knight from chivalric romance, featuring an adventure, an honor code, and a romantic encounter.[102] It is possible that a Jewish reader or listener would automatically associate Isaac with the traits of a quintessential Torah scholar, even without any mention of his own religious practices.

Even as it avoids and at times plays around with rabbinic law, this story does not ultimately vilify either rabbinic culture or courtly culture. Its happy ending of marriage between two suitable and willing youth, despite the impiety that led there, demonstrates the ability of its hero the Torah scholar-turned-knight Isaac to weather adventures and adversity, as we would expect from chivalric romance. Out of all the medieval Jewish literary characters, Isaac is as much a character from Chrétien as he is a Jewish figure. There is no evidence that the story detracts from rabbinic culture; rather, it jokes with it—prodding at its authority with a literary pointer. The story appears in *Sefer ha-Ma'asim* alongside rabbinic stories on sages of the Talmud and folktales designed to increase one's recitation of certain prayers. In other words, it was welcomed into the Jewish literary fold.

Concern with adultery unites the Jewish and Christian communities, as expressed in their own romances, in Hebrew and French, respectively. Through this reading of the French stories that inspired *Melekh Artus* and "The Poor Bachelor," the parodic, humorous, or subtly negative rewritings of the Jewish authors does not directly challenge the original intent of their source material. The Jewish readings are not anti-Christian or antithetical to the vernacular genres. The knights and courtly love genres of the texts' sources are ultimately carried through into the Hebrew versions and are used to promote expectations of marriage as a common concern across religious boundaries. When unconsummated courtly love, as in the case of Isaac and his cousin, veers into adulterous behavior, such as that displayed by Lancelot and

102. Shamma Boyarin, "At the Court of the Demon King: The Story of the Jerusalemite and Chivalric Romance," in *Medieval and Early Modern Jewish Romance*, ed. Caroline Gruenbaum and Annegret Oehme (Kalamazoo, MI: Arc Humanities, 2023), 95–106.

Guinevere, the Hebrew texts condemn its acts in the same way as their source texts.

Through its incorporation of non-Jewish source material, Hebrew romance advances the notion of an intellectual Hebrew culture in medieval northern France and Italy that would soon extend to the Jewish vernacular of Yiddish.[103] By the sixteenth century, Yiddish romance had expanded beyond the German-Jewish *Dukus Horant* (Duke Horant) to the definitively Old Yiddish romances *Vidvilt* (Wigalois) and *Bovo-Bukh* (a Yiddish translation of the Italian *Buovo d'Antona*, Bevis of Hampton).[104] In keeping with the patterns observed in Hebrew translation of French romance and seen already in *Dukus Horant*, these Yiddish stories do not add Jewish elements in their translations but rather carry over the non-Jewish plots, characters, and motifs.[105] Incorporation of Yiddish romance into early printed books allowed the dissemination of story collections such as the *Mayse Bukh* and the *Kuhbukh* (Book of Cow [Stories]), which, like *Sefer ha-Ma'asim*, contain a mix of religious tales with pious morals and secular stories based on vernacular romance and folktales. Despite some pushback about the acceptability of translations for popular consumption,[106] these popular Yiddish collections demonstrated the extent to which the Jews of Ashkenaz were ready to embrace the genre of secular literature, and romance, as a Jewish literary form.

---

103. With this understanding, I disagree with the notion that Jewish romantic literature emerged suddenly in the early modern period. See, for example, Naomi Seidman, *The Marriage Plot: Or, How Jews Fell in Love with Love, and with Literature* (Stanford, CA: Stanford University Press, 2016).

104. Annegret Oehme, *The Knight without Boundaries: Yiddish and German Arthurian* Wigalois *Adaptations* (Leiden: Brill, 2022); Elia Bokher, *Bovo d'Antona*, ed. Claudia Rosenzweig (Leiden: Brill, 2015).

105. Jerold C. Frakes, *The Emergence of Early Yiddish Literature: Cultural Translation in Ashkenaz* (Bloomington: Indiana University Press, 2017); Jerold C. Frakes, ed., "Dukus Horant," in *Early Yiddish Texts 1100–1750: With Introduction and Commentary* (Oxford: Oxford University Press, 2004), 33–43.

106. Iris Idelson-Shein, *Between the Bridge and the Barricade* (Philadelphia: University of Pennsylvania Press, 2024), https://penn.manifoldapp.org/projects/between-the-bridge-and-the-barricade.

Chapter 5

Converts and the Limits of Medieval Jewish Literature

The beginning of this book discussed instances in which Jews created secular literature, but in some cases, conversion was the only way they were able to cross literary boundaries. The literary fields of belletristic poetry and autobiography were not open to Jewish authors in Ashkenaz, and the only instances of Jewish authorship are often linked to conversion of the authors to Christianity. In other words, Jewish authors felt an encumbrance to these genres within Jewish culture; with very few examples, one of the only ways that Jewish authors could engage were when the authors themselves moved away from Judaism. These examples represent the limits of expansion into secular literary themes and genres.

Stories like *Melekh Artus* (King Arthur) and Aesopic fables demonstrate the ability of medieval Jews to engage in some secular translations. Yet there are clearly limitations to secular Jewish writing. Certain secular genres were not attempted by Jewish authors in medieval northern France, including poetry, original works of romance, music, and biographical narratives, unlike their Christian neighbors, who invented and expanded those written and performative forms of culture.[1] Jews, for

1. Douglas Kelly, *The Art of Medieval French Romance* (Madison: University of Wisconsin Press, 1992), 32–40.

example, wrote in French only in exceptional cases, implying that they did not want to or felt they could not join that cultural milieu. The few Jews who wrote in French or attempted to cross generic boundaries of poetry and autobiography, as will be shown, underwent conversion or have a vague religious identity somewhere between Judaism and Christianity. In other words, only these nontraditional Jews chose to work with non-Jewish languages and genres—as though an invisible barrier prevented traditional (i.e., nonconverted) Jews from writing in languages or scripts that were not Jewish.

The decision by medieval northern European Jews to eschew certain secular genres and non-Jewish languages likely correlates to a fear of assimilation and conversion. Writing secular poetry or recording in the Latin alphabet was too much a part of the non-Jewish literary world to be an acceptable Jewish form of text. This was expressed (silently) by the lacuna of Jewish literature in non-Jewish languages in the medieval period and reiterated by the rabbis' (albeit tepid) dismissal of romance, as seen in chapter 4. Because we cannot build an argument solely on the lack of Jewish authorship of non-Jewish-oriented texts, we will instead focus on the instances of Jews who did engage with these seemingly taboo forms of culture. Religious identity, like linguistic circumstances and historical literary history as outlined in the first few chapters of this book, had a direct influence on the literary forms produced in this period.

The link between conversion and Jewish mobility has a long history, and one that has a unique iteration in the form of thirteenth-century literature penned by Jewish converts. To take a more modern example, in 1822, the German Jew Eduard Gans was appointed to the chair of law at Berlin University, but his appointment was cancelled after his Jewish identity was revealed. He decided to baptize and was immediately approved for the position. He said to a friend, "If the state is so stupid as to forbid me to serve it in a capacity which suits my particular talents unless I profess something I do not believe—and something which the responsible minister *knows* I do not believe: all right then, it shall have its wish."[2]

His friend, the famous Jewish author Heinrich Heine, quipped that baptism was an "entry-ticket to European culture" (*Entreebillet zur europäischen Kultur*).[3] Heine himself was not immune to the draw of

---

2. Siegbert Salomon Prawer, *Heine's Jewish Comedy: A Study of His Portraits of Jews and Judaism* (Oxford: Clarendon, 1983), 12.

3. Ludwig Rosenthal, *Heinrich Heine als Jude* (Frankfurt: Ullstein Verlag, 1973), 104.

European culture and greater job prospects, and had converted shortly before his friend Gans.[4] Heine wrote scornfully about Gans's conversion in poem form, an expression of the writer's self-doubt about his own decision.[5] A poetry collection he produced later in life, the *Romanzero* (1851), contains a poem titled "Jehuda ben Halevi," after the famous medieval Spanish Hebrew poet Judah ha-Levi. In this poem, Heine reflects on Jewish tradition and modernity. In another, he refers to the martyrdoms of medieval rabbis. Despite Heine's religious breach, he did not fully separate himself from the long history of Jewish cultural traditions.[6] This chapter will reveal other complexities of culture, especially within the genre of poetry, for Jewish writers who found a foothold in the Christian literary world.

While nineteenth-century Berlin was a particularly ripe place and time for Jewish conversion, medieval northern Europe offered certain economic and social possibilities for new Christians as well. By the late thirteenth century, the Jewish communities of France and England were affected by a likely high level of conversion.[7] Although it is difficult to establish true numbers on population, it is likely that around 10 percent of the Jewish population in mid-thirteenth-century England and hundreds of French Jews in the same period converted and that voluntary conversion was part of the everyday lives of northern European Jews.[8]

Given the uncertainty about Jewish population at these periods, it is hard to determine the significance of these numbers. It was enough, however, to become a worry for contemporaneous rabbis, who mention issues about conversion often, especially as it affected the family unit.[9] These new Christians could enjoy government support, access to greater

---

4. Prawer, *Heine's Jewish Comedy*, 16.

5. Prawer, *Heine's Jewish Comedy*, 15.

6. Peter Routledge, "'Jehuda Ben Halevy' and the Restructuring of Memory within Poetic Discourse," in *Heine-Jahrbuch 2015: 54. Jahrgang*, ed. Sabine Brenner-Wilczek (Stuttgart: J. B. Metzler, 2015), 58–83, https://doi.org/10.1007/978-3-476-01400-9_4; Michael Swellander, "The Arabic-Spanish-Jewish School of Poets: Heinrich Heine's 'Jehudah Ben Halevy' and World Literature," *Germanic Review: Literature, Culture, Theory* 98, no. 1 (January 2, 2023): 33–45, https://doi.org/10.1080/00168890.2022.2161338.

7. Robert C. Stacey, "The Conversion of Jews to Christianity in Thirteenth-Century England," *Speculum* 67, no. 2 (April 1992): 263–83.

8. Paola Tartakoff, "Testing Boundaries: Jewish Conversion and Cultural Fluidity in Medieval Europe, c. 1200–1391," *Speculum* 90, no. 3 (July 2015): 734. A partner in a marriage who opted to convert to Christianity was "quite frequent": Avraham Grossman, *Pious and Rebellious: Jewish Women in Medieval Europe* (Waltham, MA: Brandeis University Press, 2004), 53, 240; Stacey, "The Conversion of Jews to Christianity in Thirteenth-Century England," 269–71.

9. For a sample of rabbinic responses concerning conversion and family life, see Grossman, *Pious and Rebellious*, 53–54, 198–99, 202–9, 205, 207, 240, 281.

job prospects, and social acceptance. Converted Jews played prominent roles in the rise of polemical literature in the thirteenth century; given their education in Hebrew and Judaism, they were in a unique position to target the Jewish faith.[10]

This does not mean that converts were opportunists striving for the next opportunity, sacrificing integrity along the way. Rather, according to William C. Jordan, they were driven by a "yearning to belong."[11] This yearning to belong to the majority culture can take many forms historically; attempting to pass oneself as part of the majority acts as protection for a persecuted minority.[12] Medieval French Jews converted for several related reasons, including a desire for more flexibility in choosing a marriage partner, general autonomy, and more opportunities for material wealth in a stable job market.[13] As Paola Tartakoff argued, medieval conversion was not the result of acculturation but rather a way to resolve personal difficulties that plagued the Jewish community.[14] On the one hand, conversion was a decision motivated by personal considerations, but on the other, it was a tactical move. Through conversion, Jews sought social, legal, and political opportunities afforded to Christians and avoided the hostility aimed at their former religion (although, in reality, newly converted Christians were not always accepted wholeheartedly).[15]

These Jewish literati and Jewish converts occupy a liminal space between Jewish and Christian literature.[16] As they transition to a new

---

10. Robert Chazan, "The Barcelona 'Disputation' of 1263: Christian Missionizing and Jewish Response," *Speculum* 52, no. 4 (October 1977): 824–42; Jeremy Cohen, "The Mentality of the Medieval Jewish Apostate: Peter Alfonsi, Hermann of Cologne, and Pablo Christiani," in *Jewish Apostasy in the Modern World*, ed. Todd M. Endelman (New York: Holmes & Meier, 1987), 20–47.

11. William C. Jordan, "Exclusion and the Yearning to Belong: Evidence from the History of Thirteenth-Century France," in *Difference and Identity in Francia and Medieval France*, ed. Meredith Cohen and Justine Firnhaber-Baker (Surrey: Ashgate, 2010), 13–24. Jordan writes, "not all converts were necessarily unprincipled opportunists" in William C. Jordan, "Adolescence and Conversion in the Middle Ages: A Research Agenda," in *Jews and Christians in Twelfth-Century Europe*, ed. Michael Alan Signer and John H. Van Engen, 77–93 (Notre Dame, IN: University of Notre Dame, 2001), 77.

12. Jordan, "Exclusion and the Yearning to Belong," 14.

13. Jordan, "Adolescence and Conversion in the Middle Ages."

14. Tartakoff, "Testing Boundaries," 731.

15. Tartakoff, "Testing Boundaries," 732.

16. Liminality, a concept popularized by the anthropologist Victor Turner, describes an in-between state occupied by those in the midst of a community ritual. Victor Turner, "Liminality and Communitas," in *The Ritual Process: Structure and Anti-Structure* (Chicago: Aldine, 1969), 94–130. We see examples of converted Jews living in a liminal space, literally, in the example of the *Domus Conversorum* (House of the Converts), a royally supported community

religion, they express their liminality through the realm of literature that is inaccessible to them before or after their transition. These exceptional cases are the subjects of this chapter. If we consider those Jews who did attempt to write in non-Jewish languages or in non-Jewish genres, we find Jewish identities that are more fluid than the identities of Hebrew authors, who are always Jewish.

Three Jewish authors from late medieval northern France and Germany wrote in the vernacular language (French or German) and in the vernacular alphabet—Herman the Jew, Hagin le Juif, and Süsskind of Trimberg—but only after converting to Christianity.[17] Only after conversion could the former Jews engage in vernacular, belletristic literary creativity.[18] We can add to our list the plausibly Jewish, or formerly Jewish, poets Mahieu le Juif and Charlot le Juif, and the Jewish convert Obadiah the Proselyte. All these authors have tenuous claims to Judaism, either as converts or referred to with a Jewish attribution; their status allows them to cross the barrier into Christian culture more easily than their Jewish counterparts. While conversion has been studied in light of its effect on polemics, on family life, and on religious practice, it does not often feature into literary discussions. This chapter showcases conversion and religious identity as an integral part of an author's identity, especially in the genres of poetry and music.

Just like the rabbinic writing about courtly love romance and secular texts, it seems that medieval rabbinic strictures did not specifically condemn music and poetry as forbidden cultural genres. We recall the rabbinic ambivalence about courtly love romance from chapter 4. On the

---

for former Jews in England. See, among others, Lauren Fogle, *The King's Converts: Jewish Conversion in Medieval London* (Lanham, MD: Lexington Books, 2018).

17. For the purposes of this chapter, I use the term "Jewish" as a reflection of their upbringing and level of Jewish education and Hebrew knowledge rather than their self-identification or religious status. The rabbis of medieval northern Europe did not agree on the protocol for determining a convert's Jewish status. For more on the status of forced converts and repentant apostates, see Rachel Furst, "A Return to Credibility? The Rehabilitation of Repentant Apostates in Medieval Ashkenaz," in *On the Word of a Jew: Religion, Reliability, and the Dynamics of Trust*, ed. Nina Caputo and Mitchell B. Hart (Bloomington: Indiana University Press, 2018), 201–21; David Malkiel, "Jews and Apostates in Medieval Europe—Boundaries Real and Imagined," *Past & Present* 194 (February 2007): 3–34; Edward Fram, "Perception and Reception of Repentant Apostates in Medieval Ashkenaz and Pre-Modern Poland," *AJS Review* 21, no. 2 (1996): 299–340.

18. There may be examples of Jewish belletristic texts that did not survive to modern day. Compare the speculations in Alan D. Deyermond, "The Lost Genre of Medieval Spanish Literature," *Hispanic Review* 43, no. 3 (1975): 231–59, https://doi.org/10.2307/472251; Alan D. Deyermond, "The Lost Literature of Medieval Spain," *La Corónica: A Journal of Medieval Hispanic Languages, Literatures, and Cultures* 5 (1976): 93–100.

one hand, rabbis admonish those who read secular romances on Shabbat. On the other hand, the rabbinic commentary on *Song of Songs* compares the biblical song to the love songs of the *trouvères*, French troubadour poets. Despite a positive comparison between the *trouvère* songs and the *Song of Songs*, the commentator ironically notes that these love songs are "customary in the non-Jewish world" (במנהג העולם, *be-minhag ha-olam*).[19] By making the comparison between *trouvères* and the *Song of Songs*, the commentator implicitly brings those secular love songs into the medieval Jewish rabbinic conversation; through his words, the love songs are linked transitively to medieval Jewish culture itself. We must also acknowledge the presence of several Hebraico-French wedding songs that challenge the assumption that medieval Jews of Ashkenaz did not perform love songs. These songs often combine bawdy humor with biblical references, and even if romantic love is not the overarching goal of the songs, their performance at weddings likely creates the atmosphere closest to the culture of the *trouvères*.

There is other evidence for Jews singing in medieval Ashkenaz outside the liturgical rite, mostly at life cycle events like weddings. They sang jubilantly at Shabbat meals and at circumcision ceremonies. As evidenced by the Hebraico-French wedding songs, they sang in the vernacular as well. The Tosafists, rabbinic commentators from northern France and likely the community that birthed *Sefer ha-Ma'asim* (Book of Tales), note that a teacher of Mishnah taught that scripture with music was a way to remember them better.[20] One rabbi even allowed a non-Jew to play music at a wedding on the Sabbath.[21]

We also know that Jews sang Hebrew songs to the melodies of vernacular songs. In the margins of the prayer book, the *Maḥzor Vitry*, written in France in 1204, next to a liturgical poem by Spanish Hebrew poet Dunash Ibn Labrat (920–990), a scribe wrote instructions to sing

19. Hanna Liss, "The Commentary on the *Song of Songs* Attributed to R. Samuel Ben Meir (Rashbam)," *Medieval Jewish Studies* 1 (August 2007): 25.

20. The *tosafot* (rabbinic additions) to Megillah 32a comments on quoting the wording of R. Shefaita on behalf of R. Yohanan about a man who happened to teach Mishnah without music: "for they were in the habit of repeating the *mishnayot* with music because people learned them by heart and in such a way they remembered more" [שהיו רגלין לשנות המשניות בזמרה לפי שהיו שונין אותם על פה ועל ידי כך היו נזכרים יותר]. See Sefaria, "Tosafot on Megilla," https://www.sefaria.org/Tosafot_on_Megillah.32a.12.1?lang=bi.

21. Guy Shaked, "The Jewish Attitude towards the Playing of Music in the Tripartite Mahzor," *Cogent Arts & Humanities* 7, no. 1 (January 1, 2020): 5, https://doi.org/10.1080/23311983.2020.1740539.

the poem to the tune of a French troubadour song.[22] Another liturgical poem in a thirteenth-century miscellany from northern France has similar instructions, to sing the Hebrew poem to the melody of a French love song. Raphael Loewe identified the composer of that melody as Moniot de Paris, who was active after 1250.[23] A French melody would seem to be an incongruous choice for this poem, which focuses on the persecutions of French Jews, but Loewe tentatively suggested that the original French song evoked a sense of lost fealty and nostalgia.[24]

Other rabbis prohibited Jews from using Christian melodies for synagogue hymns, translating Christian music into Hebrew, and singing Christian lullabies to children.[25] These prohibitions imply, as they often do, that this behavior was practiced and therefore necessitated a prohibition. In this case, however, rabbinic attitudes may have hindered the development of a genre of secular poetry and music in Ashkenaz. There is no evidence of specific Jewish melodies or examples of secular verse that may have been set to music. Although some of the source texts translated or used as foundational in medieval Ashkenaz are in metered poetical forms, Ashkenaz did not produce its own culture of secular, nonliturgical poetry. There are very few examples, with only about a dozen secular poems extant. Berechiah ha-Nakdan is one of those exceptions; he ends his fables in *Mishle Shuʿalim* (Fox Fables) with metered poetry and he produced other secular poems that circulated independently.[26] Only by the fourteenth and fifteenth centuries do these examples of secular poetry become more plentiful. A playful poem by a French Jew in this later period tells of his decision to move from France to Germany, in which he humorously suggests that German Jews are not to be counted among the Jewish people.[27]

---

22. *Maḥzor Vitry*, Jewish Theological Seminary MS 8092, fol. 38v. See Albert Evan Kohn, "Medieval Song in a Jewish Key," in *In and out, between and beyond Jewish Daily Life in Medieval Europe*, ed. Elisheva Baumgarten and Ido Noy (Jerusalem: Hebrew University of Jerusalem, 2021), 94–100.

23. Raphael Loewe, "A Thirteenth-Century Piyyut Set to French Music," *Revue des études juives* 161 (2002): 83–96.

24. Loewe, "A Thirteenth-Century Piyyut Set to French Music."

25. Shaked, "The Jewish Attitude towards the Playing of Music," 18; Gabriele L. Strauch, "Text and Context in the Reading of Medieval Literature—A Case in Point: Dukus Horant," *Exemplaria* 3, no. 1 (January 1991): 75–76.

26. For his poetry, see A. O. Brukhi, "Maḥrozet shirei tsimmudim le-Rabbi Berekhyah ha-Naqdan," *Kobez al yad* 21, no. 31 (2012): 29–46 [Hebrew]. See also the upcoming translations in volume 3 of the Posen Library of Jewish Culture and Civilization (New Haven, CT: Yale University Press).

27. T. Carmi, *The Penguin Book of Hebrew Verse* (London: Penguin, 1981), 453–54.

From the previous examples explored in this book, we may not be surprised that Ashkenaz did not develop significant amounts of secular verse. Certainly, we would not expect medieval Jews of Ashkenaz to write secular poetry in the vernacular language. Even in the more multicultural literary scene of southern Europe, Jews did not tend to write poetry in languages other than Hebrew, and never in non-Hebrew scripts. The apparent Jewishness of the few allegedly Jewish troubadour poets is mocked or questioned. One apparently Occitan Jewish poet, Bonfilh, appears in one *tenso* (a troubadour song with two interlocutors) written by Guiraut Riquier, a troubadour active in thirteenth-century Narbonne. The *tenso* likely dates to 1257–1259 and appears in a single manuscript, Paris, Bibliothèque Nationale, fr. 22543, on folio 35b, consisting of twenty-eight lines.[28] Riquier exchanges barbs with his interlocutor Bonfilh about the other poet's reasons for composing song and simultaneously insults Bonfilh's religion, writing, "*Car totz tos ditz e tos fatz son pezans / A Jesu Crist, car lon avetz esglans*" (v. 24, "but all of your words and all your acts are hateful to Jesus Christ, whom you mistreated").[29] This appears to be a reference to the medieval Christian perception of Jews as Christ's murderer. Although a generally welcoming environment for Jews, anti-Semitism in Narbonne reached its nadir in 1306 with their expulsion.[30] The debate in the poem should focus on the subject of Bonfilh's poetry, but Riquier cannot resist mentioning faith as a detraction of his opponent.

By the end of the poem, Riquier rejects Bonfilh as a professional poet: "your reply, your company: I want no more. Henceforth, my reputation is lost, and my knowledge that was so grand now diminished. For in addition to your reputation, mine has fallen into ill repute."[31] Alternatively, Bonfilh may have been in love with a Jewish woman, telling Riquier, "for my love refuses to adorate the cross" (*que jes mi dons no vol crotz adhorar*).[32] The tension between the two poets here could stem from simple literary competition rather than anti-Semitism. As we might expect in a debate

---

28. A translation appears in William D. Paden and Frances Freeman Paden, *Troubadour Poems from the South of France* (Woodbridge, UK: Boydell & Brewer, 2007), 221–22; Arie Serper, "Guiraut Riquer, Bonfils et les Juifs de Narbonne," *Romanistische Zeitschrift Fur Literaturgeschichte* 2 (1978): 421–29.

29. Serper, "Guiraut Riquer," 426.

30. Nina Caputo, "Regional History, Jewish Memory: The Purim of Narbonne," *Jewish History* 22, no. 1/2 (March 2008): 97–114.

31. Ta resposta no vuelh ni ta paria / D'est or'enan, car ma valor s'en bria. E mon sabers n'es mermatz qu'era grans, / Car ab ton pus m'en es cazuts us pans." Serper, "Guiraut Riquer," 427.

32. Serper, "Guiraut Riquer," 426.

work, *tensos* commonly end with an antagonistic tone.[33] This trend of reciprocal name-calling appears in oral societies and is dubbed flyting.[34] Ward Parks describes the literary battle of flyting: "The adversaries name and abuse one another, compare ancestries or accomplishments, debate their relative heroic merits, prognosticate on some projected competition or exploit. After a physical contest in the shape of direct combat, athletic competition, or some other feat, a winner is eventually determined; and his victory receives a ceremonialized acknowledgment, by the boasts and curses of winner and loser respectively, or through reconciliation and an exchange of gifts."[35] This appears to be exactly how Riquier and Bonfilh engage. Riquier decries his own once-elevated reputation that his fellow poet has now tarnished. Bonfilh's religion is simply another name to call him in the act of flyting, but it is only one in a list of insults.

It was not unthinkable that Jews could write poetry in thirteenth-century southern France. Stories by Crescas Caslari and Kalonymus ben Kalonymus, and poetry by Solomon da Piera and Immanuel ha-Romi, among others, remind us that Jewish writers in southern Europe were much more receptive to those literary genres. But even among those authors, their Jewish identity becomes a source of debate, especially by the fourteenth century, when conversion rates soared in southern Europe. Both Solomon da Piera, one of the latest Spanish Hebrew poets, and Joseph Benveniste, a poet from a well-known Spanish family, are rumored to have converted in the fourteenth or fifteenth century.[36]

In the north, as we might expect, Jewish poets are even rarer. We will consider four exemplary secular writers: the poets Mathieu le Juif, Charlot le Juif, and Süsskind of Trimberg, who all wrote in the vernacular in the Latin alphabet instead of Hebrew characters, and the Hebrew composer Obadiah the Proselyte, who wrote music in the non-Jewish script of musical notation. These four have in common a nontraditional connection to Judaism, which explains their ability to compose these literary forms.

Mahieu or Mathieu le Juif was apparently a convert to Christianity who wrote two known troubadour poems in the thirteenth century,

33. Paden and Paden, *Troubadour Poems from the South of France*, 221.

34. Ward Parks, *Verbal Dueling in Heroic Narrative: The Homeric and Old English Traditions* (Princeton, NJ: Princeton University Press, 1990); Walter J. Ong, *Orality and Literacy: The Technologizing of the Word*, 3rd ed. (London: Routledge, 2012), 44.

35. Parks, *Verbal Dueling in Heroic Narrative*, 3.

36. Norman Roth, *Conversos, Inquisition, and the Expulsion of the Jews from Spain* (Madison: University of Wisconsin Press, 2002), 56–57.

likely in Arras, northern France.[37] One of the earliest scholars to examine this poem designated him as a "mediocre" rhymer, a charge that has been objectively challenged.[38] His most popular song, "*Par grant franchise*," exists in eleven extant manuscripts, and three are attributable to Mahieu.[39] It appears in several redactions, including Provençal versions, attesting to its popularity. In fact, Samuel N. Rosenberg considers his song to be the most well-circulated French song not attributed to a well-known poet.[40] The content of the poem clearly resonated with listeners across the French-speaking medieval world, following transmission patterns that a mediocre poem would not achieve.

Mahieu writes in this poem:

Tricked and betrayed me—that's what you've done!
Why such ill will, madam, such spite and disdain?
For love of you, I abandoned my Lord
and turned to one that my kin wouldn't name;
and yet you laugh, you mock, you make fun!
Betrayed, abhorred, dear lady I adored,
I wish you were cursed and reviled and brought low
to feel the hurt that you've led me to know.[41]

This stanza provides literary evidence that his love for a Christian woman caused him to convert from Judaism to Christianity ("I abandoned my Lord and turned to one my kin wouldn't name").[42] Similar traces appear in his other known poem, "*Pour autrui movrai mon chant* (I'll start my song for someone else)," which exists in two manuscripts with music.[43] In "*Pour autrui*," he writes: "Come aid my suit, O Jesus Christ / new my Lord, now ever mine!"[44] Jesus as his new and everlasting lord agrees with the presumption of his conversion. One could argue, as Kirsten A. Fudeman

---

37. Arlima—Archives de littérature du Moyen Âge, "Mahieu Le Juif," accessed October 17, 2018, https://www.arlima.net/mp/mahieu_le_juif.html.

38. Alfred Jeanroy, "Une imitation d'Albert de Sisteron par Mahieu le Juif," *Romania* 27, no. 105 (1898): 148.

39. Samuel N. Rosenberg, "French Songs in Occitan Chansonniers: Mahieu le Juif in Ms. O (Rome, Biblioteca Apostolica Vaticana, Vaticani Latini 3208)," in *De Sens Rassis*, ed. Keith Busby et al. (Amsterdam: Rodopi, 2005), 568.

40. Rosenberg, "French Songs in Occitan Chansonniers," 570.

41. Samuel N. Rosenberg, "Mahieu le Juif," *Metamorphoses* 23, no. 1 (Spring 2015): 125.

42. Rosenberg, "French Songs in Occitan Chansonniers," 571.

43. Samuel N. Rosenberg and Hans Tischler, eds., "Pour Autrui Movrai Mon Chant," in *Chansons des Trouvères: Chanter m'estuet* (Paris: Librairie Générale Française, 1995), 668–71, 1042–43.

44. Rosenberg, "Mahieu le Juif," 119.

does, that "neither his subject matter nor his audience nor the script in which his work is recorded (the Latin one) justify calling his poetry 'Jewish.'"[45] But contemporaneous manuscripts attribute his works to a certain Mahieu le Juif, with the epithet implying a connection to Judaism, and his own poetry appears to speak of a grappling with faith.

Like Mahieu le Juif, another little-known poet with the "le Juif" suffix appears with tenuous connections to Judaism. The late thirteenth-century French poet Rutebeuf mentions a jongleur named Charlot (or Challot) le Juif. One of these references appears in *La desputisons de Charlot et dou Barbier de Melun* (The Disputation between Charlot and the Barber of Melun), in which Charlot engages in a repartee with his cousin Guillaume. Several mentions of faith suggest that Charlot converted from Judaism, as when Guillaume reminds his cousin, "Charlot, tu as toutes tes lois / Tu iez et juis et crestiens (Charlot, you assume all these terms, you are Jewish and Christian)."[46] Rutebeuf, like the other French poets who refer to Jewish poets, may attach the epithet "le Juif" as an insult rather than a name marking his identity. If Charlot is in fact Guillaume's cousin, there must be conversion or intermarriage to make the Jew and the Christian related. While "le juif" or "li juis" appears as a suffix for Jewish men in medieval France, it can also be applied ironically or with a malicious intent.[47] One humorous episode from Rutebeuf's *Oeuvres* called *Charlot le Juif qui chia dans la peau du lièvre* (Charlot the Jew who shat in the rabbit skin) tells of Charlot's misadventures and contributes to the overall view of the Jewish poet as the butt of a joke.[48]

But the overlying themes of faith in both Rutebeuf's *tenso* and Mahieu's own texts implies a more direct connection to Judaism than just a name. While the historical facts of Mahieu's life and his religious identity remain unknown, the reception of his work as written by a Jewish convert implies a relationship between his poetry and the Jewish faith in some as yet unidentifiable way. Conversion often led to doubt that the new member of their religious group "could authentically and entirely become (or return to being) one of their own."[49] I theorize, knowing the demographics of these literary communities around them, that Mahieu and Charlot were

45. Kirsten A. Fudeman, *Vernacular Voices: Language and Identity in Medieval French Jewish Communities* (Philadelphia: University of Pennsylvania Press, 2011), 6.

46. Rutebeuf, *Œuvres complètes*, ed. Michel Zink (Paris: Bordas, 1989), 256–57.

47. Emily Taitz, *The Jews of Medieval France: The Community of Champagne* (Westport, CT: Greenwood, 1994), 293; Fudeman, *Vernacular Voices*, 91.

48. Rutebeuf, *Œuvres complètes*, 263–71. I am grateful to Mathilda Bruckner for sharing her thoughts on this episode, especially in her chapter-in-progress on the subject.

49. Tartakoff, "Testing Boundaries," 732.

converts who had their Jewish suffixes retained by Christians suspicious of the proselytes. *Conversos*, the converted Jews of late medieval and early modern Spain, were similarly taunted for and reminded of their Jewish origins rather than respected for their new Christian religious practices.[50]

A parallel example of an unconfirmed Jewish literatus emerges from thirteenth-century Germany. The Jewish communities around the Rhineland, like the French communities, lack a defined culture of non-rabbinic literature, although a few examples can be found in Yiddish and German in Hebrew script, as in the fourteenth-century romance *Dukus Horant* (Duke Horant).[51] A pietistic group of German Jews likely were responsible for texts that espoused a comparable worldview, such as the collection in the Parma manuscript that is contemporaneous with the thirteenth-century manuscript Oxford Bodl. Or 135, with folktale stories placed intermittently in exegetical and legal contexts.[52] But one German poet, Süsskind of Trimberg, and his possible Jewish identity puts him in relief as the only Jewish, or possibly Jewish, writer of German poetry in the medieval period.

Like Jews in all medieval European Jewish communities, the Jews of Germany spoke the vernacular and wrote in Hebrew. But Süsskind of Trimberg wrote in Middle High German, distinctly not in the burgeoning Yiddish language spoken and written by German Jews in the second half of the thirteenth century, and not in the Hebrew script that defined Jewish texts in that region.[53] His command of Middle High German suggests that he had a level of education not accessible to most Germans, let alone Jews, who focused their educational content on Jewish themes.[54] His poems belong to the category of *Spruchdichtung*, didactic poetry concerned with religious and moral issues.[55] But in a thirteenth-century manuscript, the *Codex Manesse*, containing twelve of his poems, he is referred to as "Sueskint der Jude von Trimperg" ("Süsskind the Jew of Trimberg"). The manuscript features a miniature of the

50. Gregory B. Kaplan, *The Evolution of Converso Literature: The Writings of the Converted Jews of Medieval Spain* (Gainesville: University Press of Florida, 2002); Amy I. Aronson-Friedman and Gregory B. Kaplan, eds., *Marginal Voices: Studies in Converso Literature of Medieval and Golden Age Spain* (Leiden: Brill, 2012).

51. Jerold C. Frakes, ed., "Dukus Horant," in *Early Yiddish Texts 1100–1750: With Introduction and Commentary* (Oxford: Oxford University Press, 2004), 33–43.

52. Rella Kushelevsky, *Sigufim U-Pituyim: Ha-Sippur Ha-ʿivri Be-ʾashkenaz. Ms. Parma 2295 [de-Rossi 563]* (Jerusalem: Magnes, 2010).

53. Edith Wenzel, "Isolation or Symbiosis? Social and Cultural Relationships between Jews and Non-Jews in Medieval Europe," *Derekh Judaica Urbinatensia*, no. 3 (2005): 10.

54. I am grateful for Annegret Oehme's insight on this point.

55. Wenzel, "Isolation or Symbiosis?," 9–10.

presumably Jewish poet in conversation with a worldly or clerical dignitary at the city of Konstanz.[56] The name Süsskind was apparently common for Jews and not common for non-Jews.[57]

Here follows the selection of the poem that appears to designate its author as a Jew:

> I am truly on the street of fools with my poetry, since the lords won't reward me. Therefore, I shall leave their court and grow a long grey beard: From now on I shall live like the old Jews. My coat shall be long, and beneath a big hat I shall wend my way humbly, never again singing courtly songs, since the lords won't reward me.[58]

In its most literal sense, the poem tells of a man who attempts to be a courtly singer and has found his efforts rebuffed. He has decided to retreat and "live like the old Jews." The poem does not state if the author is himself one of the Jews or if he refers to the Jews as a metaphor for an insular community. The poem directly points to this tension between secular literature ("courtly songs") and his Jewish identity. Was he unable to have any success as a poet because of his religious identity? Or was he simply a mediocre Christian poet whose words did not appeal to the wealthy patrons? In the second reading, he compares himself to the bearded, hatted Jews in an act of self-pity. His comparison between outsiders and Jews points to the conscious figuring of Jews as operating outside the cultural sphere. Jews lack the "entry ticket" to mainstream German poetry, "since the lords won't reward" Jews for their literary efforts.

Although unlikely, it is not inconceivable that Süsskind, as a Jew, wrote courtly poetry in Germany. The emergence of *Dukus Horant* in a vernacular (probably Middle High German, but in Hebrew characters)

---

56. Luis Sérgio Krausz, "'Süßkind von Trimberg': An Early Paradigm of the German-Jewish Question," *Naharaiman Early Paradigm of the German-Jewish Question*, no. 1–2 (2011): 17.

57. Krausz, "Süßkind von Trimberg," 17.

58. Wenzel, "Isolation or Symbiosis?," 12:

Ich var ûf der tôren vart
mit mîner künste zwâre,
daz mir die herren nicht went geben.
des ich ir hof wil fl iehen
und wil mir einen langen bart
lân wachsen grîser hâre:
ich wil in alter juden leben
mich hinnân fürwert ziehen.
mîn mantel der sol wesen lanc,
tief under einem huote,
dêmüeteclich sol sîn mîn ganc,
und selten mê ich singe in hovelîchen sanc,
sîd mich die herren scheiden von ir guote.

suggests a Jewish engagement with secular texts in the vernacular. *Dukus Horant*, like *Melekh Artus*, recounts a heroic romance culled from German sources. Although it lacks any of the biblical references of *Melekh Artus*, it has a few Hebraisms and was written in a Hebrew script.[59] An even earlier example of a slate written in Yiddish or German in Hebrew script dates to 1349, at the latest, and was unearthed in Cologne.[60] Its writing is nearly illegible, but its visible words are enough to categorize it as a secular epic written in the popular German style of narrative poetry.[61] Another Arthurian story emerged in Yiddish in the fifteenth century, *Vidvilt* (Wigalois), and a new genre of Yiddish secular literature, including poetry, song, and plays, was born.[62] In the fourteenth century, Jews were also familiar with the love songs of the popular German poet Neidhart.[63]

At least one secular poem was produced among medieval Jewish communities in Germany, although not in Hebrew. The oldest example was composed in Middle High German in Hebrew characters (arguably an early or proto-Old Yiddish), dated to the fourteenth century. The poem survives on the first page of a commentary by Rashi (Solomon ben Isaac of Troyes).[64] The verse tells of longing for a beloved, a courtly theme once thought to be unusual in medieval Ashkenaz but one that we have proven was certainly within the cultural milieu of Jewish communities there. The poet writes:

Whither and where shall I go?
Wherever shall I turn?
I am in sin.
My heart is burning.
I cannot become happy.
There my beloved is looking,
whom I love most in this world.[65]

---

59. Jerold C. Frakes, ed., *Early Yiddish Texts 1100–1750: With Introduction and Commentary* (Oxford: Oxford University Press, 2004), 33–34.

60. Erika Timm, "Ein Neuentdeckter Literarischer Text in Hebräischen Lettern Aus Der Zeit Vor 1349," *Zeitschrift Für Deutsches Altertum* 142 (2013): 417–23. Timm provides a transcription of the letters but there are no high-resolution images to corroborate this first attempt.

61. Jerold C. Frakes, ed., *Early Yiddish Epic* (Syracuse, NY: Syracuse University Press, 2014), ix–xi.

62. Margot Behrend Valles, "Judaized Romance and Romanticized Judaization: Adaptation into Hebrew and Early Yiddish Chivalric Literature" (PhD diss., Indiana University, 2013); Wenzel, "Isolation or Symbiosis?," 19.

63. Wenzel, "Isolation or Symbiosis?," 18.

64. Edited in Frakes, *Early Yiddish Texts 1100–1750*, 64–65.

65. Translated by Annegret Oehme for volume 3, Posen Library of Jewish Culture and Civilization (New Haven, CT: Yale University Press, forthcoming).

This verse is devoid of any biblical references or Hebraisms, marking it as a truly German text. Its only claim to Judaism rests in its Hebrew script. The poet's "beloved" (ליבשט) evokes the beloved of medieval love poetry and epics, wholly removed from any beloved inspired by biblical or rabbinic texts—one might expect a reference to the language of *Song of Songs* in a Jewish text, for example. This Jewish poet, at least, could write verse in a Jewish script for a Jewish audience, but we have no proof that he or any other Jewish writer wrote poetry in German for a non-Jewish audience.

The questionable identification of Süsskind as Jewish links him with the limited examples of Mathieu, Charlot, and Bonfilh. As authors who stepped through the boundaries dividing Christian literature from Jewish literature, they became marked as Jewish, although without any scholarly consensus about their historically accurate Jewish identities.

An even less likely example of a potentially Jewish author is the looming figure of Chrétien de Troyes himself.[66] His name "Christian," an uncommon one for the period, may suggest that this was an assumed name after his conversion to emphasize his new chosen religion.[67] In *Philomena*, traditionally attributed to Chrétien, its author is named in the text as "*Crestiens li gois*," prompting scholars to translate the unknown term "*li gois*" as "the Jew."[68] The term "*li gois*" could alternatively be Chrétien's name for himself as the Hebrew גוי, "goy," or non-Jew; perhaps Chrétien was a descendant of Jews who converted.[69] But in the text itself, the term could be part of the next line of the text rather than part of the author's name.[70] The rarity of the name Chrétien can easily be explained away as being a pseudonym or descriptor, not a personal name.[71]

66. Caroline Gruenbaum, "A Not-So-Unique Text: *Melekh Artus* and Medieval Jewish Arthurian Romance," in *The Arthurian World*, ed. Victoria Coldham-Fussell, Miriam Edlich-Muth, and Renée Ward (London: Routledge, 2022), 232.

67. Matilda Tomaryn Bruckner, "Chrétien de Troyes," in *The Cambridge Companion to Medieval French Literature*, ed. Sarah Kay and Simon Gaunt (Cambridge: Cambridge University Press, 2008), 79–80, https://doi.org/10.1017/CCOL9780521861755.006; Urban T. Holmes Jr. and Amelia Klenke, *Chretien, Troyes, and the Grail* (Chapel Hill: University of North Carolina Press, 1959), 53–56; Robert Falck, "Chrétien [Crétien] de Troyes," in *Grove Music Online*, ed. Deane Root (Oxford: Oxford University Press, 2001), https://doi.org/10.1093/gmo/9781561592630.article.05698.

68. Peter Haidu, *The Philomena of Chrétien the Jew: The Semiotics of Evil*, ed. Matilda Tomaryn Bruckner (London: Modern Humanities Research Association, 2020); Urban T. Holmes Jr., *A New Interpretation of Chrétien's* Conte de Graal (Chapel Hill: University of North Carolina Press, 1948), 29–30.

69. Haidu, *The Philomena of Chrétien the Jew*.

70. Sarah Kay, "Who Was Chrétien de Troyes?," *Arthurian Literature* 15 (1997): 20–21.

71. Kay, "Who Was Chrétien de Troyes?," 6–8.

Despite the tenuous nature of claims about Chrétien's Jewishness, these theories persist. One theory about his Jewish background rests in a scene from Chrétien's unfinished romance, *Perceval*, involving a ceremonial feast. Scholars surmise that he based the feast on a Sephardic Passover seder, although the likelihood of Chrétien's familiarity with Sephardic tradition is very low given his geographical region of northern France.[72] Another work of scholarship sees themes of violence and religious persecution in *Philomena*, potentially influenced by anti-Jewish experiences.[73] Chrétien de Troyes's *Conte de Graal* (Story of the Grail) and the contemporary Jewish thinker Rashi, who also lived in the flourishing Jewish community in Troyes, were found to have similar exegetical methods.[74] These theories are unconvincing, but they all support the idea that one of the most well-known medieval French authors had a connection to Judaism.

Another unlikely venue for Jewish engagement in the medieval world was music. Music (specifically, musical notation) was a literary avenue that medieval Jews completely eschewed, across both Sepharad and Ashkenaz, with one exception: Obadiah the Proselyte, a Norman-Italian convert to Judaism in 1102, wrote musical notation in a Gregorian style in the 1120s.[75] He is the only known Jewish musical composer of the medieval period. He wrote a memoir and a set of musical compositions in Hebrew; we also have a prayer book with his name in it, and an epistle of R. Barukh of Aleppo attesting to Obadiah's worthiness to receive safe passage and hospitality on his travels.[76] Written on a common Egyptian paper of the twelfth century, his musical manuscript (Geniza ENA 4096b, at the Jewish Theological Seminary) has unique paleographic features but contains musical notations that are Lombardic or Gregorian.[77]

---

72. Eugene J. Weinraub, *Chrétien's Jewish Grail: A New Investigation of the Imagery and Significance of Chrétien de Troyes's Grail Episode Based on Medieval Hebraic Sources* (Chapel Hill: University of North Carolina Press, 1976); Leslie A. Fiedler, "Why Is the Grail Knight Jewish?," in *Aspects of Jewish Culture in the Middle Ages*, ed. Paul E. Szarmach (Albany: State University of New York Press, 1979), 151–70.

73. Haidu, *The Philomena of Chrétien the Jew*.

74. Matilda Tomaryn Bruckner, "Weaving a Tapestry from Biblical Exegesis to Romance Textuality: Caught in the Web of Chrétien's *Conte du Graal*," in *Thinking Medieval Romance*, ed. Katherine C. Little and Nicola Mcdonald (Oxford: Oxford University Press, 2018), 93–113.

75. Norman Golb, "Obadiah the Proselyte: Scribe of a Unique Twelfth-Century Hebrew Manuscript Containing Lombardic Neumes," *Journal of Religion* 45, no. 2 (1965): 153–56.

76. For descriptions, images, transcriptions, and translations of the four manuscripts, see the website devoted to Obadiah, https://johannes-obadiah.org/introduction.html, codeveloped by Gary Rendsburg and Peter Shamah, accessed October 2018.

77. Golb, "Obadiah the Proselyte," 153.

To explain this phenomenon, we can consider his biography. Obadiah was born Johannes of Oppido in Italy around 1070. He converted to Judaism in 1102; traveled through Syria, Palestine, and Iraq; and learned to write Hebrew while in the East. He settled in Egypt to write his memoirs and music. In other words, ENA 4096b is written with mixed styles by a proselyte who was born and raised as a Christian in Italy, learned how to write Hebrew in Baghdad, and settled in Egypt.[78] Although his works are not the product of Ashkenaz, Obadiah's blending of European, Jewish, and Egyptian styles makes him an ideal example of how texts and culture traveled through different religious communities.

In a letter of recommendation for Obadiah that he might receive safe passage during his travels, a certain Rabbi Barukh writes that Obadiah "is expert in the reading of their [Christian] books. Because of his understanding of what he read in the books of their error, he returned to the Lord of Israel with all his heart, all his soul and with all his strength, and became a proselyte in a law-court."[79] It was through the act of reading that Obadiah discovered the faults of Christianity. Obadiah also differentiates himself from his Christian brother Rogerius in his memoir. "Rogerius became a man who sought the sword and warfare, whereas Johannes became a man seeking knowledge and wisdom in books."[80] At an early age, Rogerius's predilection for war contrasts with Johannes—the future Jew—and his quest for knowledge. We are reminded of the Christian knights in *Melekh Artus*, who also seek the sword and warfare, in comparison with the Jewish author, who does not participate in the knightly activities but only writes about them. Reading, literacy, and literary analysis are hallmarks of the Jewish figures like Johannes/Obadiah in opposition to the Christian ones.

Obadiah's literary innovation does not lie in the content of his texts. His musical compositions consist of verses of biblical books strung together, called *florilegia*, and is a traditional way to form Hebrew poetry. His innovation, then, rests in its form, which is highly unusual, and stands as the singular example of its kind, of Hebrew verse written with

78. Golb, "Obadiah the Proselyte," 155.

79. Bodleian Library, MS. Heb. a. 3, folio 1a, translated by Norman Golb, "The Autograph Memoirs of Obadiah the Proselyte of Oppido Lucano and the Epistle of Barukh b. Isaac of Aleppo," in *Giovanni-Obadiah da Oppido: Proselito, Viaggiatore e Musicista Della'eta Normanna*, ed. Mauro Perani and Antonio De Rosa (Florence: Giuntina, 2004), 17, and available at https://johannes-obadiah.org.

80. רוייריוס איש דורש חרב ומלחמות ויהנס<א>, איש דורש דעת ובינה ספרים. From Kaufman MS 134, folio 1, recto, available at https://johannes-obadiah.org, with translation by Norman Golb.

musical notation. Traditional Hebrew cantillation consists of marks that denote relative pitch and length of note. When the ninth- and tenth-century Masoretes added vowels to canonical, biblical Hebrew texts, they included cantillation marks above and below the letters. These marks are roughly equivalent to *neumes*, or marks for musical notation.

These supra- and subliner cantillation marks do not provide melodies, which are often regional. Musical phrases and traditional melodies also differ throughout parts of the biblical text. They are passed down aurally and not placed into musical notation—the first Hebrew musical notation, apart from Obadiah, dates only to the seventeenth century.

Obadiah's music is not cantillated but rather fitted with Italian musical notation. Three main features designate it as Italian: its ruling, its ligatures, and its custos marks. It has a clef and dry point ruling. The clef runs from the first letter of the Hebrew alphabet (*aleph*) through the sixth letter, but unfortunately there is no way of knowing which note *aleph* corresponds to, which would change the entire pitch of the song. It is likely that the song is based in C, according to common Italian notation of Obadiah's time. The dry point ruled staff lines on Obadiah's manuscripts were also a common feature.[81]

Obadiah's song also has ligatures, which are backward from a Roman script and modern musical perspective, although they read perfectly normally with a right-to-left Hebrew script. Obadiah's text also features stemless note heads, which were typical in twelfth-century Italy. It also has custos marks, another common feature of Italian notation; they are marginal notes that indicate the note on the following line of the manuscript. In his song titled "*Barukh ha-gever* (Blessed is the man)," the last line of the folio has a custos mark, which suggests more lines of poetry that are not extant. None of these features are found on Hebrew music consistently until the nineteenth century (see figure 5).[82]

Obadiah's unique position as a former monk and a new Jew allows him to translate his Christian musical experience into a Hebrew framework. This brief discussion on his contribution to medieval Jewish literary culture rests on the premise that his musical notation can be read and understood as a text—or at least, as a textual object. This interpretation

81. I am thoroughly indebted to Eleanor Giraud for her insights on the musical practices of Obadiah and his Italian contemporaries.

82. Edwin Seroussi, "The Jewish Liturgical Music Printing Revolution: A Preliminary Assessment," in *Textual Transmission in Contemporary Jewish Cultures*, ed. Avriel Bar-Levav and Uzi Rebhun (Oxford: Oxford University Press, 2020), 100–136.

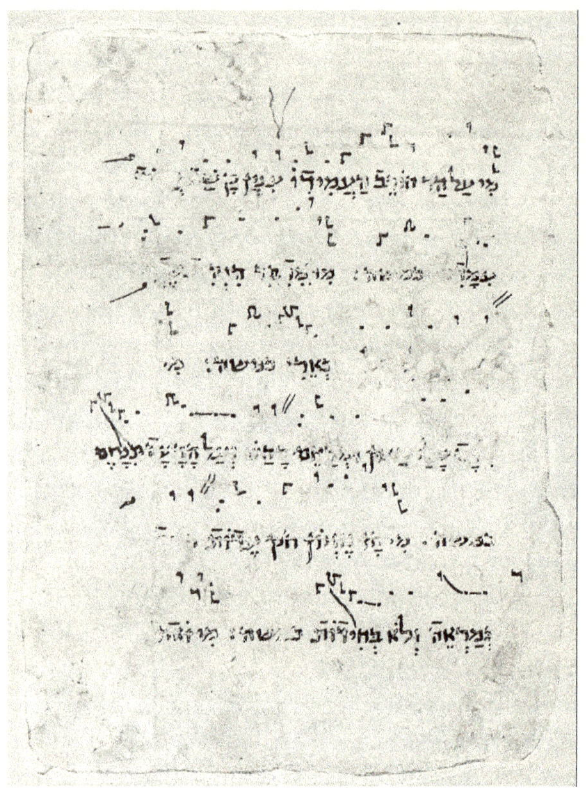

FIGURE 5. Obadiah the Proselyte, "The Praise of Moses." Early twelfth century. Courtesy of the Jewish Theological Seminary ENA 4096b recto.

is in keeping with scholarship on art and text as intrinsically linked in the medieval period.[83]

A particular conversion narrative of an Ashkenazi Jew appears in Latin, another non-Jewish written language like Middle High German or Old French, and it gives significant evidence about the relationship between literary arts, conversion, and identity. A certain "Herman

83. Suzanne Lewis, *Reading Images: Narrative Discourse and Reception in the Thirteenth-Century Illuminated Apocalypse* (Cambridge: Cambridge University Press, 1995); Marco Mostert and Mariëlle Hageman, eds., *Reading Images and Texts: Medieval Images and Texts as Forms of Communication*. Papers from the Third Utrecht Symposium on Medieval Literacy, Utrecht, December 7-9, 2000, Utrecht Studies in Medieval Literacy 8 (Turnhout: Brepols, 2005); Susan L. Ward, "Visual Environment of Jewish Learning in Twelfth-Century Rouen," *IMAGES: A Journal of Jewish Art and Visual Culture* 11, no. 1 (December 5, 2018): 43–56.

the former Jew" (*Hermannus quondam Judaeus*) wrote his *Opusculum de conversione sua* (A Short Work about His Conversion) in Latin in the twelfth century.[84] It is an autobiography detailing his early Jewish life and his conversion to Christianity. Debates in the twentieth century raged about Herman's identity. Did he exist? Was he ever Jewish, or was he simply an example for Christians on how to develop techniques for converts? As Jean-Claude Schmitt, in the most recent study on Herman, concludes, we cannot answer these questions conclusively in the medieval period: "Whether one turns to hagiography, history, or literature, the conclusion, then, is the same with varying degrees: there is never any whole truth or fiction."[85] Schmitt claims the only certainties are that the text is "a work of Latin Christianity in the form of an autobiography."[86] This book is not concerned with Herman's actual (a)historical presence. Instead, we view his autobiography as another example of a Jew crossing literary boundaries, this time through the liminal space of a convert, who emphasized the role of Jewish and non-Jewish literary languages in his conversion process.

The story follows Herman from his early life as the Jewish Judas ben David ha-Levi in Cologne through his conversion and acceptance into the Augustinian order. Herman tells us that, when he was thirteen, he has a dream about the reigning emperor Henry V (1105–1125), who gave him a white horse, a purse of gold, a silk baldric, and wealthy objects. The emperor invited him to eat a meal at his table. Judas wakes, excited about the prospects of his dream, but his uncle Isaac gave him an unsatisfactory, "carnal" interpretation: that Judas would have a rich marriage and a great fortune. Throughout his adolescence, Judas attends bishops' sermons and has conversations with Christian clerics, who make him question the Jewish interpretation of the Old Testament. He persists in his blind adherence to Judaism despite many episodes that shake his resolve, including the apparently divine smiting down of a Jew who accuses Judas of being a secret Christian. He asks recluses to pray for him, which appears to be the final push to his acceptance of Christianity. When Judas is traveling to Mainz, he strikes up a conversation with a messenger. The messenger mentions

84. Jean-Claude Schmitt, *The Conversion of Herman the Jew: Autobiography, History, and Fiction in the Twelfth Century*, trans. Alex J. Novikoff (Philadelphia: University of Pennsylvania Press, 2013), 1.

85. Schmitt, *The Conversion of Herman the Jew*, 41.

86. Schmitt, *The Conversion of Herman the Jew*, 43.

that he has a secret letter to deliver to certain Jews in Mainz, not realizing that those Jews are Judas's own relatives. Herman immediately realizes that the Jews of his hometown Cologne had written a letter to the Jews of Mainz telling them of Judas's intended conversion to Christianity. He guesses the letter's contents before reading it:

> Then—miraculously, but most true, as God is witness—I announced to him the contents and meaning of those letters, solely from the conjecture of my heart, as though I had read them or learned about them from another source. This happened, not by chance, but by the inspiration and providence of God, who engineered events so as to "snatch me" out from the most malign "expectations of the people of the Jews" [cf. Acts 12:11] and to resolve to a glorious outcome the holy business I had undertaken. Receiving the letters that he extended to me, I unfolded them and read them over, wherein I found, as I had suspected, the most malign accusations against me by the Jews. And with the greatest exultation I gave thanks to God for my deliverance and burned those pestiferous writings in the fire.[87]

The letters here take on much greater meaning than the simple correspondence between two Jewish communities. Written in Hebrew, the letters become, by virtue of their language, Jewish documents that may be inaccessible to the messenger. Hebrew was a crucial axis upon which the tenuous relationship between Christianity and Jewish scripture spun. The biographer of the thirteenth-century Dominican friar Raymond de Penaforte wrote similarly about the role of Hebrew for the friar's conversion program:

> With [Penaforte's] advice and approval, certain friars were thus instructed in the Hebrew language, so that they could overcome the malice and the errors of the Jews, who might not longer, as they had been accustomed to do in the past, audaciously deny the true text and the glosses of their own sages which might agree with our own saints in these matters pertaining to the Catholic faith. Moreover, [the friars studied Hebrew] so that the falsehoods and corruptions which they [the Jews] had inserted in many places in the Bible to hide the mysteries of the Passion and other sacraments of the faith, might be revealed through their authentic scriptural

87. Schmitt, *The Conversion of Herman the Jew*, 229.

> texts—which is all meant to confuse them [the Jews] greatly and confirm the Christian faith.[88]

Hebrew allowed the friars to confront directly the interpretations of Scripture that divided them from Jews, attacking Jewish theology on a literal plane. In fact, the Jews who converted to Christianity played an outsized role in polemics based on their knowledge of both Hebrew and Latin, a vital asset for a debate over text-based theology. The proselytes Petrus Alfonsi and Pablo Christiani both engaged in debates that targeted Jewish interpretation of Hebrew texts, using their Jewish education to support their new faith.[89]

Herman's acquisition of Latin crucially informs his progress up the Christian ladder of authority. He writes near the end of his text:

> I also took up the yoke of learning the Latin language and became, with God's assistance, so proficient within five years that the charity of the brethren judged me fit to take holy orders and kindly drew me to them. I humbly and justly felt that I was unworthy and protested that I was hardly suited for this. I modestly refused as much as I dared and as much as was proper. But "God, who always gives grace to the humble" [1 Peter 5:5], seeing me choose the lowest place among his followers, saw it fitting to say to me, "Friend, move up higher" [Luke 14:10]. Exalting in his call, not with prideful swelling but "in trembling," as it is written [Psalms 2:11], I climbed the canonical orders until I reached the office of priestly excellence. Then, for the first time, I understood the dream that I had seen before my conversion and that I inserted at the beginning of this short work prefiguring my future.[90]

In this section, we understand that Herman's knowledge of Latin is the last step before he begins the process of priesthood. Learning Latin directly leads to the brothers' acceptance of him into the orders. Throughout the autobiography, Herman quotes from the Latin versions of the biblical texts and includes references to the New Testament.

---

88. Cohen, "The Mentality of the Medieval Jewish Apostate," 38.

89. Petrus Alfonsi used his dual identity in his writing, arguing against his former, Jewish self. David A. Wacks, "Conflicted Identity and Colonial Adaptation in Petrus Alfonsi's 'Dialogus Contra Judaeos' and 'Disciplina Clericalis,'" in *Marginal Voices: Studies in Converso Literature of Medieval and Golden Age Spain*, ed. Amy I. Aronson-Friedman and Gregory B. Kaplan (Leiden: Brill, 2012), 69–90; Cohen, "The Mentality of the Medieval Jewish Apostate."

90. Schmitt, *The Conversion of Herman the Jew*, 236; Gerlinde Niemeyer, ed., *Hermannus Quondam Judaeus: Opusculum de Conversione Sua* (Weimar: H. Böhlaus Nachfolger, 1963), 122.

His decision to learn Latin affects not only his religious vocation, but also his language of thought; he writes his text in Latin, and his devotional frame of reference has become Latin rather than Hebrew. When he delivers his nephew to a monastery to enact the boy's own conversion, Herman explains, "I brought the boy so that they might instruct him in the sacred letters" (*commendato eis puero, ut sacris per eos litteris imbueretur*).[91] For Herman, Latin and Christianity are firmly inseparable, and in fact his new religion relies on the Latin language. R. Barukh's emphasis on Obadiah's literacy echoes the idea that religious faith has a reciprocal relationship with book learning.

Herman can interpret his dream only after he has learned Latin and gained a priestly position. In his book on dreams in the Middle Ages, Steven Kruger writes, "granted the illumination necessary to Christian exegesis, Hermann can now give an elaborate allegorical reading of his dream that drives home its significance for his spiritual life."[92] The "illumination" Herman gains gradually throughout his conversion process has many components, but the catalyst for this final stage is his acquisition of Latin. He displays the intertwined relationship between written language and religious identity for medieval Jews who normally wrote and spoke in different languages, one Jewish and the other not, and the instances in which they deviated from their expected linguistic choices by writing in languages other than Hebrew.

We have established Jewish links to Latin previously (especially in chapter 2), but it is worth repeating here. The rare cases of translation between Hebrew and Latin occur for medical, scientific, and philosophical texts, but almost never for literary works, especially in northern Europe.[93] (Yet again, our famed literatus Berechiah ha-Nakdan may be the only exception who knew and engaged with Latin sources.[94])

91. Niemeyer, *Hermannus Quondam Judaeus*, 116.

92. Steven F. Kruger, *Dreaming in the Middle Ages* (New York: Cambridge University Press, 1992), 163.

93. Gad Freudenthal, "Arabic and Latin Cultures as Resources for the Hebrew Translation Movement," in *Science in Medieval Jewish Cultures*, ed. Gad Freudenthal (Cambridge: Cambridge University Press, 2012), 74–105; Eve de Visscher, "Hebrew, Latin, French, English: Multilingualism in Jewish-Christian Encounters," in *Multilingualism in Medieval Britain (c. 1066–1520): Sources and Analysis*, ed. Judith Jefferson and Ad Putter (Turnhout: Brepols, 2013), 89–104; Resianne Fontaine and Gad Freudenthal, eds., *Latin-into-Hebrew: Texts and Studies* (Leiden: Brill, 2013).

94. Berechiah ben Natronai Ha-Nakdan, *Berakhyah Ben Natronai Ha-Nakdan: Sefer Ko'aḥ Ha-Avanim (On the Virtue of the Stones); Hebrew Text and English Translation; with Lexicological Analysis of the Romance Terminology and Source Study*, ed. Gerrit Bos and Julia Zwink, Études sur le Judaïsme Médiéval, vol. 40 (Leiden: Brill, 2010); Tamás Visi, "Science and Religion in Ashkenaz: Berechiah Ben Natronai Ha-Naqdan and His Predecessors," in *Berechiah Ben Natronai*

Hebrew-to-Latin translations are also overwhelmingly associated with conversion, as we have seen in other genres in this chapter. We can consider two other examples of converts who engaged in translations from Latin to Hebrew, Doeg the Edomite and Jean Avignon (born Moses ben Samuel de Roquemaure), although both translators operated in the southern literary sphere.

The twelfth-century translator Doeg is the first known of a set of translators from Latin to Hebrew based out of the Midi.[95] He was able to produce twenty-four translations of medical texts, a number that is quite astonishing given the scarcity of translations from Hebrew to Latin in the century before him and after him. In general, medieval Jews received most of their medical knowledge from Arabic texts, Jewish and non-Jewish, rather than from Latin culture.[96]

Doeg had converted to Christianity, learned Latin, completed his translation project, and began to regret his decision, as we learn from the introductions to his translations. His name for himself, Doeg the Edomite, refers to a biblical and Talmudic figure who was learned but also a foreigner, villain, and murderer.[97] In exceptional Hebrew, he writes about his betrayal to his faith. His command of medical terms confirms that he was a physician, which might have explained his access to Latin, and the high level of his Hebrew implies he may have been drawing on existing Latin-to-Hebrew translations, now lost.[98] He refers to Jews in positive terms throughout his introductions, and his own self-deprecating pseudonym paints him as a convert who regretted his decision. His translation projects reflect a deep concern for the welfare of sick Jews because he embarks on a program to prevent Jews from taking medicine that was not permissible under Jewish dietary law.[99] Like Süsskind and Herman before him, his conversion became an entry ticket to the world of Latin.

An early fourteenth-century convert, Jean of Avignon (born Moses ben Samuel de Roquemaure) translated Bernardus of Gordon's *Lilium Medicinae* (Lily of Medicine) in Seville in 1360. He also retained a

Ha-Naqdan's Works and Their Reception, ed. Tamás Visi, Tovi Bibring, and Daniel Soukup (Turnhout: Brepols, 2019), 87–118.

95. Gad Freudenthal, "The Father of the Latin-into-Hebrew Translations: 'Doeg the Edomite,' the Twelfth-Century Repentant Convert," in *Latin-into-Hebrew: Texts and Studies*, ed. Resianne Fontaine and Gad Freudenthal (Leiden: Brill, 2013), 105–20.

96. Freudenthal, "The Father of the Latin-into-Hebrew Translations," 111–12.

97. Freudenthal, "The Father of the Latin-into-Hebrew Translations," 108.

98. Freudenthal, "The Father of the Latin-into-Hebrew Translations," 108.

99. Freudenthal, "The Father of the Latin-into-Hebrew Translations," 110.

relationship with Jews after his conversion because he translated into Hebrew for a Jewish audience.[100] The discovery of an early fourteenth-century Latin text in Hebrew, with a parallel column in a Hebrew translation, is based on Arnaldus de Villa Nova's *Speculum mediciniae* (Mirror of Medicine).[101] Medical translations are the most common example of transmission between Latin and Hebrew in the medieval period. Gad Freudenthal posits that the medical field allowed for more collaboration between faiths because medicine is a universal need.[102]

In cases of converts who produce Hebrew to Latin translations, the translator could sever his ties to the Jewish community, as in the case of John of Capua, an apostate to Christianity in the late thirteenth century. John of Capua translated the popular Arabic collection of folktales *Kalila we-Dimna* (Kalila and Dimna) from an early thirteenth-century Hebrew version. His Latin version, *Directorium humanae vitae, alas parabola antiquorum sapientum* (The Guide of Human Life, or the Proverbs of the Ancient Sages), became the exemplar for many subsequent vernacular translations.[103] A connection between conversion and translation is not unique to this proselyte's translation of the text. *Kalila we-Dimna* was originally translated from Persian to Arabic and thereafter transmitted to the entire Western European world by a Zoroastrian convert to Islam, Abdallah ibn al-Muqaffa'.[104] Like John of Capua, ibn al-Muqaffa' used his unique education on both sides of the religious divide to make him a vital textual intermediary.

John of Capua's scholarship is shaky; his translation reveals a mediocre understanding of Hebrew and a "detestable" Latin.[105] We cannot determine the exact dates of the Hebrew version from which John of

100. Naama Cohen-Hanegbi, "Transmitting Medicine across Religions: Jean of Avignon's Hebrew Translation of the Lilium Medicine," in *Latin-into-Hebrew: Texts and Studies*, ed. Resianne Fontaine and Gad Freudenthal (Leiden: Brill, 2013), 122.

101. Michael McVaugh and Susan Einbinder, "Latin into Hebrew—Twice Over! Presenting Latin Scholastic Medicine to a Jewish Audience," in *Latin-into-Hebrew: Texts and Studies*, ed. Resianne Fontaine and Gad Freudenthal (Leiden: Brill, 2013), 31–44; Cyril Aslanov, "Latin in Hebrew Letters: The Transliteration/Transcription/Translation of a Compendium of Arnaldus de Villa Nova's Speculum Mediciniae," in *Latin-into-Hebrew: Texts and Studies*, ed. Resianne Fontaine and Gad Freudenthal (Leiden: Brill, 2013), 45–58.

102. Freudenthal, "The Father of the Latin-into-Hebrew Translations," 112.

103. John of Capua, *Directorium vitae humanae alias parabola antiquorum sapientum: version latine du livre de Kalilah et Dimnah, 1er fascicule*, ed Joseph Derenbourg (Paris: Vieweg, 1887).

104. David A. Wacks, "The Performativity of Ibn Al-Muqaffa 's Kalīla Wa-Dimna and Al-Maqāmāt Al-Luzūmiyya of Al-Saraqustī," *Journal of Arabic Literature* 34, no. 1/2 (April 2003): 181–82.

105. John of Capua, *Directorium vitae humanae*, xvi.

Capua translated, although a sixteenth-century version refers to a medieval "Rabbi Joel" as the producer of the Hebrew urtext. John of Capua tells us in his introduction that he dedicates his translation to Cardinal Matthew Rubens Ursinus, who was cardinal between 1263 and 1305. This places the Hebrew translation, whether produced by "Rabbi Joel" or another unattributed hand, at the beginning of the twelfth century.[106] There was also an incomplete Hebrew version produced in the late twelfth or early thirteenth century by R. Jacob ben Eleazer of Toledo as a translation from Arabic.[107] Capua, where John likely converted in 1265, appears to be a place ripe with proselytes.

When Abraham Abulafia, a noted mystic, visited the city between 1260 and 1271, he was troubled by the disloyalty to Judaism among Jewish youth there.[108] John of Capua writes in the first line of his introduction: "This is the work of John of Capua, who, after fumbling around in the shadows of Jewish ritual, had been called through solely divine inspiration to the unshakeable and true state of orthodox faith."[109] He continues that he writes this text in order to introduce Christian audiences, in Latin, to the many texts circulating in Hebrew. He retains respect for his source text, referring to *Kalila we-Dimna* as a "work for men of intelligence" (although it is not clear if he means *his* translated work or the original version).[110] But his intent is fully Christian. He ends his prologue by lauding Matthew and invoking Mary's grace. He also writes about his gratitude for being a member of the Christian faith in another of his texts, a Latin version of ibn Zuhr's *Kitab al-Taysir* (Book of Simplification Concerning Therapeutics and Diet), dedicated to the Archbishop Martin d'Oliveira (active 1292–1313).[111] He even dedicates his translation of Maimonides' *On the Regimen of Health* to Pope Boniface VIII (pope from 1294 to 1303)![112] He is not a repentant convert like Doeg but has unabashedly accepted his new religion. John of Capua's decision to dedicate his translations to Christian authorities in the highest positions of power likely reflects a certain amount of insecurity because he is

106. John of Capua, *Directorium vitae humanae*, xiv.

107. J. Derenbourg, *Deux Versions Hebraique Du Livre de Kalilah et Dimnah* (Paris: Vieweg, 1881), vii.

108. John of Capua, *Directorium vitae humanae*, xv.

109. "*Verbum Johannis de Capua, post tenebrarum olim palpationem ritus iudaici divina sola inspiratione ad firmum et verum statum orthodoxe fidei revocati.*" John of Capua, *Directorium vitae humanae*, 3.

110. John of Capua, *Directorium vitae humanae*, 3.

111. John of Capua, *Directorium vitae humanae*, xiv.

112. John of Capua, *Directorium vitae humanae*, xiv.

still establishing himself as a Christian who contributes to their faith. A thirteenth-century French poet, tentatively identified as a convert from Judaism by William C. Jordan, expresses similar ideas. The poet continually agonizes over his inability to be recognized fully by the members of his new faith.[113] He writes, "To you, sweet honored virgin, I pray and request . . . that [your son] grant vengeance for me on those who have denied me Christian faith, since I truly believe in him who made sky and dew."[114] The poet struggles to establish himself in the Christian community despite his heartfelt association with its religious tenets.

What makes John of Capua's translation of *Kalila we-Dimna* so noteworthy compared to Jacob ben Eleazer's translation of the same text from Arabic into Hebrew in the thirteenth century? John of Capua translates into the Christian language of Latin, a project that places him firmly and permanently as a member of the Christian literary community. Ben Eleazer works with two languages accessible to the Jewish community; Arabic was a language that Spanish Jews in Castile, where he operated, were still reading and writing.[115] In his *Takhemoni*, the famed Jewish poet and author Judah al-Ḥarizi insists on the superiority of Hebrew over Arabic, both languages in which Jewish authors worked in al-Ḥarizi's twelfth-century Islamic literary spheres. But even Judah al-Ḥarizi ended his life as a professional Arabic poet, where the profession was more lucrative, without renouncing his faith. Like ben Eleazer, al-Ḥarizi lived in a uniquely multicultural environment, where, according to Ross Brann, "Muslim elites may not have feared contact with Jewish literary and religious intellectuals," a reflection of the "permeability of the cultural boundaries between Muslim and Jew."[116] There was no permeability between Latin and Hebrew in thirteenth-century northern Europe.

One well-known Ashkenazi rabbi, Eliezer ben Joel ha-Levi of Bonn (1140–1225), reports his father's fascinating response to the question of a convert to Judaism who continued to study the Bible in Latin. His father, Joel ha-Levi of Bonn, had explained:

> One day, I, the undersigned, found him sitting and copying a book of the Pentateuch from an invalid book of Christian priests.

113. Jordan, "Exclusion and the Yearning to Belong."

114. Jordan, "Exclusion and the Yearning to Belong," 19.

115. For a succinct overview of language in medieval Castile, see Elaine R. Miller, *Jewish Multiglossia: Hebrew, Arabic, and Castilian in Medieval Spain* (Newark, DE: Juan de la Cuesta, 2000).

116. Ross Brann, *Power in the Portrayal: Representations of Jews and Muslims in Eleventh- and Twelfth-Century Islamic Spain* (Princeton, NJ: Princeton University Press, 2002), 159.

> I said to him, "What is that in your hand?" [see Exodus 4:2]. He answered me as follows, "I know the language of priests, but I do not know the holy tongue. Thus, for me it is like a commentary. In addition, the sages of Speyer lent me books of priests for copying, and they did not object. If it displeases you, I will return from it [see Numbers 22:34], and I will do so no more." I replied, "You should know that I consider this an evil deed." He then asked me to write on his behalf to my teachers in Speyer; perhaps they would find a lenient ruling for him.[117]

As he continues in his response, Joel rules that any reading in Latin is not allowed, even if the material is scripture. For him, Latin represents a non-Jewish language that cannot be made acceptable for any form of Jewish literature. We see, however, that Joel's response was not necessarily the majority because the convert believed he would find a more sympathetic response from the rabbis of Speyer. The question of Latin literacy and religious identity among the rabbis was not so simple.

Another case of a converted literatus is that of Hagin le Juif, who prepared in the late thirteenth century a French translation of Abraham Ibn Ezra's *Beginning of Wisdom* (*Reshit Hokhmah* in Hebrew, or *Comencement de sapience* in the French). It is the only translation of a Hebrew text into French in the late medieval period. The French texts are Paris, Bibliothèque nationale de France, fonds français, 24276, fols. 1a–66a, and 1351, folios. 1a–66a. They were produced considerably earlier than any of the extant manuscripts of Ibn Ezra's *Reshit Hokhmah* (Beginning of Wisdom) in Hebrew, making the French version a viable resource for English translations of the Hebrew text.[118]

Abraham Ibn Ezra (ca.1089–ca.1161) was a known transmitter of Arabic science and astrology in twelfth-century Europe, especially through his travels in Italy, France, and England. He wrote biblical commentaries; religious and secular poetry; religious-theological monographs and grammatical treatises; and scientific treatises in mathematics, astronomy, scientific instruments. His decision to write almost exclusively in Hebrew represents a literary shift from Jewish literature written in Judeo-Arabic to Hebrew—a natural consequence of the large-scale

---

117. See the forthcoming translation by Avi Steinhart in volume 3 of the Posen Library for Jewish Culture and Civilization, used here with permission.

118. Avraham Ben-Me'ir Ibn-ʿEzra, *Abraham Ibn Ezra's Introductions to Astrology: A Parallel Hebrew-English Critical Edition of the* Book of the Beginning of Wisdom *and the* Book of the Judgments of the Zodiacal Signs, ed. Shelomoh Sela (Leiden: Brill, 2017), 39.

migrations of Jews from Muslim Spain to Christian Spain and Latin Europe in the late twelfth century after the Almohad invasion.[119] *Reshit Hokhmah* and *Mishpetei ha-Mazzalot* (Rules of the Zodiacal Signs, another of his treatises) were also available to Christians in the second half of the thirteenth century via translations into Old French, Latin, Old Spanish, and Catalan.[120] Like Ibn Ezra's other texts, *Reshit Hokhmah* was based partially on Arabic philosophical texts.[121] In the body of *Reshit Hokhmah*, he refers to himself as "Abraham, translator of this book." He clearly engages in an editorial translation, not a word-for-word translation, with emendations to the original.[122]

Thanks to a colophon by the scribe at the end of the French text of *Comencement de sapience* (Beginning of Wisdom), we know a significant amount about the unique situation that produced the translation. The scribe writes:

> Ci define li livers de comencement de sapience que fist Abraham Even Aze ou Aezera qui est interpretes maistre de aide que translata Hagins li Juis de ebrieu en romans et Obers de Mondidier escrivoit le romans et *du fait* a Malines en la meson sire Henri Bate et fu fines l'en de grace 1273.
>
> This concludes the book of the *Beginning of Wisdom* which was made by Abraham Ibn Ezra, which means "one to give assistance," translated by Hagin le Juif from Hebrew to *romance* [French] and Obers de Mondidier wrote in *romance* and was made in Malines at the house of Sir Henri Bate, and was completed in the year 1273.
>
> [Paris, Bibliothèque Nationale, fr 1351, fol. 66r]

This Henri Bate, a student of theology and the arts at the University of Paris, was active at the end of the thirteenth century. Bate used *Comencement de sapience* as the basis for his Latin translation, produced in Orvieto in 1292. Hagin le Juif was the translator, but the scribe was Obert de Montdider, who spoke the Picard dialect. He was not incredibly

119. Gad Freudenthal, "Abraham Ibn Ezra and Judah Ibn Tibbon as Cultural Intermediaries: Early Stages in the Introduction of Non-Rabbinic Learning into Provence in the Mid-Twelfth Century," in *Exchange and Transmission across Cultural Boundaries: Philosophy, Mysticism and Science in the Mediterranean World = Yedaʿ Ḥotseh Gevulot Tarbut: Filosofyah, Misṭiḳah u-Madaʿ Be-Agan Ha-Yam Ha-Tikhon*, ed. Haggai Ben-Shammai, Shaul Shaked, Sarah Stroumsa, and Shlomo Pines (Jerusalem: Israel Academy of Sciences and Humanities, 2013), 53–64; Ibn-ʿEzra, *Abraham Ibn Ezra's Introductions to Astrology*, 1.

120. See the editor's introduction in Ibn-ʿEzra, *Abraham Ibn Ezra's Introductions to Astrology*, 2.

121. Ibn-ʿEzra, *Abraham Ibn Ezra's Introductions to Astrology*, ix.

122. Ibn-ʿEzra, *Abraham Ibn Ezra's Introductions to Astrology*, 11.

talented, which suggests that Hagin did not know how to write in French, for if only a question of transcribing more beautifully, he would have hired a better calligrapher than Obert.[123] It is possible that Hagin also translated Ibn Ezra's *Mishpetei ha-Mazzalot* into Old French, which was then used as an exemplar for a Latin translation whose source is currently unknown.[124]

We do not know what motivated Hagin to transcribe the text for Henri Bate. Perhaps financial incentives helped in arranging the relationship. It is entirely possible, and, I would argue, most logical, that Hagin was a convert to Christianity who was using his Hebrew skills to assist the scholar. The false etymology of Abraham Ibn Ezra's name suggests that one of the men involved was attempting to understand Hebrew linguistics. Obers de Mondidier's, or Hagin's, description of Ibn Ezra as "maistre de aide" comes from his translation of "ezra", עזרא, as related to the Hebrew word for help, עזרה.[125] This mistake, regardless of who suggested the etymology, further suggests that these learned scholars were engaging closely with translations between the vernacular and Hebrew. This text had even more circulation in the Christian world; recent scholarship has identified the hand of the glosses in the manuscript as belonging to Peter of Limoges, a late thirteenth-century theologian. It is suggested that Bate sent his own copy to Peter of Limoges at the end of 1273.[126]

This brings us back to the question of acculturation affecting conversion, of medieval Jews needing an entry ticket. While it was easier for Jews to enter into Christian belletristic or literary society after conversion, this does not mean that they converted for this express purpose. Herman's description of his experience applies to all our authors. He becomes drawn to Christianity through faith-based experience—but learning the textual language of Latin finally allows him to cross the border into the priesthood. His conversion occurs not because of Latin alone but with Latin as the final catalyst. This is also the case with Doeg, Jean of Avignon, and the vernacular poets. Already interested in Christianity for a variety of reasons, including desire for a woman or

123. As referenced in Kirsten A. Fudeman, "Comencement de Sapience: Hebrew Astrology in French," *Cornell Working Papers in Linguistics* 17 (Fall 1999): 21.

124. Ibn-ʿEzra, *Abraham Ibn Ezra's Introductions to Astrology*, 37.

125. Raphael Levy, "A Note on the Latin Translators of Ibn Ezra," *Isis* 37, no. 3/4 (1947): 154.

126. David Juste, "Bate's Nativitas in Context," in *The Astrological Autobiography of a Medieval Philosopher: Henry Bate's Nativitas (1280–81)*, ed. Steven Vanden Broecke, Carlos Steel, David Juste, and Shlomo Sela (Leuven: Leuven University Press, 2018), 73–74.

religious-based experiences, our authors learn Latin or vernacular poetry because of their interest, not as a cause. We recall Mahieu le Juif's words: "Come aid my suit, O Jesus Christ / new my Lord, now ever mine!"[127] Mahieu has chosen Jesus as his lord to help him win over his lover.

Despite the social intermingling that occurred in medieval northern Europe among disparate groups, for the Jewish community, certain forms of literature were directly correlated to the act of conversion and a cultural form that they could not share with the majority. Conversion, like Heinrich Heine's quip suggests, becomes an entry ticket for literary access.

But why only certain forms of literature? Despite medieval Jews crossing borders to engage with the literary narrative genres of romance and folktales, they were not able to engage fully with vernacular or secular poetry or musical notation. There seems to be an innate difference between narrative stories, which were acceptable to translate into Hebrew, and the more literary, artistic genres of poetry and music, which were not popular. It could be that poetry and music were linked in Christian culture to performance, and Jewish culture did not have court musicians or performative poetry outside the synagogue. This fits, considering that Hebrew poetry in the medieval period (in Ashkenaz) was restricted to liturgical use, for singing in the specific performative setting of the synagogue or for a ceremony such as a wedding. There would be no physical space for reciting secular poetry or musical notation. This confirms Obadiah's ability to transpose Western musical notation into Hebrew poetry because the poetry he chooses consists of verses from psalms and is not secular. It could have been recited in a synagogue setting, even if no one could read it besides him. This may have been his attempt to record and recall melodies from his past.

For some reason, poetry, autobiography, and music were even more of a barrier for Jewish authors than the borrowing and translating of themes discussed in previous chapters such as romance and ethics. There is no singular explanation to explain this discrepancy.

If we continue examining the Hebrew and Jewish writing communities in Italy and Germany, Jews began in the late medieval and early modern periods to write original works of poetry and romance, such as the Hebrew sonnets of Immanuel ha-Romi and the Yiddish epic *Vidvilt* (Wigalois). The few Yiddish examples already examined, such as *Dukus Horant* and the secular verse, both come from the late fourteenth

127. Rosenberg, "Mahieu le Juif," 119.

century, at the later end of the medieval period. This type of literature likely began to be more universally accepted only in regions where Jews had settled for a significant amount of time. Only after several hundred years did Jews become comfortable enough with the vernacular to pen original works in those languages. In France, however, the Jews faced continual expulsions until the fourteenth century, when they were expelled until the seventeenth century. If allowed to stay continuously throughout the medieval period, it is certainly possible that they would have been able to develop their own culture and engaged with original compositions in poetry, music, and chronicle.

Conclusion

Finding a Place for Literature of Ashkenaz

In season one of a popular Israeli television show about Orthodox singles in modern-day Jerusalem titled *Srugim* ("Knitted"), after the style of knitted yarmulkes the male characters wear as a sign of their religious observance, two main characters plan to watch a Monty Python marathon at the local movie theater.[1] Although typical television drama antics interrupt their intended viewing, it is not because of any opposition to the secular content of the movies. The main characters of *Srugim* do not see any conflict between their observance and the decidedly nonkosher irreverence of British comedy. With its satirical knights and feudal exchanges, *Monty Python and the Holy Grail*, the most famous film of the corpus, has a transcendent appeal.

In a scene in a later episode, however, the main characters dine with a guest, a student who studies in a religious academy (yeshiva). Over the Shabbat meal, a character references the "Soup Nazi" character from the American television show *Seinfeld*, but the yeshiva student does not grasp

1. Laizy Shapiro, dir., *Srugim*. Season 1, Episode 2, "Sippurei Savta (Grandmother's Stories)" (Israel: Yes TV, aired June 30, 2008). The show aired from 2008 to 2012 in Israel and is now available in America on Amazon Prime and other streaming platforms.

the reference.[2] This exchange is meant to demonstrate alienation between his more conservative worldview and the progressive, still religiously devout main characters who enjoy aspects of non-Orthodox culture.

Despite the main characters' ready acceptance of Monty Python, the presence of the yeshiva student hints at an overarching division within Judaism between those who avoid non-Jewish culture and those who embrace it. This division appeared within reception of *Srugim* itself; the laxity of some characters vis-à-vis rabbinic law prompted one prominent religious leader in Israel to proclaim a ban against the show. He said, "Of course it is forbidden to watch the show. There is bad language and licentiousness. . . . The show has plenty of cheap, low, and stupid content, and it is a disgrace to the Religious Zionist community. To learn about how one should act, a person should read the [Jewish ethical text] *Path of the Upright*."[3] That ethical text, also known as *Mesillat Yesharim*, was written by Rabbi Moshe Chaim Luzzatto (1707–1746) as a guide to pious life that relies heavily on biblical text and rabbinic discussions.[4] This plea to read proper literature dovetails with comparable rabbinic authoritative responses seen throughout the medieval period.

This tension between pop culture and piety has existed whenever Judaism found itself side by side with a comparative culture—that is, almost throughout its entire history. The modern rabbi's condemnation of *Srugim* has late antique, medieval, and early modern parallels when rabbis scorned non-Jewish literature, stories, and music. One of the genres that most entranced medieval Jews, however, was the same as the one that entranced *Srugim*'s Jewish characters who wanted to watch *Monty Python and the Holy Grail*: the stories of King Arthur and his knights, courtly love, and chivalric romance. These stories appeared in medieval Hebrew and Yiddish folktales, manuscript art, poetry, and more.

While the modern rabbi himself might not have understood the popular culture references of *Monty Python* and *Seinfeld*, and he did not condemn the show based on its incorporation of non-Jewish culture,

2. Laizy Shapiro, dir., *Srugim*. Season 1, Episode 7, "Tafsiq Le'fahed (You/She Will Stop Being Afraid)" (Israel: Yes TV, aired August 4, 2008).

3. Kobi Nakshoni, "*Harav Aviner Neged Srugim: Albon letzibur dati* (Rabbi Aviner against *Srugim*: A Shame for the Religious Community)," *Yediot Ahronot*, September 3, 2008, www.ynet.co.il/articles/0,7340,L-3591417,00.html, cited and translated in Shayna Weiss, "Frum with Benefits: Israeli Television, Globalization, and Srugim's American Appeal," *Jewish Film & New Media* 4, no. 1 (2016): 74, https://doi.org/10.13110/jewifilmnewmedi.4.1.0068.

4. Moses Hayyim Luzzatto, *Mesillat Yesharim: The Path of the Upright*, trans. Mordecai Menahem Kaplan (Philadelphia: Jewish Publication Society, 2010), http://muse.jhu.edu/pub/199/monograph/book/2307.

he believed that the lifestyle of the show's characters reflected low moral value. This lifestyle includes forays into non-Jewish cultural forms. Yet his comments did not detract from the show's popularity among religious and non-religious audiences, Jewish and non-Jewish, Israeli and non-Israeli, as one of the most popular Hebrew shows of the previous decades.[5] As this book has expressed, medieval rabbinic authority also failed to eradicate Jewish interest in non-Jewish culture and sometimes even incorporated external material into its own educational system.

This book has examined in particular the role of nonliturgical literature in and from Ashkenaz, especially the development of a mini corpus of translations from non-Jewish material. These texts spanned the twelfth and thirteenth centuries, and this development paralleled, although did not come close to reaching, the output in southern France and Spain of translations, original works of narrative and poetry, and other nonrabbinic works by Jewish authors. Ashkenaz may have lacked the systemic translation movements of their neighbors in the south, but it nonetheless produced important works that revealed Jewish engagement with non-Jewish, secular literature. Despite many trailblazing studies about Ashkenazi cultural engagement with the outside world, especially by Joseph Dan and Eli Yassif, and more recently Elisheva Baumgarten and Rella Kushelevsky, the idea of Ashkenaz as a literary center has not quite reached universal acceptance.

The salient reasons for the lesser literary output from Ashkenaz have already been outlined elsewhere in this book, and they include: (1) the forced expulsions of Jews from England and northern France, leading to instability and migration of texts, culture, and people; (2) lack of institutional (patronized) support for literary arts; (3) rabbinic pushback against some forms of literature, such as nonliturgical music; and (4) limited linguistic access to Arabic literature. Although less voluminous and less often transmitted than that of Sepharad, the belletristic literature of Ashkenaz clearly deserves its own analysis.

Here, I focused on texts from Ashkenaz that are critical examples of this type of engagement: a chivalric romance, a translation of French animals, and folktales with themes from romance. I show that this engagement may have occurred through oral and textual channels from

5. Weiss, "Frum with Benefits."

the vernacular source language into Hebrew, and the myriad ways that transmission and translation was complicated by restricted literacy among Jewish people. These texts are little studied outside the disciplinary confines of medieval Jewish literature (often further subdivided geographically into scholarship on Sepharad and scholarship on Ashkenaz), but they have enormous implications for the study of medieval literature broadly.

My brief mention of rabbinic texts prove that this literary engagement took place even through more religious avenues. In the pietistic manual *Sefer Ḥasidim* (Book of the Pious), its authors use the legends of Alexander the Great, transmit non-Jewish folktales, and use vernacular terminology such as "dragon" and "witch." Many stories from *Sefer ha-Ma'asim* (Book of Tales), although not exclusively a rabbinic code but certainly one with piety as a driving force, firmly attest to the ways that non-Jewish literary topoi featured in everyday religious observances. This should not surprise us, knowing as we do that medieval religious observance was also a staple of nonliturgical literature among Christians, even if its content appears to be secular. This explains the phenomenon of the Lancelot-Grail Cycle absorbing religious motifs such as the Holy Grail, and the typology of the lion as a Christ-like figure in Chrétien de Troyes' *Yvain, ou le chevalier au lion* (Yvain, or the Knight with the Lion).[6]

A tangential story collection that did not receive enough of my attention is Parma, Biblioteca Palatina, Cod. 2295 (de-Rossi 563), containing thirteen tales with midrashic, talmudic, and halakhic foundations.[7] Parma 2295 dates to the end of the thirteenth century, almost half a century after Bodl. Or 135. Unlike *Sefer ha-Ma'asim*, the collection of tales in Parma 2295 is not bound with any other story collection; the texts within the manuscript are religiously oriented, in the tradition of commentaries and midrash.[8] Kushelevsky argues that the folktales in

6. Peter Haidu, *Lion-Queue-Coupée: L'écart Symbolique Chez Chrétien de Troyes* (Geneva: Droz, 1975).

7. Rella Kushelevsky, *Sigufim U-Pituyim: Ha-Sippur Ha-'ivri Be-ashkenaz. Ms. Parma 2295 [de-Rossi 563]* (Jerusalem: Magnes, 2010); Rella Kushelevsky, "The Image of Woman in Transition from East to West: The Tale of R. Meir and His Friend's Wife in the Book of Comfort and in Manuscript Parma 2295 de Rossi 563," *Aschkenas* 11, no. 1 (January 2001): 9–38. For a similar story collection that warrants further attention, see Eli Yassif, ed., *Me'ah Sipurim Ḥaser Eḥad: Agadot Ketav-Yad Yerushalayim Ba-Folklor Ha-Yehudi Shel Yeme Ha-Benayim* (Tel Aviv: Haim Rubin Tel Aviv University Press, 2013).

8. Malachi Beit-Arié, *Hebrew Manuscripts in the Biblioteca Palatina in Parma Catalogue: Palaeographical and Codiocological Descriptions*, ed. Benjamin Richler (Jerusalem: Jewish National and University Library, 2001), no. 1541.

Parma 2295 have a pietistic origin, copied from another manuscript from 1161 to 1290.[9] A similar fourteenth-century folktale collection, *Sefer ha-Maʿasiyot* (Book of Exempla), also has a pious-historical chronology but has had limited scholarship, leaving its date, location, and source texts unknown.[10] Future studies of those stories will continue to reveal how, or if, they, like *Sefer ha-Ma'asim*, borrow from vernacular stories of their day.

For all these Hebrew texts, it is tedious and difficult to locate vernacular influence because the Jewish authors of northern Europe kept this information tightly concealed, with no overt attributions to their source material. In each of the texts surveyed in this book, the authors never mention the Christian authors from whom they borrow, in sharp contrast to, for example, the Lancelot-Grail Cycle, which attributes its material variously to Walter Map, Robert de Boron, and Jesus Christ.[11] The closest we have to attribution are references to the vernacular origin of certain words (*la'az*), or, in *Mishle Shuʿalim* (Fox Fables), attribution to the "Arabic sage" who is the source for some of the adages at the end of the fables. In *Melekh Artus* (King Arthur), a gloss on the first word of the first folio writes "l'distruzione" ("on the destruction") in Hebrew characters, which is a vernacular translation of the Hebrew words that begin the text. Next to his gloss, the scribe has written in Hebrew, *bi-la'az*: "in the vernacular."[12] In lieu of a prologue, the scribe of Oxford, Bodl. Or 135 simply writes one rhymed hemistich at the beginning of his story collection, "with the help of God who makes miracles, I will begin to write my tales."[13] But none of the Hebrew authors writing narrative in northern Europe mention specific texts or authors by name. This also contradicts the attribution in Marie de

9. Kushelevsky, *Sigufim U-Pituyim*.

10. Moses Gaster, *The Exempla of the Rabbis: Being a Collection of Exempla, Apologues and Tales Culled from Hebrew Manuscripts and Rare Hebrew Books* (London: Asia Publishing, 1924). *Sefer ha-Maʿasiyot* has been dated to the twelfth or thirteenth century, but it is not clear where it originated.

11. Joshua Byron Smith, *Walter Map and the Matter of Britain* (Philadelphia: University of Pennsylvania Press, 2017); Carol Chase, "'Or Dist Li Contes': Narrative Interventions and the Implied Audience in the *Estoire del Saint Graal*," in *The Lancelot-Grail Cycle: Text and Transformations*, ed. William W. Kibler (Austin: University of Texas Press, 1994), 117–38.

12. Vatican Library, Urbinati ebraici. 48, fol. 75r, https://digi.vatlib.it/view/MSS_Urb.ebr.48.

13. בעזת הא' עושה ניסים אחל לכתוב מעשים. Rella Kushelevsky, *Tales in Context: Sefer Ha-Ma'asim in Medieval Northern France* (Detroit, MI: Wayne State University Press, 2017), 87.

France, who explicitly mentions (apocryphal) authors in her epilogue to the *Ysopet*, writing:

> *Esope* is this book's name,
> After the one who translated and wrote it down,
> From Greek into Latin he turned it.
> King Alfred, who loved it so,
> Then translated it into English.
> I have put it into French verse,
> Just as I found it, exactly.[14]

Here, we see another stark example that contrasts with the Ashkenazic hesitation to engage with majority literature and to acknowledge the non-Jewish origins of their work. While Marie de France takes authority from authors who came before her, Jewish translators did not bolster their work with the authority of non-Jewish writing. In medieval Ashkenaz, the true authorities were rabbinic thinkers and other Jewish figures of the past.

The lack of attribution was not common in the south. In southern Italy, for example, Hebrew translators named their Christian authors overtly. Contacts with Latin culture were "consistently flaunted" in public, and authors retained positive references to Christian authorities present in their texts rather than excising them.[15] The farther north one moved, the less acceptable it was to reference Latinate texts. The naturally multicultural atmosphere of the south proved fertile ground for translations and cross-cultural exchange.

We see this exemplified in the works of an Italian-Jewish poet. According to a Hebrew poem by Immanuel ha-Romi in early fourteenth-century Italy, his patron commissioned a poem from him as a Hebrew version of an existing Christian work: "I saw among the poems of the Christians /

---

14. Marie de France, *Fables*, ed. Harriet Spiegel (Toronto: University of Toronto Press, 1987), 256–57:

> Esope apel'um cest livre
> Qu'il translate e fist escrire,
> Del griu en latin le turna.
> Li reis Alfrez, que mut l'ama
> Le translata puis en engleis,
> E jeo l'ai rimee en franceis,
> Si cum jeo poi plus proprement.

15. Gad Freudenthal, "Arabic and Latin Cultures as Resources for the Hebrew Translation Movement," in *Science in Medieval Jewish Cultures*, ed. Gad Freudenthal (Cambridge: Cambridge University Press, 2012), 88.

a poem which I had never seen before among the Hebrews / and it was a poem that recalled all the labor and kingdoms and lands / and all languages and wisdom arranged in this one poem / so I hoped for one like it in the Hebrew language."[16] In his oeuvre, ha-Romi offers the first Hebrew versions of secular sonnets, complete with the romantic and erotic themes present in the vernacular versions. The poem cited above represents the dramatic differences between the literature explored in this book and the literature produced in southern Jewish communities in the thirteenth century and later. Immanuel ha-Romi refers to a patron, an opportunity lacking from the north, and mentions that the Christian poet's content of "labor and kingdoms and lands" inspired the patron to commission one similar in Hebrew. This process did not occur in Ashkenaz. The only literature emerging from that region was self-motivated and occasionally produced as part of institutional rabbinic culture (possibly with *Sefer ha-Ma'asim*, for example).

We have outlined the major forms and functions of medieval Jewish literature in Ashkenaz, and a few outstanding points are worth mentioning. Because this book was a comprehensive look at nonrabbinic and nonbiblical literature in and from northern Jewish communities, I eschewed exegetical texts such as rabbinic midrash or legal codes, in which external influences also played a role in their literary themes and content. The *Chronicle of Moses* is one salient example, an early medieval midrash about Moses in the form of a historical romance, and the story of "King Solomon and the Queen of Sheba" similarly relies on biblical material to form its sweeping narrative.[17] Philosophy was not a major focus either—but this field, like science and medicine, did not feature significantly into the Ashkenazi literary scene, mostly because its authors were unable to translate from Arabic and Latin source texts.[18]

16. Immanuel Ha-Romi, *Maḥbarot*, ed. Dov Yarden (Jerusalem: Mossad Bialik, 1957), 174. My translation, in consultation with Dvora Bregman, *The Golden Way: The Hebrew Sonnet during the Renaissance and the Baroque*, trans. Ann Brener (Tempe: Arizona Center for Medieval and Renaissance Studies, 2006), 16.

17. See, for example, Eleazer ben Asher ha-Levi, *Sefer Ha-Zikhronot, Hu Divre Ha-Yamim Li-Yeraḥmi'el*, ed. Eli Yassif (Ramat Gan: Tel Aviv University, 2001); *Solomon and Sheba*, ed. J. B. Pritchard (London: Phaidon, 1974); Jacob Lassner, *Demonizing the Queen of Sheba: Boundaries of Gender and Culture in Postbiblical Judaism and Medieval Islam* (Chicago: University of Chicago Press, 1993); Eli Yassif, "The Throne and the Queen: A New Version and Interpretation of the Romance of Solomon and the Queen of Sheba," in *Festschrift for Rella Kushelevsky* (Ramat Gan: Bar Ilan University, forthcoming).

18. Mauro Zonta, "Medieval Hebrew Translations of Philosophical and Scientific Texts: A Chronological Table," in *Science in Medieval Jewish Cultures*, ed. Gad Freudenthal (Cambridge: Cambridge University Press, 2012), 17–73; Gad Freudenthal and Ruth Glasner, "Patterns of

While some Jews of Ashkenaz read Latin, I have been unable to prove any direct engagement with Arabic among Ashkenazi authors.[19]

By restricting myself to Ashkenaz, I naturally did not fully engage with texts from Sepharad that perform similar acts of translation and transmission into Jewish culture, such as *Sefer ha-Meshalim* (Book of Tales), *Sefer ha-Qadmoni* (Book of Fables), *Kalila we-Dimna* (Kalila and Dimna), *Minḥat Yehudah sone ha-Nashim* (Judah the Misogynist), and many others. These texts borrow from Arabic and Castilian narrative themes, especially in the form of the Arabic *maqama* and Castilian romance.[20] The precedent of Sephardic belletristic literary borrowing was present already in tenth-century poetry that used Arabic poetics for Hebrew verse, and so it comes as no surprise that later Sephardic authors felt no compunctions about continuing to incorporate non-Jewish literature into their works.

I anticipate that the literature of Ashkenaz will find its place, both inside and outside the scholarly field of Jewish studies, as a valuable contribution to medieval culture. Its growing acceptance within Jewish studies has enabled more scholars to publicize the wonders of this fascinating body of literature. Berechiah ha-Nakdan's animal fables, King Arthur's Jewish knights, and courageous sons of Torah deserve their own recognition as worthwhile literary creations, standing side by side with their vernacular counterparts. These Jewish literary creations were forged with Jewish tradition, vernacular language, and the cultural background of medieval northern Europe that together resulted in unique amalgamations that reveal much about the milieu in which they were formed.

Translation Movements," in *De L'Antiquité Tardive au Moyen Age: Études de Logique Aristolelicienne et de Philosophie Grecque, Syriaque, Arabe et Latine Offertes à Henri Hugonnard-Roche*, ed. Elisa Coda and Martini Bonadeo (Paris: Librairie Philosophique J. Vrin, 2014), 245–52.

19. The prolific translator and author Abraham ibn Ezra, who lived and was active in southern Europe, composed Arabic and Latin translations while on Ashkenazi soil in England and Rouen, so it is possible that he engaged with Ashkenazi authors while he was there. See Shlomo Sela and Gad Freudenthal, "Abraham Ibn Ezra's Scholarly Writings: A Chronological Listing," *Aleph* 6 (2006): 13.

20. Raymond P. Scheindlin, "Fawns of the Palace and Fawns of the Field," *Prooftexts* 6, no. 3 (1986): 189–203; David A. Wacks, "The Performativity of Ibn Al-Muqaffa's Kalīla Wa-Dimna and Al-Maqāmāt Al-Luzūmiyya of Al- Saraqustī," *Journal of Arabic Literature* 34, no. 1/2 (April 2003): 181–82; Sara Offenberg, "Isaac Ibn Sahula and King Alfonso X: Possible Connections between the Book Meshal Haqadmoni and the Cantigas de Santa Maria," *Arts and Social Sciences Journal* 5, no. 2 (2014): 1–7; Tovi Bibring, "Fairies, Lovers, and Glass Palaces: French Influences on Thirteenth-Century Hebrew Poetry in Spain—the Case of Ya'akov Ben El'azar's Ninth Mahberet," *Jewish Quarterly Review* 107, no. 3 (Summer 2017): 297–322.

Appendix

Literary, Scientific, and Philosophical Texts and Translations Produced in Ashkenazi Communities in the Medieval Period (ca. 1000–ca. 1400)

This list includes all the "literary" texts produced in Ashkenaz or in Ashkenazi communities in the medieval period. I am indebted to the work of Gad Freudenthal, Shlomo Sela, and Mauro Zonta for data on many of the works listed here.[1] This list does not include functional texts such as *piyyut* (liturgical poetry, including *selichot*, penitential poetry), legal and rabbinic texts (i.e., responsa, commentaries, or theological texts), liturgy, or documentary texts such as ethical wills or chronicles that feature into rabbinic works. I have also included here scientific and medical works and philosophical works. If any texts are missing, the omission is likely unintentional.

1. Mauro Zonta, "Medieval Hebrew Translations of Philosophical and Scientific Texts: A Chronological Table," in *Science in Medieval Jewish Cultures*, ed. Gad Freudenthal (Cambridge: Cambridge University Press, 2012), 17–73; Shlomo Sela and Gad Freudenthal, "Abraham Ibn Ezra's Scholarly Writings: A Chronological Listing," *Aleph* 6 (2006): 13.

DATE	TITLE	AUTHOR OR TRANSLATOR	LOCATION (WRITTEN)	CONTENTS	LANGUAGE
12th century	Abū l-Faraj Harun, *Guidance to the Reading (of the Bible)*[a]	Unknown	Mainz, Germany	Translation from Arabic	Hebrew
Second half of the 12th century	Travelogue[b]	Jacob, son of Nathanel ha-Cohen	Germany	Travelogue	Hebrew
1160	Ahmad Ibn al-Muthannā, *Commentary on al-Khwārizmī's Astronomical Tables*[c]	Abraham Ibn Ezra	England	Translation from Arabic	Hebrew
13th century	Joseph Kimhi, *Sefer ha-Galuy*[d]	Copied and annotated by "Benjamin"	England	Biblical lexicography	Hebrew
ca. 1200	*Dodi ve-nechdi* (Uncle and Nephew)[e]	Berechiah ha-Nakdan	Normandy?	Translation/ paraphrase from Latin	Hebrew
ca. 1200	*Mishle Shuʿalim* (Fox Fables)[f]	Berechiah ha-Nakdan	Normandy?	Aesopic fables	Hebrew
ca. 1200	Philosophical poems[g]	Berechiah ha-Nakdan	France?	Poems	Hebrew
ca. 1200	*Sefer koḥot ha-avanim* (Book of the Virtues of Stones)[h]	Berechiah ha-Nakdan	France?	Lapidary	Hebrew
ca. 1200	Travelogue[i]	Followers of Petachiah of Regensburg	Germany	Travelogue	Hebrew
Second half of the 13th century	Aristotle, *Book on Animals* (*Historia, De partibus*, and *De generatione animalium*), Arabic trans. by Pseudo-Yaḥya Ibn al-Biṭrīq, from the Latin trans. by Michael Scotus[j]	Unknown	Northern France	Translation from Arabic	Hebrew
Second half of the 13th century	"To the hill of frankincense"[k]	Unknown	Champagne, France or Lorraine	Macaronic wedding song/poem	Hebrew and Hebraico-French
Late 13th century	Poems[l]	"Menahem of Saltwharf"	England	Debate poetry	Hebrew
1279	*Melekh Artus* (King Arthur)[m]	Unknown	Northern Italy?	Translations of Arthurian legends	Hebrew
End of the 13th century	Parma 2295[n]	Unknown	Northern France	Story collection	Hebrew
ca. 1300	*Fevres* (Fevers)[o]	Unknown	Champagne or Burgundy	Medical text	Hebraico-French

DATE	TITLE	AUTHOR OR TRANSLATOR	LOCATION (WRITTEN)	CONTENTS	LANGUAGE
14th century	"Whither and where shall I go?"[p]	Unknown	Germany	Poem	German in Hebrew characters, or Yiddish
1349	Slate[q]	Unknown	Cologne, Germany	Arthurian legend?	German in Hebrew characters, or Yiddish
1382	*Dukus Horant*[r]	Unknown	Germany	Arthurian legend	German in Hebrew characters, or Yiddish
14th or 15th century	"When I left France"[s]	Unknown	Germany	Poem	Hebrew

a Giulio Busi, *Horayat Ha-Qore'. Una Grammatica Ebraica Del Secolo X* (Frankfurt: Verlag Peter Lang, 1984); Ilan Eldar, "Mukhtasar (an Abridgement of) Hidayat al-Qari: A Grammatical Treatise Discovered in the Genizah," in *Genizah Research after Ninety Years: The Case of Judaeo-Arabic*, ed. Joshua Blau and Stefan C. Reif (Cambridge: Cambridge University Press, 1992), 67–73.

b Elkan Nathan Adler, *Jewish Travellers in the Middle Ages: 19 Firsthand Accounts* (New York: Dover, 1987), 92–100.

c Bernard R. Goldstein, ed., *Ibn Al-Muthanna's Commentary on the Astronomical Tables of al-Khawarizmi* (New Haven, CT: Yale University Press, 1967).

d Pinchas Roth, "A Hebrew Debate Poem from Medieval England," *Early Middle English* 2, no. 2 (2020): 84–85.

e Berechiah ben Natronai Ha-Nakdan, *Dodi Ve-Nechdi*, ed. and trans. Hermann Gollancz (Oxford: Oxford University Press, 1920).

f Berechiah ben Natronai Ha-Nakdan, *Mishlei Shualim*, ed. A. M. Habermann (Tel Aviv: Schocken, 1946); Haim Schwarzbaum, *The Mishle Shu'alim (Fox Fables) of Rabbi Berechiah Ha-Nakdan* (Jerusalem: Institute for Jewish and Arab Folklore Research, 1979).

g Aviyah Unna Baruchi, "A Series of Paronomasia Poems by R. Berechiah Ha-Nakdan," *Kovetz al Yad* 21 (2012): 27–46.

h Berechiah ben Natronai Ha-Nakdan, *Berakhyah Ben Natronai Ha-Nakdan: Sefer Ko'aḥ Ha-Avanim (On the Virtue of the Stones); Hebrew Text and English Translation; with Lexicological Analysis of the Romance Terminology and Source Study*, ed. Gerrit Bos and Julia Zwink, Études sur le Judaïsme Médiéval, vol. 40 (Leiden: Brill, 2010).

i Abraham Benisch, ed., *Sibbuv R. Petahya: Travels of Rabbi Petachia of Ratisbon*, trans. Abraham Benisch (London: Trubner, 1856).

j Giuseppe Furlani, "Le Antiche Versioni Araba, Latina Ed Ebraica del de Partibus Animalium di Aristotele," *Rivista Degli Studi Orientali* 9, no. 3 (1922): 237–57; Mauro Zonta, "The Zoological Writings in the Hebrew Tradition," in *Aristotle's Animals in the Middle Ages and Renaissance*, ed. Carlos G. Steel, Guy Guldentops, and Pieter Beullens (Leuven: Leuven University Press, 1999), 44–68.

k Kirsten A. Fudeman, "'They Have Ears, but Do Not Hear': Gendered Access to Hebrew and the Medieval Hebrew-French Wedding Song," *Jewish Quarterly Review*, no. 4 (2006): 542–67.

l Roth, "A Hebrew Debate Poem from Medieval England."

m Curt Leviant, *King Artus: A Hebrew Arthurian Romance of 1279* (Syracuse, NY: Syracuse University Press, 2003); Moses Gaster, "The History of the Destruction of the Round Table as Told in Hebrew in the Year 1279," *Folk Lore* 20 (1909): 272–94.

n Rella Kushelevsky, *Sigufim U-Pituyim: Ha-Sippur Ha-'ivri Be-'ashkenaz. Ms. Parma 2295 [de-Rossi 563]* (Jerusalem: Magnes, 2010).

o Julia Zwink, "Étude Lexicographique Du Traité Anonyme 'Fevres': Une Compilation Médicale En Ancien Français, Écrite En Caractères Hébraïques," *Panace@* 7, no. 24 (2006): 250–60.

p Jerold C. Frakes, ed., *Early Yiddish Texts 1100–1750: With Introduction and Commentary* (Oxford: Oxford University Press, 2004), 64–65.

q Erika Timm, "Ein Neuentdeckter Literarischer Text in Hebräischen Lettern Aus Der Zeit Vor 1349," *Zeitschrift Für Deutsches Altertum* 142 (2013): 417–23; Jerold C. Frakes, ed., *Early Yiddish Epic* (Syracuse, NY: Syracuse University Press, 2014), ix–xi.

r Jerold C. Frakes, ed., "Dukus Horant," in *Early Yiddish Texts 1100–1750: With Introduction and Commentary* (Oxford: Oxford University Press, 2004), 33–43.

s T. Carmi, *The Penguin Book of Hebrew Verse* (London: Penguin, 1981), 453–54.

Bibliography

Abrahams, Israel, ed. *Hebrew Ethical Wills*. Philadelphia: Jewish Publication Society, 2006.

Adler, Elkan Nathan. *Jewish Travellers in the Middle Ages: 19 Firsthand Accounts*. New York: Dover, 1987.

Agus, Irving A. *Urban Civilization in Pre-Crusade Europe: A Study of Organized Town-Life in Northwestern Europe during the Tenth and Eleventh Centuries Based on the Responsa Literature*. 2 vols. Brill: New York, 1965.

Alexander-Frizer, Tamar. *The Heart Is a Mirror: The Sephardic Folktale*. Detroit, MI: Wayne State University Press, 2008.

Amer, Sahar. "Marie de France Rewrites Genesis: The Image of Woman in Marie de France's Fables." *Neophilologus* 81, no. 4 (October 1997): 489–99.

Amodio, Mark C., ed. *New Directions in Oral Theory: Essays on Ancient and Medieval Literatures*. Tempe: Arizona Center for Medieval and Renaissance Studies, 2005.

Angerer, Michael Lysander. "Translatio Studii as Literary Innovation: Marie de France's Fresne and the Cultural Authority of Translation." *Exemplaria* 34, no. 4 (October 2, 2022): 341–62. https://doi.org/10.1080/10412573.2022.2144489.

Arlima—Archives de littérature du Moyen Âge. "Mahieu Le Juif." Accessed October 17, 2018. https://www.arlima.net/mp/mahieu_le_juif.html.

Armstrong, Dorsey. *Gender and the Chivalric Community of Malory's Morte d'Arthur*. Gainesville: University Press of Florida, 2003.

Aronson-Friedman, Amy I., and Gregory B. Kaplan, eds. *Marginal Voices: Studies in Converso Literature of Medieval and Golden Age Spain*. Leiden: Brill, 2012.

Aslanov, Cyril. "Can the Language of Mishlei Shu'alim Give Us a Clue about Berechiah Ha-Naqdan's Geographical Origin?" In *Berechiah Ben Natronai Ha-Naqdan's Works and Their Reception*, edited by Tamás Visi, Tovi Bibring, and Daniel Soukup, 75–84. Turnhout: Brepols, 2019.

Aslanov, Cyril. "Latin in Hebrew Letters: The Transliteration/Transcription/Translation of a Compendium of Arnaldus de Villa Nova's Speculum Mediciniae." In *Latin-into-Hebrew: Texts and Studies*, edited by Resianne Fontaine and Gad Freudenthal, 45–58. Leiden: Brill, 2013.

Attia, Elodie. *The Masorah of Elijah Ha-Naqdan. An Edition of Ashkenazic Micrographical Notes*. Open Access. Materiale Textkulturen 11. Berlin: De Gruyter, 2015.

Banitt, Menachem, ed. *Le Glossaire de Leipzig*. 4 vols. Jerusalem: Académie nationale des sciences et des lettres d'Israël, 1995.

Banitt, Menachem. "Une Langue-Fantôme: Le Judéo-Français." *Revue de Linguistique Romane* 27 (1963): 245–94.

Baskin, Judith R. "Dolce of Worms: The Lives and Deaths of an Exemplary Medieval Jewish Woman and Her Daughters." In *Judaism in Practice: From the Middle Ages through the Early Modern Period*, edited by Lawrence Fine, 429–37. Princeton, NJ: Princeton University Press, 2001.

Baskin, Judith R. "Some Parallels in the Education of Medieval Jewish and Christian Women." *Jewish History* 5, no. 1 (1991): 41–51.

Baum, Ilil. "Hebrew-Catalan Medieval Wedding Songs: Satirical Functions of the Hebrew Component and Other Linguistic Aspects." *Journal of Jewish Languages* 4, no. 2 (August 16, 2016): 166–202.

Baumgarten, Elisheva. *Mothers and Children: Jewish Family Life in Medieval Europe*. Princeton, NJ: Princeton University Press, 2004.

Baumgarten, Elisheva. *Practicing Piety in Medieval Ashkenaz: Men, Women, and Everyday Religious Observance*. Jewish Culture and Contexts. Philadelphia: University of Pennsylvania Press, 2014.

Baumgarten, Elisheva. "Shared Stories and Religious Rhetoric: R. Judah the Pious, Peter the Chanter and a Drought." *Medieval Encounters* 18, no. 1 (January 2012): 36–54.

Beit-Arié, Malachi. "Book Production." In *The Cambridge History of Judaism*, edited by Robert Chazan, 535–54. Cambridge: Cambridge University Press, 2018. https://doi.org/10.1017/9781139048880.021.

Beit-Arié, Malachi. *Hebrew Codicology: Historical and Comparative Typology of Hebrew Medieval Codices Based on the Documentation of the Extant Dated Manuscripts in Quantitative Approach*. Jerusalem: National Library of Israel, 2017. http://web.nli.org.il/sites/NLI/English/collections/manuscripts/hebrewcodicology/Pages/default.aspx.

Beit-Arié, Malachi. *Hebrew Manuscripts from East to West: A Comparative Codicology*. London: British Library, 1992.

Beit-Arié, Malachi. *Hebrew Manuscripts in the Biblioteca Palatina in Parma Catalogue: Palaeographical and Codiocological Descriptions*, edited by Benjamin Richler. Jerusalem: Jewish National and University Library, 2001.

Beit-Arié, Malachi. "Ms Oxford, Bodleian Library, Bodl. Or. 135: On the Margins of the Article by E. Yassif [Heb.]." *Tarbiz* 54, no. 4 (July 1, 1985): 631–34.

Beit-Arié, Malachi. "Publication and Reproduction of Literary Texts in Medieval Jewish Civilization: Jewish Scribality and Its Impact on the Texts Transmitted." In *Transmitting Jewish Traditions: Orality, Textuality, and Cultural Diffusion*, edited by Yaakov Elman and Israel Gershoni, 225–47. New Haven, CT: Yale University Press, 2000.

Beit-Arié, Malachi. *Unveiled Faces of Medieval Hebrew Books: The Evolution of Manuscript Production—Progression or Regression?* Jerusalem: Hebrew University Magnes Press, 2003.

Ben-Amos, Dan. "Jewish Folk Literature." *Oral Tradition* 14 (1999): 140–274.

Benisch, Abraham, ed. *Sibbuv R. Petahya: Travels of Rabbi Petachia of Ratisbon*, translated by Abraham Benisch. London: Trubner, 1856.

Berger, David. "Gilbert Crispin, Alan of Lille, and Jacob Ben Reuben: A Study in the Transmission of Medieval Polemic." *Speculum* 49, no. 1 (1974): 34–47. https://doi.org/10.2307/2856550.

Berger, David. "Mission to the Jews and Jewish-Christian Contacts in the Polemical Literature in the High Middle Ages." *American Historical Review* 91, no. 3 (1986): 576–91.

Berger, Michael S. *Rabbinic Authority*. Oxford: Oxford University Press, 1998.

Bettan, Israel. *Studies in Jewish Preaching: Middle Ages*. Lanham, MD: Hebrew Union College Press, 1987.

Biale, David. *Eros and the Jews: From Biblical Israel to Contemporary America*. Berkeley: University of California Press, 1997.

Biale, David. *Not in the Heavens: The Tradition of Jewish Secular Thought*. Princeton, NJ: Princeton University Press, 2010. https://press.princeton.edu/books/hardcover/9780691147239/not-in-the-heavens.

Biale, David. *Power and Powerlessness in Jewish History*. New York: Schocken, 1986.

Bibring, Tovi. "Le chemin corrigé: Moralités inédites dans la fable 'La souris et la grenouille' de Marie de France et 'Rat avec Rainette et Aigle' de Berekiah Hanaqdan." In *Le récit exemplaire: 1200–1800*, edited by Véronique Duché-Gavet and Madeleine Jeay, 37–58. Colloques, congrès et conférences sur la Renaissance européenne 67. Paris: Classiques Garnier, 2011.

Bibring, Tovi. "Fairies, Lovers, and Glass Palaces: French Influences on Thirteenth-Century Hebrew Poetry in Spain—the Case of Ya'akov Ben El'azar's Ninth Mahberet." *Jewish Quarterly Review* 107, no. 3 (Summer 2017): 297–322.

Bibring, Tovi. "A Medieval Hebrew French Kiss: Courtly Ideals and the Love Story of Sahar and Kima by Ya'akov Ben El'azar." *Jewish Quarterly Review* 109, no. 1 (Winter 2019): 24–37.

Bibring, Tovi. "Vengeance, Justice et Repentir dans la Fable 'Le Riche et le Serpent' de Berrechia Ben Natronaï Hankdan." In *La Fable Avant La Fontaine*, edited by Jeanne-Marie Boivin, Jacqueline Toulet-Cerquiglini, and Laurence Harf-Lancner, 247–58. Paris: Droz, 2011.

Bibring, Tovi. " 'Would That My Words Were Inscribed': Berechiah Ha-Naqdan's 'Mišlei Šu'alim' and European Fable Traditions." In *Latin-into-Hebrew: Texts and Studies*, edited by Resianne Fontaine and Gad Freudenthal, 309–29. Leiden: Brill, 2013.

Bin Gorion, Emanuel, ed. *Mimekor Yisrael: Selected Classical Jewish Folktales*. Bloomington: Indiana University Press, 1990.

Bloch, R. Howard. *The Anonymous Marie de France*. Chicago: University of Chicago Press, 2011.

Blondheim, D. S. *Les Parlers Judéo-Romans et la Vetus Latina: Étude sur les rapports entre les traductions bibliques en langue Romane des Juifs au Moyen Âge et les anciennes versions*. Cambridge: Cambridge University Press, 1925.

Blondheim, D. S. *Poèmes judéo-français du moyen âge*. Paris: Champion, 1927.

Blumenfeld-Kosinski, Renate, Duncan Robertson, and Nancy Bradley Warren, eds. *The Vernacular Spirit*. New York: Palgrave Macmillan, 2002.

Bokher, Elia. *Bovo d'Antona*, edited by Claudia Rosenzweig. Leiden: Brill, 2015.

Boyarin, Adrienne Williams. *The Christian Jew and the Unmarked Jewess: The Polemics of Sameness in Medieval English Anti-Judaism*. Philadelphia: University of Pennsylvania Press, 2020.

Boyarin, Daniel. *Intertextuality and the Reading of Midrash*. Bloomington: Indiana University Press, 1990.

Boyarin, Shamma. "At the Court of the Demon King: The Story of the Jerusalemite and Chivalric Romance." In *Medieval and Early Modern Jewish Romance*, edited by Caroline Gruenbaum and Annegret Oehme, 95–106. Kalamazoo, MI: Arc Humanities, 2023.

Boyarin, Shamma. "Hebrew Alexander Romance and Astrological Questions: Alexander, Aristotle, and the Medieval Jewish Audience." In *Alexander the Great in the Middle Ages*, edited by Markus Stock, 88–103. Toronto: University of Toronto Press, 2016.

Brann, Ross. "The Arabized Jews." In *The Literature of Al-Andalus*, edited by Maria Menocal, Raymond P. Scheindlin, and Michael Sells, 435–54. Cambridge: Cambridge University Press, 2000.

Brann, Ross. *Power in the Portrayal: Representations of Jews and Muslims in Eleventh- and Twelfth-Century Islamic Spain*. Princeton, NJ: Princeton University Press, 2002.

Brantley, Jessica. *Reading in the Wilderness: Private Devotion and Public Performance in Late Medieval England*. Chicago: University of Chicago Press, 2008.

Bregman, Dvora. *The Golden Way: The Hebrew Sonnet during the Renaissance and the Baroque*, translated by Ann Brener. Tempe: Arizona Center for Medieval and Renaissance Studies, 2006.

Brisman, Shimeon. *A History and Guide to Judaic Dictionaries and Concordances*. New York: KTAV, 2000.

Brucker, Charles. "The Fables of Marie de France and the Mirror of Princes." In *A Companion to Marie de France*, edited by Logan E. Whalen, 209–35. Leiden: Brill, 2014.

Bruckner, Matilda Tomaryn. "Chrétien de Troyes." In *The Cambridge Companion to Medieval French Literature*, edited by Sarah Kay and Simon Gaunt, 79–94. Cambridge: Cambridge University Press, 2008. https://doi.org/10.1017/CCOL9780521861755.006.

Bruckner, Matilda Tomaryn. "Weaving a Tapestry from Biblical Exegesis to Romance Textuality: Caught in the Web of Chrétien's *Conte du Graal*." In *Thinking Medieval Romance*, edited by Katherine C. Little and Nicola Mcdonald, 93–113. Oxford: Oxford University Press, 2018.

Brukhi, A. O. "Maḥrozet shirei tsimmudim le-Rabbi Berekhyah ha-Naqdan." *Kobez al yad* 21, no. 31 (2012): 29–46.

Brundage, James. *Law, Sex, and Christian Society in Medieval Europe*. Chicago: University of Chicago Press, 1987.

Bryant, Nigel, ed. *Merlin and the Grail: Joseph of Arimathea, Merlin, Perceval: The Trilogy of Prose Romances Attributed to Robert de Boron*. Woodbridge, UK: D. S. Brewer, 2003.

Burke, Peter, and R. Po-chia Hsia, eds. *Cultural Translation in Early Modern Europe*. Cambridge: Cambridge University Press, 2007.

Busby, Keith. "Arthuriana in the Italian Regions of Medieval Francophonia." In *The Arthur of the Italians*, edited by Gloria Allaire and F. Regina Psaki, 11–20. Cardiff: University of Wales Press, 2014.

Busby, Keith. "The Manuscripts of Marie de France." In *A Companion to Marie de France*, edited by Logan E. Whalen, 303–18. Leiden: Brill, 2014.

Busby, Keith. "Romance, French." In *The Oxford Dictionary of the Middle Ages*. Oxford: Oxford University Press, 2010. http://www.oxfordreference.com/view/10.1093/acref/9780198662624.001.0001/acref-9780198662624-e-5062.

Busi, Giulio. *Horayat Ha-Qore'. Una Grammatica Ebraica Del Secolo X.* Frankfurt: Verlag Peter Lang, 1984.

Butterfield, Ardis. *Poetry and Music in Medieval France: From Jean Renart to Guillaume de Machaut.* Cambridge: Cambridge University Press, 2002.

Bynum, Caroline Walker. *Holy Feast and Holy Fast: The Religious Significance of Food to Medieval Women.* Berkeley: University of California Press, 1987.

Campbell, Emma, and Robert Mills, eds. *Rethinking Medieval Translation: Ethics, Politics, Theory.* Cambridge: D. S. Brewer, 2012.

Campbell, Killis, ed. *The Seven Sages of Rome.* Boston: Ginn, 1907.

Capellanus, Andreas. *The Art of Courtly Love*, translated by John Jay Perry. New York: Columbia University Press, 1941.

Caputo, Nina. "Regional History, Jewish Memory: The Purim of Narbonne." *Jewish History* 22, no. 1/2 (March 2008): 97–114.

Carlson, David. "Religion and Romance: The Languages of Love in the Treatises of Gerard of Liege and the Case of Andreas Capellanus." In *Poetics of Love in the Middle Ages: Texts and Contexts*, edited by Moshe Lazar and Norris J. Lacy, 81–92. Fairfax: University of Virginia Press, 1989.

Carmi, T. *The Penguin Book of Hebrew Verse.* London: Penguin, 1981.

Carruthers, Mary. *The Book of Memory: A Study of Memory in Medieval Culture.* Cambridge: Cambridge University Press, 1992.

Chase, Carol. "'Or Dist Li Contes': Narrative Interventions and the Implied Audience in the *Estoire del Saint Graal*." In *The Lancelot-Grail Cycle: Text and Transformations*, edited by William W. Kibler, 117–38. Austin: University of Texas Press, 1994.

Chazan, Robert. "The Barcelona 'Disputation' of 1263: Christian Missionizing and Jewish Response." *Speculum* 52, no. 4 (October 1977): 824–42.

Chazan, Robert. *Daggers of Faith: Thirteenth-Century Christian Missionizing and Jewish Response.* Berkeley: University of California Press, 1989.

Chazan, Robert. *Fashioning Jewish Identity in Medieval Western Christendom.* Cambridge: Cambridge University Press, 2004.

Chazan, Robert. *God, Humanity and History: The Hebrew First Crusade Narratives.* Berkeley: University of California Press, 2000.

Chernick, Michael. "Marie de France in the Synagogue." *Exemplaria* 19, no. 1 (Spring 2007): 183–205.

Cherniss, Michael D. "The Literary Comedy of Andreas Capellanus." *Modern Philology* 72, no. 3 (1975): 223–37.

Chrétien de Troyes. *Le chevalier au lion ou le roman d'Yvain*, edited and translated by David F. Hult. Paris: Librairie Générale Française, 2009.

Chrétien de Troyes. *The Complete Romances of Chrétien de Troyes*, translated by David Staines. Bloomington: Indiana University Press, 1991.

Chrétien de Troyes. *Erec and Enide*, translated by Ruth Harwood Cline. Athens: University of Georgia Press, 2000.

Cohen, Jeremy. *The Friars and the Jews: The Evolution of Medieval Anti-Judaism*. Ithaca, NY: Cornell University Press, 1984.

Cohen, Jeremy. "The Mentality of the Medieval Jewish Apostate: Peter Alfonsi, Hermann of Cologne, and Pablo Christiani." In *Jewish Apostasy in the Modern World*, edited by Todd M. Endelman, 20–47. New York: Holmes & Meier, 1987.

Cohen-Hanegbi, Naama. "Transmitting Medicine across Religions: Jean of Avignon's Hebrew Translation of the Lilium Medicine." In *Latin-into-Hebrew: Texts and Studies*, edited by Resianne Fontaine and Gad Freudenthal, 121–59. Leiden: Brill, 2013.

Coldham-Fussell, Victoria, Miriam Edlich-Muth, and Renée Ward, eds. *The Arthurian World*. London: Routledge, 2022.

Coleman, Joyce. *Public Reading and the Reading Public in Late Medieval England and France*. Cambridge: Cambridge University Press, 1996.

Conlee, John, ed. *Prose Merlin*. Kalamazoo, MI: Medieval Institute Publications, 1998.

Corley, Corin, trans. *Lancelot of the Lake*. Oxford: Oxford University Press, 2008.

Cuffel, Alexandra. *Gendering Disgust in Medieval Religious Polemic*. Notre Dame, IN: University of Notre Dame Press, 2007.

Dan, Joseph. *Ha-sipur ha-'ivri bi-yeme ha-benayim: 'iyunim be-toldotaṿ* [The Hebrew Story in the Middle Ages]. Jerusalem: Keter, 1974.

Dan, Joseph. "Hebrew Versions of Medieval Prose Romances." *Hebrew University Studies in Literature* 6 (1978): 1–9.

Dan, Joseph. "Rabbi Judah the Pious and Caesarius of Heisterbach: Common Motifs in Their Stories." *Scripta Hierosolymitana* 22 (1971): 18–27.

Darling, Linda T. "Mirrors for Princes in Europe and the Middle East: A Case of Historiographical Incommensurability." In *East Meets West in the Middle Ages and Early Modern Times: Transcultural Experiences in the Premodern World*, edited by Albrecht Classen, 223–42. Berlin: de Gruyter, 2013. https://www.academia.edu/4117152/Mirrors_for_Princes_in_Europe_and_the_Middle_East_A_Case_of_Historiographical_Incommensurability.

Darmesteter, Arsène, and D. S. Blondheim. *Les Gloses Françaises Dans Les Commentaires Talmudiques de Raschi*. Paris: Champion, 1929.

Davidson, Israel. "Parody in Jewish Literature." PhD diss., Columbia University, 1907.

Decter, Jonathan P. "Belles-Lettres." In *The Cambridge History of Judaism*, edited by Robert Chazan, 787–812. Cambridge: Cambridge University Press, 2018.

Decter, Jonathan. "The Rendering of Qur'anic Quotations in Hebrew Translations of Islamic Texts." *Jewish Quarterly Review* 96, no. 3 (Summer 2006): 336–58.

Delcorno Branca, Daniela. "La tradizione della Mort Artu in Italia." *Critica del testo* 7, no. 1 (2004): 1000–1023. https://doi.org/10.1400/118417.

Derenbourg, J. *Deux Versions Hebraique Du Livre de Kalilah et Dimnah*. Paris: Vieweg, 1881.

Deyermond, Alan D. "The Lost Genre of Medieval Spanish Literature." *Hispanic Review* 43, no. 3 (1975): 231–59. https://doi.org/10.2307/472251.

Deyermond, Alan D. "The Lost Literature of Medieval Spain." *La Corónica: A Journal of Medieval Hispanic Languages, Literatures, and Cultures* 5 (1976): 93–100.

Doane, A. N., and Carol Braun Pasternak, eds. *Vox Intexta: Orality and Textuality in the Middle Ages*. Madison: University of Wisconsin Press, 1991.

Drori, Itamar. "The Power of the Tongue: A Medieval Hebrew Story from Midrashic Literature." *Fabula* 58, no. 3–4 (January 10, 2017): 319–34.

Drory, Rina. "The Maqama." In *The Literature of Al-Andalus*, edited by Maria Rosa Menocal, Raymond P. Scheindlin, and Michael Sells, 190–210. Cambridge: Cambridge University Press, 2000.

Drory, Rina. *Reshit Ha-Maga'im Shel Ha-Sifrut Ha-Yehudit 'im Ha-Sifrut Ha-'Arvit Ba-Me'ah Ha-'aśirit* [The Emergence of Jewish-Arabic Literary Contacts at the Beginning of the Tenth Century]. Tel Aviv: Ha-Kibutz ha-Meuhad, 1988.

Drukker, Tamar S. "A Thirteenth-Century Arthurian Tale in Hebrew: A Unique Literary Exchange." *Medieval Encounters* 15, no. 1 (March 2009): 114–29.

Duggan, Joseph J. *The Romances of Chrétien de Troyes*. New Haven, CT: Yale University Press, 2001.

Duval, Frédéric. *Le Français Médiéval*. Turnhout: Brepols, 2009.

Einbinder, Susan. "The Troyes Laments: Jewish Martyrology in Hebrew and Old French." *Viator* 30 (January 1, 1999): 201–30.

Einbinder, Susan L. *Beautiful Death: Jewish Poetry and Martyrdom in Medieval France*. Princeton, NJ: Princeton University Press, 2002.

Einbinder, Susan L. "Meir b. Elijah of Norwich: Persecution and Poetry among Medieval English Jews." *Journal of Medieval History* 26, no. 2 (2000): 145–62.

Einbinder, Susan L. *No Place of Rest: Jewish Literature, Expulsion, and the Memory of Medieval France*. Philadelphia: University of Pennsylvania Press, 2008.

Einbinder, Susan L. "A Proper Diet: Medicine and History in Crescas Caslari's 'Esther.'" *Speculum* 80, no. 2 (2005): 437–63.

Elbaum, Jacob. "Yalqut Shim'oni and the Medieval Midrashic Anthology." In *The Anthology in Jewish Literature*, edited by David Stern, 159–75. Oxford: Oxford University Press, 2004.

Eldar, Ilan. "Mukhtasar (an Abridgement of) Hidayat al-Qari: A Grammatical Treatise Discovered in the Genizah." In *Genizah Research after Ninety Years: The Case of Judaeo-Arabic*, edited by Joshua Blau and Stefan C. Reif, 67–73. Cambridge: Cambridge University Press, 1992.

Eleazer ben Asher ha-Levi. *Sefer Ha-Zikhronot, Hu Divre Ha-Yamim Li-Yeraḥmi'el*, edited by Eli Yassif. Ramat Gan: Tel Aviv University, 2001.

Elman, Yaakov, and I. Gershoni, eds. *Transmitting Jewish Traditions: Orality, Textuality, and Cultural Diffusion*. New Haven, CT: Yale University Press, 2000.

Emanuel, Simcha. "The Lost Halakhic Books of the Tosaphists [Heb.]." PhD diss., Hebrew University of Jerusalem, 1993.

Epstein, Morris. "'Mishle Sendebar': New Light on the Transmission of Folklore from East to West." *Proceedings of the American Academy for Jewish Research* 27 (1958): 1–17. https://doi.org/10.2307/3622494.

Epstein, Morris, ed. and trans. *Tales of Sendebar*. Philadelphia: Jewish Publication Society, 1967.

Falck, Robert. "Chrétien [Crétien] de Troyes." In *Grove Music Online*, edited by Deane Root. Vol. 1. Oxford: Oxford University Press, 2001. https://doi.org/10.1093/gmo/9781561592630.article.05698.

Ferguson, Charles A. "Diglossia." *WORD* 15, no. 2 (January 1959): 325–40.

Fiedler, Leslie A. "Why Is the Grail Knight Jewish?" In *Aspects of Jewish Culture in the Middle Ages*, edited by Paul E. Szarmach, 151–70. Albany: State University of New York Press, 1979.

Finkelstein, Louis. *Jewish Self-Government in the Middle Ages*. New York: Jewish Theological Seminary of America, 1924.

Finnegan, Ruth H. *Literacy and Orality: Studies in the Technology of Communication*. New York: Blackwell, 1988.

Fishman, Joshua A. "Bilingualism with and without Diglossia; Diglossia with and without Bilingualism." *Journal of Social Issues* 23, no. 2 (April 1967): 29–38.

Fishman, Talya. *Becoming the People of the Talmud: Oral Torah as Written Tradition in Medieval Jewish Cultures*. Philadelphia: University of Pennsylvania Press, 2011.

Fishman, Talya. "A Medieval Parody of Misogyny: Judah Ibn Shabbetai's 'Minhat Yehudah Sone Hanashim.'" *Prooftexts* 8, no. 1 (1988): 89–111.

Fishman, Talya. "The Rhineland Pietists' Sacralization of Oral Torah." *Jewish Quarterly Review*, no. 1 (2006): 9.

Fogle, Lauren. *The King's Converts: Jewish Conversion in Medieval London*. Lanham, MD: Lexington Books, 2018.

Foley, John Miles. *How to Read an Oral Poem*. Urbana: University of Illinois Press, 2002.

Fontaine, Resianne, and Gad Freudenthal, eds. *Latin-into-Hebrew: Texts and Studies*. Leiden: Brill, 2013.

Frakes, Jerold C., ed. *Early Yiddish Epic*. Syracuse, NY: Syracuse University Press, 2014.

Frakes, Jerold C., ed. "Dukus Horant." In *Early Yiddish Texts 1100–1750: With Introduction and Commentary*, 33–43. Oxford: Oxford University Press, 2004.

Frakes, Jerold C., trans. "Dukus Horant." In *Early Yiddish Epic*. Syracuse, NY: Syracuse University Press, 2014.

Frakes, Jerold C., ed. *Early Yiddish Texts 1100–1750: With Introduction and Commentary*. Oxford: Oxford University Press, 2004.

Frakes, Jerold C. *The Emergence of Early Yiddish Literature: Cultural Translation in Ashkenaz*. Bloomington: Indiana University Press, 2017.

Fram, Edward. "Perception and Reception of Repentant Apostates in Medieval Ashkenaz and Pre-Modern Poland." *AJS Review* 21, no. 2 (1996): 299–340.

Frappier, Jean. *La mort le roi Artu: roman du XIIIe siècle*. Paris: Librairie Droz, 1996.

Freudenthal, Gad. "Abraham Ibn Ezra and Judah Ibn Tibbon as Cultural Intermediaries: Early Stages in the Introduction of Non-Rabbinic Learning into Provence in the Mid-Twelfth Century." In *Exchange and Transmission across Cultural Boundaries: Philosophy, Mysticism and Science in the Mediterranean World = Yedaʿ Ḥotseh Gevulot Tarbut: Filosofyah, Misṭiḳah u-Madaʿ Be-Agan*

Ha-Yam Ha-Tikhon, edited by Haggai Ben-Shammai, Shaul Shaked, Sarah Stroumsa, and Shlomo Pines, 52–81. Jerusalem: Israel Academy of Sciences and Humanities, 2013.

Freudenthal, Gad. "Arabic and Latin Cultures as Resources for the Hebrew Translation Movement." In *Science in Medieval Jewish Cultures*, edited by Gad Freudenthal, 74–105. Cambridge: Cambridge University Press, 2012.

Freudenthal, Gad. "'Arav and Edom as Cultural Resources for Medieval Judaism: Contrasting Attitudes towards Arabic and Latin Learning in the Midi and in Italy." In *Late Medieval Jewish Identities: Iberia and Beyond*, edited by Carmen Caballero-Navas and Esperanza Alfonso, 123–56. New York: Palgrave Macmillan, 2010.

Freudenthal, Gad. "The Father of the Latin-into-Hebrew Translations: 'Doeg the Edomite,' the Twelfth-Century Repentant Convert." In *Latin-into-Hebrew: Texts and Studies*, edited by Resianne Fontaine and Gad Freudenthal, 105–20. Leiden: Brill, 2013.

Freudenthal, Gad, and Ruth Glasner. "Patterns of Translation Movements." In *De L'Antiquité Tardive au Moyen Age: Études de Logique Aristolelicienne et de Philosophie Grecque, Syriaque, Arabe et Latine Offertes à Henri Hugonnard-Roche*, edited by Elisa Coda and Martini Bonadeo, 245–52. Paris: Librairie Philosophique J. Vrin, 2014.

Freudenthal, Gad, and Jean-Marc Mandosio. "Old French into Hebrew in Twelfth-Century Tsarfat: Medieval Hebrew Versions of Marbode's Lapidary." *Aleph* 14, no. 1 (January 2014): 11–187.

Freudenthal, Gad, Michael McVaugh, and Katelyn Mesler. "Twelfth-Century Latin Medicine in Hebrew Garb: Doeg the Edomite as a Cultural Intermediary." *Medieval Encounters* 26, no. 3 (September 24, 2020): 226–84. https://doi.org/10.1163/15700674-12340072.

Friend, Albert C. "The Tale of the Captive Bird and the Traveler: Nequam, Berechiah, and Chaucer's Squire's Tale." *Medievalia et Humanistica* 1 (1970): 57–65.

Frojmovic, Eva. "Jewish Scribes and Christian Illuminators: Interstitial Encounters and Cultural Negotiation." In *Between Judaism and Christianity: Art Historical Essays in Honor of Elisheva (Elisabeth) Revel-Neher*, edited by Elisabeth Revel-Neher, Katrin Kogman-Appel, and Mati Meyer, 281–306. Leiden: Brill, 2009.

Fudeman, Kirsten A. "Comencement de Sapience: Hebrew Astrology in French." *Cornell Working Papers in Linguistics* 17 (Fall 1999): 21–29.

Fudeman, Kirsten A. "Restoring a Vernacular Jewish Voice: The Old French Elegy of Troyes." *Jewish Studies Quarterly* 15, no. 3 (September 1, 2008): 190–221.

Fudeman, Kirsten A. "'They Have Ears, but Do Not Hear': Gendered Access to Hebrew and the Medieval Hebrew-French Wedding Song." *Jewish Quarterly Review*, no. 4 (2006): 542–67.

Fudeman, Kirsten A. *Vernacular Voices: Language and Identity in Medieval French Jewish Communities*. Philadelphia: University of Pennsylvania Press, 2011.

Fuks, Lajb. *The Oldest Known Literary Documents of Yiddish Literature (c. 1382)*. Leiden: Brill, 1957. http://archive.org/details/oldestknownliter0002fuks.

Furlani, Giuseppe. "Le Antiche Versioni Araba, Latina Ed Ebraica del de Partibus Animalium di Aristotele." *Rivista Degli Studi Orientali* 9, no. 3 (1922): 237–57.

Furst, Rachel. "A Return to Credibility? The Rehabilitation of Repentant Apostates in Medieval Ashkenaz." In *On the Word of a Jew: Religion, Reliability, and the Dynamics of Trust*, edited by Nina Caputo and Mitchell B. Hart, 201–21. Bloomington: Indiana University Press, 2018.

Gaster, Moses. *The Exempla of the Rabbis: Being a Collection of Exempla, Apologues and Tales Culled from Hebrew Manuscripts and Rare Hebrew Books*. London: Asia Publishing, 1924.

Gaster, Moses. "The History of the Destruction of the Round Table as Told in Hebrew in the Year 1279." *Folk Lore* 20 (1909): 272–94.

Gaunt, Simon. *Retelling the Tale: An Introduction to French Medieval Literature*. London: Duckworth, 2001.

Gilliam, Terry, and Terry Jones, dir. *Monty Python and the Holy Grail*. London: Python (Monty) Pictures Limited, 1975.

Goitein, S. D. *A Mediterranean Society: The Jewish Communities of the Arab World as Portrayed in the Documents of the Cairo Geniza*. 6 vols. Berkeley: University of California Press, 1967.

Golb, Norman. "The Autograph Memoirs of Obadiah the Proselyte of Oppido Lucano and the Epistle of Barukh b. Isaac of Aleppo." In *Giovanni-Obadiah da Oppido: Proselito, Viaggiatore e Musicista Della'eta Normanna*, edited by Mauro Perani and Antonio De Rosa, i–24. Florence: Giuntina, 2004.

Golb, Norman. *The Jews in Medieval Normandy: A Social and Intellectual History*. Cambridge: Cambridge University Press, 1998.

Golb, Norman. "Obadiah the Proselyte: Scribe of a Unique Twelfth-Century Hebrew Manuscript Containing Lombardic Neumes." *Journal of Religion* 45, no. 2 (1965): 153–56.

Goldstein, Bernard R., ed. *Ibn Al-Muthanna's Commentary on the Astronomical Tables of al-Khawarizmi*. New Haven, CT: Yale University Press, 1967.

Goldwyn, Adam J. "Arthur in the East: Cross-Cultural Translations of Arthurian Romance in Greek and Hebrew, Including a New Translation of 'O Presbus Ippotes' (The Old Knight)." *Latch* 5 (January 2012): 75–105.

Goodwin, Deborah L. *Take Hold of the Robe of a Jew: Herbert of Bosham's Christian Hebraism*. Leiden: Brill, 2006.

Gorlach, Marina L., Jeffrey H. Taylor, and Leslie A. Taylor. "The Hebrew Translations of Boethius's *De Consolatione Philosophiae*." In *Vernacular Traditions of Boethius's* De Consolatione Philosophiae, edited by Noel Harold Kaylor Jr. and Philip Edward Phillips, 125–42. Kalamazoo, MI: Medieval Institute Publications, 2016.

Groos, Arthur, and Norris J. Lacy. *Perceval/Parzival: A Casebook*. London: Routledge, 2012.

Grossman, Avraham. "Bekhor Shor, Joseph Ben Isaac." In *Encyclopaedia Judaica*, edited by Michael Berenbaum and Fred Skolnik, 276–77. Detroit, MI: Macmillian, 2007.

Grossman, Avraham. *The Early Sages of Ashkenaz*. Jerusalem: Magnes, 2001.

Grossman, Avraham. *Pious and Rebellious: Jewish Women in Medieval Europe*. Waltham, MA: Brandeis University Press, 2004.

Gruenbaum, Caroline. "A Not-So-Unique Text: *Melekh Artus* and Medieval Jewish Arthurian Romance." In *The Arthurian World*, edited by Victoria Coldham-Fussell, Miriam Edlich-Muth, and Renée Ward, 127–40. London: Routledge, 2022.

Gruenbaum, Caroline. "The Quest for the 'Charity Dish': Interpretation in the Hebrew Arthurian Translation Melekh Artus (1279, Northern Italy)." *Medieval Encounters* 26, no. 6 (February 2021): 517–42.

Gruenbaum, Caroline, and Annegret Oehme, eds. *Medieval and Early Modern Jewish Romance*. Kalamazoo, MI: Arc Humanities, 2023.

Guerreau-Jalabert, Anita. *Index des motifs narratifs dans les romans arthuriens français en vers: XIIe–XIIIe siècles*. Geneva: Droz, 1992.

Hadas, Moses. "Introduction." In Berechiah ben Natronai Ha-Nakdan, *The Mishle Shu'alim (Fox Fables) of Rabbi Berechiah Ha-Nakdan*, translated by Haim Schwarzbaum. Jerusalem: Institute for Jewish and Arab Folklore Research, 1979.

Haidu, Peter. *Lion-Queue-Coupée: L'écart Symbolique Chez Chrétien de Troyes*. Geneva: Droz, 1975.

Haidu, Peter. *The Philomena of Chrétien the Jew: The Semiotics of Evil*, edited by Matilda Tomaryn Bruckner. London: Modern Humanities Research Association, 2020.

Halkin, Abraham Solomon, and Angel Saenz-Badillos. "Translation and Translators." In *Encyclopaedia Judaica*, edited by Michael Berenbaum and Fred Skolnik, vol. 20, 94–102. Detroit, MI: Macmillan Reference, 2007.

Ha-Nakdan, Berechiah ben Natronai. *Berakhyah Ben Natronai Ha-Nakdan: Sefer Ko'aḥ Ha-Avanim (On the Virtue of the Stones); Hebrew Text and English Translation; with Lexicological Analysis of the Romance Terminology and Source Study*, edited by Gerrit Bos and Julia Zwink. Études sur le Judaïsme Médiéval, vol. 40. Leiden: Brill, 2010.

Ha-Nakdan, Berechiah ben Natronai. *A Commentary on the Book of Job: From a Hebrew Manuscript in the University Library, Cambridge*, translated by S. A. Hirsch. London: Williams & Norgate, 1905.

Ha-Nakdan, Berechiah ben Natronai. *Dodi Ve-Nechdi*, edited and translated by Hermann Gollancz. Oxford: Oxford University Press, 1920.

Ha-Nakdan, Berechiah ben Natronai. *The Ethical Treatises of Berachya Son of Rabbi Natronai Ha-Nakdan, Being the Compendium and the Masref*, edited and translated by Hermann Gollancz. London: D. Nutt, 1902.

Ha-Nakdan, Berechiah ben Natronai. *Fables of a Jewish Aesop: Translated from the Fox Fables of Berechiah Ha-Nakdan*, translated by Moses Hadas. New York: Columbia University Press, 1967.

Ha-Nakdan, Berechiah ben Natronai. *Mishlei Shualim*, edited by A. M. Habermann. Tel Aviv: Schocken, 1946.

Ha-Romi, Immanuel. *Maḥbarot*, edited by Dov Yarden. Jerusalem: Mossad Bialik, 1957.

Harvey, Steven. "The Introductions of Thirteenth-Century Arabic-to-Hebrew Translators of Philosophic and Scientific Texts." In *Vehicles of Transmission, Translation, and Transformation in Medieval Textual Culture*, edited by Robert Wisnovsky, Faith Wallis, Jamie C. Fumo, and Carlos Fraenkel, vol. 4, 223–34. Turnhout: Brepols, 2011.

Hasan-Rokem, Galit. *Web of Life: Folklore and Midrash in Rabbinic Literature*. Stanford, CA: Stanford University Press, 2000.

Heijkant, Marie-José. "From France to Italy: The Tristan Texts." In *The Arthur of the Italians*, edited by Gloria Allaire and F. Regina Psaki, 41–68. Cardiff: University of Wales Press, 2014.

Heller, Marvin J. *Studies in the Making of the Early Hebrew Book*. Leiden: Brill, 2007.

Holmes, Urban T., Jr. *A New Interpretation of Chrétien's* Conte de Graal. Chapel Hill: University of North Carolina Press, 1948.

Holmes, Urban T., Jr., and Amelia Klenke. *Chretien, Troyes, and the Grail*. Chapel Hill: University of North Carolina Press, 1959.

Hook, David. *The Arthur of the Iberians: The Arthurian Legends in the Spanish and Portuguese Worlds*. Cardiff: University of Wales Press, 2015.

Hudson, Alan. "Outline of a Theory of Diglossia." *International Journal of the Sociology of Language* 2002, no. 157(2006): 1–48.

Ibn Saqbel, Solomon. "Asher in the Harem." In *Rabbinic Fantasies: Imaginative Narratives from Classical Hebrew Literature*, edited by Mark Jay Mirsky and David Stern, translated by Raymond P. Scheindlin, 253–67. New Haven, CT: Yale University Press, 1990.

Ibn-ʿEzra, Avraham Ben-Meʾir. *Abraham Ibn Ezra's Introductions to Astrology: A Parallel Hebrew-English Critical Edition of the* Book of the Beginning of Wisdom *and the* Book of the Judgments of the Zodiacal Signs, edited by Shelomoh Sela. Leiden: Brill, 2017.

Idelson-Shein, Iris. *Between the Bridge and the Barricade*. Philadelphia: University of Pennsylvania Press, 2024. https://penn.manifoldapp.org/projects/between-the-bridge-and-the-barricade.

Jacobowitz-Efron, Leon. "The Linguistic Provenance of the Hebrew *King Arthur* (1279) Reassessed." *Journal of the International Arthurian Society* 12, no. 1 (September 1, 2024): 62–86. https://doi.org/10.1515/jias-2024-0003.

Jambeck, Karen K. "The 'Fables' of Marie de France: A Mirror of Princes." In *In Quest of Marie de France: A Twelfth-Century Poet*, edited by Chantal Anne-Marie Maréchal, 59–106. Lewiston, NY: Mellen, 1992.

Jánošíková, Magdaléna. "Fox Fables in the Early Modern Era: The Fables That Ashkenaz Read in Hebrew." In *Berechiah Ben Natronai Ha-Naqdan's Works and Their Reception*, edited by Tovi Bibring, Tamás Visi, and Daniel Soukup, 189–203. Turnhout: Brepols, 2019.

Japhet, Sara. "Did Rashbam Know the Vulgate Latin Translation of the Song of Songs?" *Textus* 24 (2009): 263–85.

Jauss, Hans Robert. *Toward an Aesthetic of Reception*. Minneapolis: University of Minnesota Press, 1982.

Jeanroy, Alfred. "Une imitation d'Albert de Sisteron par Mahieu le Juif." *Romania* 27, no. 105 (1898): 148–50.

John of Capua. *Directorium vitae humanae alias parabola antiquorum sapientum: version latine du livre de Kalilah et Dimnah, 1er fascicule*, edited by Joseph Derenbourg. Paris: Vieweg, 1887.

Johnson, Joseph. "Animal Speech and Human Handwriting in the *Ysopet* of Marie and the Roman de Renart." PhD diss., New York University, 2017.

Jordan, William C. "Adolescence and Conversion in the Middle Ages: A Research Agenda." In *Jews and Christians in Twelfth-Century Europe*, edited by Michael Alan Signer and John H. Van Engen, 77–93. Notre Dame, IN: University of Notre Dame, 2001.

Jordan, William C. "Exclusion and the Yearning to Belong: Evidence from the History of Thirteenth-Century France." In *Difference and Identity in Francia and Medieval France*, edited by Meredith Cohen and Justine Firnhaber-Baker, 13–24. Surrey: Ashgate, 2010.

Juste, David. "Bate's Nativitas in Context." In *The Astrological Autobiography of a Medieval Philosopher: Henry Bate's Nativitas (1280–81)*, edited by Steven Vanden Broecke, Carlos Steel, David Juste, and Shlomo Sela, 65–85. Leuven: Leuven University Press, 2018.

Kalinke, Marianne E., ed. *The Arthur of the North: The Arthurian Legend in the Norse and Rus' Realms*. Cardiff: University of Wales Press, 2011.

Kalonymus ben Kalonymus. *Iggeret Ba'alei Hayyim*, edited by Yisrael Toporovsky. Jerusalem: Mossad ha-Rav Kook, 1949.

Kanarfogel, Ephraim. *The Intellectual History and Rabbinic Culture of Medieval Ashkenaz*. Detroit, MI: Wayne State University Press, 2013.

Kanarfogel, Ephraim. *Jewish Education and Society in the High Middle Ages*. Detroit, MI: Wayne State University Press, 2007.

Kanarfogel, Ephraim. *Peering through the Lattices: Mystical, Magical, and Pietistic Dimensions in the Tosafist Period*. Detroit, MI: Wayne State University Press, 2000.

Kaplan, Gregory B. *The Evolution of Converso Literature: The Writings of the Converted Jews of Medieval Spain*. Gainesville: University Press of Florida, 2002.

Kaplan, Yosef, ed. *The Early Modern Era, 1500–1750*. Vol. 5. New Haven, CT: Yale University Press, 2023.

Karo, Joseph. *Shulchan Arukh Orach Chayim*. Maginei Eretz: Lemberg, 1893.

Kay, Sarah. "Who Was Chrétien de Troyes?" *Arthurian Literature* 15 (1997): 1–35.

Kazis, Israel, ed. *The Book of the Gests of Alexander of Macedon*, translated by Israel Kazis. Cambridge: Medieval Academy of America, 1962.

Kelly, Douglas. *The Art of Medieval French Romance*. Madison: University of Wisconsin Press, 1992.

Kelly, Douglas. *Chrétien de Troyes: An Analytic Bibliography*. London: Grant & Cutler, 1976.

Khan, Geoffrey. "Learning to Read Biblical Hebrew in the Middle Ages: The Transition from Oral Standard to Written Standard." In *Jewish Education from Antiquity to the Middle Ages: Studies in Honour of Philip S. Alexander*, edited by George J. Brooke and Renate Smithuis, 269–95. Boston: Brill, 2017.

Kimhi, Joseph. *The Book of the Covenant of Joseph Kimhi*, translated by Frank Talmage. Toronto: Pontifical Institute of Mediaeval Studies, 1972.

Kinoshita, Sharon. "Translatio/n, Empire, and the Worlding of Medieval Literature: The Travels of Kalila Wa Dimna." *Postcolonial Studies* 11, no. 4 (December 2008): 371–85.

Kiwitt, Marc. "The Problem of Judeo-French: Between Language and Cultural Dynamics." *International Journal of the Sociology of Language* 2014, no. 226 (March 2014): 25–56. https://doi.org/10.1515/ijsl-2013-0074.

Kiwitt, Marc, and Stephen Dörr. "Judeo-French." In *Handbook of Jewish Languages*, edited by Lily Kahn and Aaron D. Rubin, 138–77. Leiden: Brill, 2015.

Klepper, Deeana Copeland. *The Insight of Unbelievers: Nicholas of Lyra and Christian Reading of Jewish Text in the Later Middle Ages*. Philadelphia: University of Pennsylvania Press, 2010.

Kohn, Albert Evan. "Medieval Song in a Jewish Key." In *In and out, between and beyond Jewish Daily Life in Medieval Europe*, edited by Elisheva Baumgarten and Ido Noy, 94–100. Jerusalem: Hebrew University of Jerusalem, 2021.

Kozodoy, Maud. "The Hebrew Bible as Weapon of Faith in Late Medieval Iberia: Irony, Satire, and Scriptural Allusion in Profiat Duran's *Al Tehi Ka-Avotekha*." *Jewish Studies Quarterly* 18, no. 2 (June 2011): 185–201. https://doi.org/info:doi/10.1628/094457011796019674.

Kozodoy, Maud. *The Secret Faith of Maestre Honoratus, Profayt Duran and Jewish Identity in Late Medieval Iberia*. Philadelphia: University of Pennsylvania Press, 2015. https://doi.org/10.9783/9780812291810.

Krausz, Luis Sérgio. "'Süßkind von Trimberg': An Early Paradigm of the German-Jewish Question." *Naharaiman Early Paradigm of the German-Jewish Question*, no. 1–2 (2011): 17–35.

Krueger, Roberta L., ed. *The Cambridge Companion to Medieval Romance*. Cambridge: Cambridge University Press, 2000.

Kruger, Steven F. *Dreaming in the Middle Ages*. New York: Cambridge University Press, 1992.

Krummel, Miriamne Ara. *The Medieval Postcolonial Jew, in and out of Time*. Ann Arbor: University of Michigan Press, 2022.

Kugel, James L. *In Potiphar's House*. San Francisco: Harper, 1990.

Kushelevsky, Rella. "Chastity versus Courtly Love in 'The Poor Bachelor and His Rich Maiden Cousin.'" *Jewish Studies Quarterly* 20 (2013): 61–82.

Kushelevsky, Rella. "The Image of Woman in Transition from East to West: The Tale of R. Meir and His Friend's Wife in the Book of Comfort and in Manuscript Parma 2295 de Rossi 563." *Aschkenas* 11, no. 1 (January 2001): 9–38.

Kushelevsky, Rella. "Jews Reading Arthurian Romances from the Middle Ages: On the Reception of Chrétien de Troyes's *Yvain, the Knight of the Lion*, Based on Manuscript JTS Rab. 1164." *AJS Review* 42, no. 2 (November 2018): 381–401.

Kushelevsky, Rella. "'King Artus' as a Jewish Romance: Horizons of Expectation and Genre Configurations." In *Medieval and Early Modern Romance*, edited by Caroline Gruenbaum and Annegret Oehme (Kalamazoo, MI: Arc Humanities, 2023), 107–28.

Kushelevsky, Rella. "R. Berechiah's Imprint on *Sefer Ha-Ma'asim*: The Reception of *Mishlei Shu'alim*." In *Berechiah Ben Natronai Ha-Naqdan's Works and Their Reception*, edited by Tamás Visi, Tovi Bibring, and Daniel Soukup, 141–61. Turnhout: Brepols, 2019.

Kushelevsky, Rella. *Sigufim U-Pituyim: Ha-Sippur Ha-'ivri Be-'ashkenaz. Ms. Parma 2295 [de-Rossi 563]*. Jerusalem: Magnes, 2010.

Kushelevsky, Rella. *Tales in Context: Sefer Ha-Ma'asim in Medieval Northern France*. Detroit, MI: Wayne State University Press, 2017.

Lacerenza, Giancarlo. "'Melek Artûs': I Temi Arturiani Ebraizzati Nel "«Sefer Ha-Sˇmad»." In *Macrotesti Fra Oriente e Occidente: 4. Colloquio Internazionale, Vico Equense, 26–29 Ottobre 2000*, edited by Giovanna Carbonaro, Natalia L. Tornesello, and Eliana Creazzo, 101–18. Soveria Mannelli (Catanzaro): Rubbettino, 2003.

Lacy, Norris J. *Lancelot-Grail: The Death of Arthur*. Vol. 7. Cambridge: D. S. Brewer, 2010.

Lacy, Norris J., ed. *Lancelot-Grail: The Old French Arthurian Vulgate and Post-Vulgate in Translation*. 10 vols. Cambridge: D. S. Brewer, 2010.

Lacy, Norris J. *Lancelot-Grail: The Quest for the Holy Grail*. Woodbridge, UK: Boydell & Brewer, 2010.

Lacy, Norris J., and James J. Wilhelm, eds. *The Romance of Arthur: An Anthology of Medieval Texts in Translation*. London: Routledge, 2012.

Lambert, Mayer, and Louis Brandin. *Glossaire hébreu-français du XIIIe siècle: recueil de mots hébreux bibliques avec traduction française*. Paris: E. Leroux, 1905.

Langermann, Y. Tzvi. "Was There Science in Ashkenaz?" *Simon Dubnow Institute Yearbook* 8 (2009): 1–26.

Larrington, Carolyne. "Gender/Queer Studies." In *Handbook of Arthurian Romance: King Arthur's Court in Medieval European Literature*, edited by Leah Tether, Johnny McFadyen, Keith Busby, and Ad Putter, 259–72. Berlin: De Gruyter, 2017.

Lassner, Jacob. *Demonizing the Queen of Sheba: Boundaries of Gender and Culture in Postbiblical Judaism and Medieval Islam*. Chicago: University of Chicago Press, 1993.

Lehnardt, Andreas, ed. *European Genizah: Newly Discovered Hebrew Binding Fragments in Context*. Leiden: Brill, 2020.

Lehnardt, Andreas, ed. *"Genizat Germania": Hebrew and Aramaic Binding Fragments from Germany in Context*. Leiden: Brill, 2010.

Lehnardt, Andreas. "'I Saw in a Town Violence and Strife': An Unknown Ashkenazic *Maqama* Found in a Binding Fragment." In *Berechiah Ben Natronai Ha-Naqdan's Works and Their Reception*, edited by Tamás Visi, Tovi Bibring, and Daniel Soukup, 163–85. Turnhout: Brepols, 2019. https://doi.org/10.1484/M.BEHE-EB.5.117468.

Lévi, Israel, ed. *Le roman d'Alexandre: texte hébreu anonyme*. Paris: Librairie A. Durlacher, 1887.

Lévi, Israel. "Un recueil de contes juives inédits." *Revue des études juives* 34–35 (1897): 458–76.

Leviant, Curt. *King Artus: A Hebrew Arthurian Romance of 1279*. Syracuse, NY: Syracuse University Press, 2003.

Levinson, Eyal. "Adolescence and Masculinities in Jewish Society in Medieval Ashkenaz [Heb.]." PhD diss., Hebrew University of Jerusalem, 2017.

Levinson, Eyal. *Gender and Sexuality in Ashkenaz in the Middle Ages*. Jerusalem: Shazar, 2022.

Levinson, Joshua. *Ha-Sipur She-Lo' Supar: Omanut Ha-Sipur Ha-Mikra'i Hamurhav Be-Midreshe Hazal* [The Twice-Told Tale: A Poetics of the Exegetical Narrative in Rabbinic Midrash]. Jerusalem: Magnes, 2005.

Levy, Raphael. "A Note on the Latin Translators of Ibn Ezra." *Isis* 37, no. 3/4 (1947): 153–55.

Levy Willard, Denis. *Le Livre Dans la Société Juive Medievale de la France du Nord.* Paris: Editions du Cerf, 2008.

Lewis, Suzanne. *Reading Images: Narrative Discourse and Reception in the Thirteenth-Century Illuminated Apocalypse.* Cambridge: Cambridge University Press, 1995.

Liss, Hanna. "The Commentary on the *Song of Songs* Attributed to R. Samuel Ben Meir (Rashbam)." *Medieval Jewish Studies* 1 (August 2007): 1–27.

Liss, Hanna. *Creating Fictional Worlds: Peshaṭ-Exegesis and Narrativity in Rashbam's Commentary on the Torah.* Leiden: Brill, 2011.

Loewe, Raphael. "The Mediaeval Christian Hebraists of England: Herbert of Bosham and Earlier Scholars." *Transactions* 17 (1951): 225–49.

Loewe, Raphael. "The Mediaeval Christian Hebraists of England: The Superscriptio Lincolniensis." *Hebrew Union College Annual* 28 (1957): 205–52.

Loewe, Raphael. "A Thirteenth-Century Piyyut Set to French Music." *Revue des études juives* 161 (2002): 83–96.

Loomis, Roger Sherman. *The Grail: From Celtic Myth to Christian Symbol.* New York: Columbia University Press, 1963.

Luzzatto, Moses Hayyim. *Mesillat Yesharim: The Path of the Upright*, translated by Mordecai Menahem Kaplan. Philadelphia: Jewish Publication Society, 2010. http://muse.jhu.edu/pub/199/monograph/book/2307.

Magin, Christine. "Armed Jews in Legal Sources from the High and Late Middle Ages." *Jewish Studies* 41 (2002): 67–81.

Malkiel, David. "Jews and Apostates in Medieval Europe—Boundaries Real and Imagined." *Past & Present* 194 (February 2007): 3–34.

Malkiel, David. *Reconstructing Ashkenaz: The Human Face of Franco-German Jewry, 1000–1250.* Stanford, CA: Stanford University Press, 2009.

Manekin, Charles H., Y. Tzvi Langermann, and Hans Hinrich Biesterfeldt, eds. *Moritz Steinschneider: The Hebrew Translations of the Middle Ages and the Jews as Transmitters.* Dordrecht: Springer Netherlands, 2013.

Maor, Noga Roguin, Ariel Roguin, and Nathan Roguin. "Medieval Roots of the Myth of Jewish Male Menstruation." *Rambam Maimonides Medical Journal* 12, no. 4 (October 25, 2021): e0033. https://doi.org/10.5041/RMMJ.10454.

Marcus, Ivan G., ed. *A Facsimile Edition of Sefer Hasidim, MS Parma H 3280.* Jerusalem: Hebrew University Dinur Center, 1985.

Marcus, Ivan G. "From Politics to Martyrdom: Shifting Paradigms in the Hebrew Narratives of the 1096 Crusade Riots." *Prooftexts* 2, no. 1 (1982): 40–52.

Marcus, Ivan G. *Rituals of Childhood: Jewish Acculturation in Medieval Europe.* New Haven, CT: Yale University Press, 1996.

Marcus, Ivan G. "Why Is This Knight Different? A Jewish Self-Representation in Medieval Europe." In *Tov Elem—Memory, Community and Gender in Medieval and Early Jewish Societies: Essays in Honor of Robert Bonfil*, edited by Elisheva Baumgarten, Amnon Raz-Krakotzkin, and Roni Weinstein, 139–52. Jerusalem: Bialik Institute, 2011.

Marie de France. *Die Fabeln Der Marie de France*, edited by Karl Warnke. Halle: Niemeyer, 1898.

Marie de France. *Fables*, edited by Harriet Spiegel. Toronto: University of Toronto Press, 1987.

Marroum, Marianne. "'Kalila Wa Dimna': Inception, Appropriation, and Transmimesis." *Comparative Literature Studies* 48, no. 4 (December 2011): 512–40.

McVaugh, Michael, and Susan Einbinder. "Latin into Hebrew—Twice Over! Presenting Latin Scholastic Medicine to a Jewish Audience." In *Latin-into-Hebrew: Texts and Studies*, edited by Resianne Fontaine and Gad Freudenthal, 31–44. Leiden: Brill, 2013.

Meir ben Barukh of Rothenberg. *Shaarei Teshuvot*, edited by Moses Bloch. Berlin: Itskovski, 1891.

Meir of Norwich. *Into the Light: The Medieval Hebrew Poetry of Meir of Norwich*, edited by Ellman Crasnow and Bente Elsworth, translated by Keiron Pim. Norwich: East Publishing, 2013.

Mikva, Rachel S. "'Midrash vaYosha' and the Development of Narrative in Medieval Jewish Exegesis." PhD diss., Jewish Theological Seminary of America, 2008.

Miller, Elaine R. *Jewish Multiglossia: Hebrew, Arabic, and Castilian in Medieval Spain*. Newark, DE: Juan de la Cuesta, 2000.

Moses ben Isaac Hanessiah. *Sefer Ha-Shoham*, edited by Benjamin Klar. London: Jewish Historical Society of England, 1947.

Mostert, Marco, and Mariëlle Hageman, eds. *Reading Images and Texts: Medieval Images and Texts as Forms of Communication*. Papers from the Third Utrecht Symposium on Medieval Literacy, Utrecht, December 7–9, 2000. Utrecht Studies in Medieval Literacy 8. Turnhout: Brepols, 2005.

Mundill, Robin R. *The King's Jews: Money, Massacre and Exodus in Medieval England*. London: Continuum, 2010.

Nahon, Gerard. "Orality and Literacy: The French Tosaphists." In *Studies in Medieval Jewish Intellectual and Social History: Festschrift in Honor of Robert Chazan*, edited by Elliot R. Wolfson, Lawrence H. Schiffman, and David Engel, 145–68. Leiden: Brill, 2012.

Narkiss, Bezalel. *Hebrew Illuminated Manuscripts*. New York: Encyclopedia Judaica, 1969.

Navarro Peiro, Angeles. "La Versión Hebrea de 'Calila y Dimna' de Ya'aqob Ben El'azar." *Jewish Studies at the Turn of the Twentieth Century* 1 (1999): 468–75.

Needler, Howard. "Refiguring the Middle Ages: Reflections on Hebrew Romances." *New Literary History* 8, no. 2 (1977): 235–55.

Newman, Barbara. *Medieval Crossover: Reading the Secular against the Sacred*. Notre Dame, IN: University of Notre Dame Press, 2013.

Niemeyer, Gerlinde, ed. *Hermannus Quondam Judaeus: Opusculum de Conversione Sua*. Weimar: H. Böhlaus Nachfolger, 1963.

Nisse, Ruth. *Jacob's Shipwreck: Diaspora, Translation, and Jewish-Christian Relations in Medieval England*. Ithaca, NY: Cornell University Press, 2017.

Noble, Peter S. *Love and Marriage in Chrétien de Troyes*. Cardiff: University of Wales Press, 1982.

Nothaft, C. Philipp E. "The Meaning of Judaeus and the Myth of Jewish Male Menses in a Late Medieval Astronomical School Text." *European Journal of Jewish Studies* 7, no. 1 (2013): 73–93.

Noy, Dov. "What Is Jewish about the Jewish Folktale?" In *Miriam's Tambourine: Jewish Folktales from around the World*, edited by Howard Schwartz, xv–xviii. Oxford: Oxford University Press, 1988.

Oehme, Annegret. "Angelic Giants and Monstrous Kings in the Old Yiddish Dukus Horant." *Euphorion* 116, no. 3 (2022): 345–66.

Oehme, Annegret. *The Knight without Boundaries: Yiddish and German Arthurian* Wigalois *Adaptations*. Leiden: Brill, 2022.

Oettinger, Ayelet. "Criticism of the Estates in Judah Al-Ḥarizi's Book of Taḥkemoni and in European-Christian Literature of the Thirteenth Century: Affinity and Distinction." In *Studies in Medieval Jewish Poetry: A Message upon the Garden*, edited by Alessandro Guetta and Masha Itzhaki, 85–115. Leiden: Brill, 2009.

Oettinger, Ayelet. "Maqama." In *Encyclopedia of Jewish Folklore and Traditions*, edited by Ḥaya Bar-Itzhak and Raphael Patai, 352–53. London: Routledge, 2013.

Oettinger, Ayelet. "Parody as a Satirical Weapon in Yehudah Al-Harizi's *Book of the Tahkhemoni* [Heb.]." In *Mittuv Yosef: Yosef Tobi Jubilee Volume*, edited by Ayelet Oettinger and Danny Bar-Maoz, 299–322. Jerusalem: A. Stern, 2011.

Offenberg, Sara. "Isaac Ibn Sahula and King Alfonso X: Possible Connections between the Book Meshal Haqadmoni and the Cantigas de Santa Maria." *Arts and Social Sciences Journal* 5, no. 2 (2014): 1–7.

Offenberg, Sara. "Jacob the Knight in Ezekiel's Chariot: Imagined Identity in a Micrography Decoration of an Ashkenazic Bible." *AJS Review* 40, no. 1 (April 2016): 1–16.

Offenberg, Sara. "A Jewish Knight in Shining Armour: Messianic Narrative and Imagination in Ashkenazic Illuminated Manuscripts." *University of Toronto Journal of Jewish Thought* 4 (2014): 1–14.

Olszowy-Schlanger, Judith. "The Science of Language among Medieval Jews." In *Science in Medieval Jewish Cultures*, edited by Gad Freudenthal, 359–424. Cambridge: Cambridge University Press, 2012.

Ong, Walter J. *Orality and Literacy: The Technologizing of the Word*. 3rd ed. London: Routledge, 2012.

Ong, Walter J. "Orality, Literacy, and Medieval Textualization." *New Literary History* 16, no. 1 (1984): 1–12.

Paden, William D., and Frances Freeman Paden. *Troubadour Poems from the South of France*. Woodbridge, UK: Boydell & Brewer, 2007.

Pagis, Dan. *Al Sod Hatum: Le-Toldot Ha-Hidah Ha-'Ivrit Be-Italyah Uve-Holand*. Jerusalem: Magnes, 1986.

Paris, Gaston. "Études Sur Les Romans de La Table Ronde: *Lancelot du Lac*." *Romania* 12 (1883): 459–534.

Parks, Ward. "The Textualization of Orality in Literary Criticism." In *Vox Intexta: Orality and Textuality in the Middle Ages*, edited by A. N. Doane and Carol Braun Pasternak, 46–61. Madison: University of Wisconsin Press, 1991.

Parks, Ward. *Verbal Dueling in Heroic Narrative: The Homeric and Old English Traditions*. Princeton, NJ: Princeton University Press, 1990.

Patai, Raphael. *Encyclopedia of Jewish Folklore and Traditions*. London: Routledge, 2015.

Penkower, Jordan S. "The End of Rashi's Commentary on Job: The Manuscripts and the Printed Editions." *Jewish Studies Quarterly* 10, no. 1 (2003): 18–48.

Prawer, Siegbert Salomon. *Heine's Jewish Comedy: A Study of His Portraits of Jews and Judaism*. Oxford: Clarendon, 1983.

Predelli, Maria Bendinelli, ed. *La Struzione Della Tavola Ritonda*. Florence: Societa Editrice Fiorentina, 2015.

Psaki, Regina, and Gloria Allaire, eds. *The Arthur of the Italians: The Arthurian Legend in Medieval Italian Literature and Culture*. Cardiff: University of Wales Press, 2014.

Refael-Vivante, Revital. "The Influence of 'Kalila and Dimna' on Medieval Hebrew Fable Literature." In *Énoncés Sapientiels et Littérature Exemplaire*, edited by Marie-Sol Ortolá, 45–79. Lorraine, France: Presses Universitaires de Lorraine, 2013.

Refael-Vivante, Revital. "Of Lions and Foxes: Power and Rule in Hebrew Medieval Fables." *Revista de Paz y Conflictos*, no. 2 (2009): 24–43.

Reif, Stefan C. "Aspects of Mediaeval Jewish Literacy." In *The Uses of Literacy in Early Medieval Europe*, edited by Rosamond McKitterick, 134–55. Cambridge: Cambridge University Press, 1990.

Reynolds, Suzanne. *Medieval Reading: Grammar, Rhetoric and the Classical Text*. Cambridge: Cambridge University Press, 1996.

Rice, Nicole R. *Lay Piety and Religious Discipline in Middle English Literature*. Cambridge: Cambridge University Press, 2009.

Riera i Sans, Jaume, ed. *Cants de noces dels jueus catalans*. Barcelona: Curial, 1974.

Robinson, Cynthia. "Arthur in the Alhambra? Narrative and Nasrid Courtly Self-Fashioning in the Hall of Justice Ceiling Paintings." *Medieval Encounters* 14, no. 2–3 (January 1, 2008): 164–98.

Rosen, Tova. "The *Muwashshah*." In *The Literature of Al-Andalus*, edited by Maria Rosa Menocal, Raymond P. Scheindlin, and Michael Sells, 163–89. Cambridge: Cambridge University Press, 2000.

Rosen, Tova. *Unveiling Eve: Reading Gender in Medieval Hebrew Literature*. Philadelphia: University of Pennsylvania Press, 2003.

Rosenberg, Bruce A. "Folklore Methodology and Medieval Literature." *Journal of the Folklore Institute* 13, no. 3 (1976): 311–25.

Rosenberg, Samuel N. "French Songs in Occitan Chansonniers: Mahieu le Juif in Ms. O (Rome, Biblioteca Apostolica Vaticana, Vaticani Latini 3208)." In *De Sens Rassis*, edited by Keith Busby, Bernard Guidot, Logan E. Whalen, Raymond C. La Charité, and Virginia A. La Charité, 567–75. Amsterdam: Rodopi, 2005.

Rosenberg, Samuel N. "Mahieu le Juif." *Metamorphoses* 23, no. 1 (Spring 2015): 118–25.

Rosenberg, Samuel N. "The Medieval Hebrew-French Wedding Song." *Shofar* 11 (1992): 22–37.

Rosenberg, Samuel N., and Hans Tischler, eds. "Pour Autrui Movrai Mon Chant." In *Chansons des Trouvères: Chanter m'estuet*, 668–71, 1042–43. Paris: Librairie Générale Française, 1995.

Rosenthal, Ludwig. *Heinrich Heine als Jude*. Frankfurt: Ullstein Verlag, 1973.

Roth, Norman. *Conversos, Inquisition, and the Expulsion of the Jews from Spain*. Madison: University of Wisconsin Press, 2002.

Roth, Pinchas. "A Hebrew Debate Poem from Medieval England." *Early Middle English* 2, no. 2 (2020): 83–89.

Rotman, David. "At the Limits of Reality: The Marvelous in Medieval Ashkenazi Hebrew Folktales." *Jewish Studies Quarterly* 20, no. 2 (June 2013): 101–28.

Routledge, Peter. "'Jehuda Ben Halevy' and the Restructuring of Memory within Poetic Discourse." In *Heine-Jahrbuch 2015: 54. Jahrgang*, edited by Sabine Brenner-Wilczek, 58–83. Stuttgart: J. B. Metzler, 2015. https://doi.org/10.1007/978-3-476-01400-9_4.

Rovang, Paul R. "Hebraizing Arthurian Romance: The Originality of Melech Artus." *Arthuriana* 19, no. 2 (2009): 3–9.

Rubenstein, Jeffrey L. *The Culture of the Babylonian Talmud*. Baltimore, MD: Johns Hopkins University Press, 2005.

Rubenstein, Jeffrey L. "From Mythic Motifs to Sustained Myth: The Revision of Rabbinic Traditions in Medieval Midrashim." *Harvard Theological Review* 89, no. 2 (April 1996): 131–59.

Rubenstein, Jeffrey L. *Stories of the Babylonian Talmud*. Baltimore, MD: Johns Hopkins University Press, 2010.

Rubenstein, Jeffrey L. *Talmudic Stories: Narrative Art, Composition, and Culture*. Baltimore, MD: Johns Hopkins University Press, 1999.

Rubin, Aaron D. "Judeo-Italian." In *Handbook of Jewish Languages*, edited by Lily Kahn and Aaron D. Rubin, 297–364. Leiden: Brill, 2015.

Rubin, Miri, ed. *Medieval Christianity in Practice*. Princeton, NJ: Princeton University Press, 2009.

Runte, Hans R., J. Keith Wikeley, and Anthony J. Farrell, eds. *The Seven Sages of Rome and the Book of Sindbad: An Analytical Bibliography*. New York: Garland, 1984.

Rutebeuf. *Œuvres complètes*, edited by Michel Zink. Paris: Bordas, 1989.

Sáenz-Badillos, Angel. *A History of the Hebrew Language*. Cambridge: Cambridge University Press, 2012.

Saltzstein, Jennifer. *The Refrain and the Rise of the Vernacular in Medieval French Music and Poetry*. Rochester, NY: D. S. Brewer, 2013.

Samely, Alexander. *Forms of Rabbinic Thought and Literature*. Oxford: Oxford University Press, 2007.

Saperstein, Marc. "Italian Jewish Preaching: An Overview." In *Preachers of the Italian Ghetto*, edited by David B. Ruderman, 22–40. Berkeley: University of California Press, 1992.

Saperstein, Marc. "The Sermon as Oral Performance." In *Transmitting Jewish Traditions*, edited by David D. Gilmore, 248–77. New Haven, CT: Yale University Press, 2000.

Sargent-Baur, Barbara N. *The Romance of Tristran by Béroul and Béroul II: A Diplomatic Edition and a Critical Edition*. Toronto: University of Toronto Press, 2015.

Scheindlin, Raymond P. "Fawns of the Palace and Fawns of the Field." *Prooftexts* 6, no. 3 (1986): 189–203.

Scheindlin, Raymond P. *Wine, Women, and Death: Medieval Hebrew Poems on the Good Life*. Oxford: Oxford University Press, 1986.

Schiffman, Harold F. "Diglossia as a Sociolinguistic Situation." In *The Handbook of Sociolinguistics*, edited by Florian Coulmas, 205–16. Oxford: Blackwell, 1997. https://onlinelibrary-wiley-com.proxy.library.nyu.edu/doi/pdf/10.1002/9781405166256.ch12.

Schirmann, Jefim. "The Function of the Hebrew Poet in Medieval Spain." *Jewish Social Studies* 16, no. 3 (1954): 235–52.

Schmitt, Jean-Claude. *The Conversion of Herman the Jew: Autobiography, History, and Fiction in the Twelfth Century*, translated by Alex J. Novikoff. Philadelphia: University of Pennsylvania Press, 2013.

Schüler, M. "Die hebraische Version der Sage von Arthur und Lanzelot aus den Jahre 1279." *Archiv für das Studium der neueren Sprachen und Literaturen* 122 (1909): 51–63.

Schwan, Eduard, and Dietrich Behrens. *Grammaire de l'ancien français*, translated by Oscar Bloch. Leipzig: O. R. Reisland, 1913.

Schwarzbaum, Haim. *The Mishle Shu'alim (Fox Fables) of Rabbi Berechiah Ha-Nakdan*. Jerusalem: Institute for Jewish and Arab Folklore Research, 1979.

Seidman, Naomi. *The Marriage Plot: Or, How Jews Fell in Love with Love, and with Literature*. Stanford, CA: Stanford University Press, 2016.

Sela, Shlomo, and Gad Freudenthal. "Abraham Ibn Ezra's Scholarly Writings: A Chronological Listing." *Aleph* 6 (2006): 13.

Sermoneta, Giuseppe. *Un Glossario Filosofico Ebraico-Italiano Del XIII Secolo*. Rome: Edizioni dell'Ateneo, 1969.

Seroussi, Edwin. "The Jewish Liturgical Music Printing Revolution: A Preliminary Assessment." In *Textual Transmission in Contemporary Jewish Cultures*, edited by Avriel Bar-Levav and Uzi Rebhun, 100–136. Oxford: Oxford University Press, 2020.

Serper, Arie. "Guiraut Riquer, Bonfils et les Juifs de Narbonne." *Romanistische Zeitschrift Fur Literaturgeschichte* 2 (1978): 421–29.

Shaked, Guy. "The Jewish Attitude towards the Playing of Music in the Tripartite Mahzor." *Cogent Arts & Humanities* 7, no. 1 (January 1, 2020): 1740539. https://doi.org/10.1080/23311983.2020.1740539.

Shapiro, Laizy, dir. *Srugim*. Season 1, Episode 2, "Sippurei Savta (Grandmother's Stories)." Israel: Yes TV, aired June 30, 2008.

Shapiro, Laizy, dir. *Srugim*. Season 1, Episode 7, "Tafsiq Le'fahed (You/She Will Stop Being Afraid)." Israel: Yes TV, aired August 4, 2008.

Shatzmiller, Joseph. *Cultural Exchange: Jews, Christians, and Art in the Medieval Marketplace*. Princeton, NJ: Princeton University Press, 2013.

Shoaf, Judith, trans. and ed. *Quest of the Holy Grail*. Peterborough, Canada: Broadview, 2018.

Shukry, Zipporah. "The Wolf and the Fox in the Well." *Laographia* 22 (1964): 491–97.

Shyovitz, David I. *A Remembrance of His Wonders: Nature and the Supernatural in Medieval Ashkenaz*. Philadelphia: University of Pennsylvania Press, 2017.

Sirat, Colette. *Hebrew Manuscripts of the Middle Ages*, edited and translated by Nicholas de Lange. Cambridge: Cambridge University Press, 2002.

Sklar, Elizabeth Sherr, and Donald L. Hoffman, eds. *King Arthur in Popular Culture*. Jefferson, NC: McFarland, 2002.

Smalley, Beryl. *The Study of the Bible in the Middle Ages*. Notre Dame, IN: University of Notre Dame Press, 1964.

Smith, Joshua Byron. *Walter Map and the Matter of Britain*. Philadelphia: University of Pennsylvania Press, 2017.

Solomon and Sheba, edited by J. B. Pritchard. London: Phaidon, 1974.

Sommer, Heinrich Oskar. *L'estoire de Merlin*. Vol. II. Washington: Carnegie Institution of Washington, 1909.

Soukup, Daniel. "Melchior Hanel (1627–1689) and His Latin Translation of Mishlei Shu'alim in the Context of the Respublica Litteraria." In *Berechiah Ben Natronai Ha-Naqdan's Works and Their Reception*, edited by Tamás Visi, Tovi Bibring, and Daniel Soukup, 205–19. Turnhout: Brepols, 2019. https://doi.org/10.1484/M.BEHE-EB.5.117470.

Speer, Mary B., ed. *Le Roman Des Sept Sages de Rome: A Critical Edition of the Two Verse Redactions of a Twelfth-Century Romance*. Lexington, KY: French Forum, 1989.

Spiegel, Gabrielle M. *Romancing the Past: The Rise of Vernacular Prose Historiography in Thirteenth-Century France*. Berkeley: University of California Press, 1995.

Stacey, Robert C. "The Conversion of Jews to Christianity in Thirteenth-Century England." *Speculum* 67, no. 2 (April 1992): 263–83.

Steinmetz, Ralf-Henning, ed. *Die Historia von Den Sieben Weisen Meistern Und Dem Kaiser Diocletianus*. Tübingen: Niemeyer, 2001.

Steinschneider, Moritz. *Die hebraeischen Übersetzungen des Mittelalters und die Juden als Dolmetscher* [The Hebrew Translations of the Middle Ages and the Jews as Translators]. Berlin: Kommissionsverlag des Bibliographischen Bureaus, 1893.

Stern, David. *Parables in Midrash: Narrative and Exegesis in Rabbinic Literature*. Cambridge, MA: Harvard University Press, 1991.

Stern, David, and Mark Jay Mirsky, eds. "The Alphabet of Ben Sira." In *Rabbinic Fantasies: Imaginative Narratives from Classical Hebrew Literature*, translated by Norman Bronznick 167–202. New Haven, CT: Yale University Press, 1990.

Stock, Brian. *Listening for the Text: On the Uses of the Past*. Philadelphia: University of Pennsylvania Press, 1990.

Strauch, Gabriele L. "Text and Context in the Reading of Medieval Literature—A Case in Point: Dukus Horant." *Exemplaria* 3, no. 1 (January 1991): 67–94.

Swellander, Michael. "The Arabic-Spanish-Jewish School of Poets: Heinrich Heine's 'Jehudah Ben Halevy' and World Literature." *Germanic Review: Literature, Culture, Theory* 98, no. 1 (January 2, 2023): 33–45. https://doi.org/10.1080/00168890.2022.2161338.

Taitz, Emily. *The Jews of Medieval France: The Community of Champagne*. Westport, CT: Greenwood, 1994.

Tartakoff, Paola. "Testing Boundaries: Jewish Conversion and Cultural Fluidity in Medieval Europe, c. 1200–1391." *Speculum* 90, no. 3 (July 2015): 728–62.

Ta-Shma, Israel. *Creativity and Tradition: Studies in Medieval Rabbinic Scholarship, Literature and Thought*. Cambridge, MA: Harvard University Press, 2007.

Téné, David, ed. *Sefer Ha-Hassagah, Hu'Kitab al-Mustahlaq, Le-R. Yonah Ibn Janah, Be-Targumo Ha-'ivri Sel Ovadiyyah Ha-Sefaradi*. Jerusalem: Academy of the Hebrew Language and Bialik Institute, 2006.

Thompson, Stith. *The Folktale*. Berkeley: University of California Press, 1977.

Thompson, Stith. *Motif-Index of Folk-Literature: A Classification of Narrative Elements in Folktales, Ballads, Myths, Fables, Medieval Romances, Exempla, Fabliaux, Jest-Books and Local Legends*. Bloomington: Indiana University Press, 1955.

Timm, Erika. "Ein Neuentdeckter Literarischer Text in Hebräischen Lettern Aus Der Zeit Vor 1349." *Zeitschrift Für Deutsches Altertum* 142 (2013): 417–23.

Ṭobi, Joseph. *Between Hebrew and Arabic Poetry: Studies in Spanish Medieval Hebrew Poetry*. Leiden: Brill, 2010.

Ṭobi, Joseph. "The Religious Element in the War Poems of Samuel Ha-Nagid and in the Arabic Panegyrics in Andalusia." In *Between Hebrew and Arabic Poetry: Studies in Spanish Medieval Hebrew Poetry*, 93–114. Leiden: Brill, 2010.

Turner, Victor. "Liminality and Communitas." In *The Ritual Process: Structure and Anti-Structure*, 94–130. Chicago: Aldine, 1969.

Unna Baruchi, Aviyah. "A Series of Paronomasia Poems by R. Berechiah Ha-Nakdan." *Kovetz al Yad* 21 (2012): 27–46.

Urbach, Ephraim E. *Ba'ale ha-tosafot: toldotehem, ḥiburehem, shiṭatam*. Jerusalem: Mosad Bi'aliḳ, 1968.

Valles, Margot Behrend. "Judaized Romance and Romanticized Judaization: Adaptation into Hebrew and Early Yiddish Chivalric Literature." PhD diss., Indiana University, 2013.

Visi, Tamás. "Berechiah Ben Naṭronai Ha-Naqdan's *Dodi ve-Neḵdi* and the Transfer of Scientific Knowledge from Latin to Hebrew in the Twelfth Century." *Aleph* 14, no. 2 (July 2014): 9–73.

Visi, Tamás. "Introduction." In *Berechiah Ben Natronai Ha-Naqdan's Works and Their Reception*, edited by Tamás Visi, Tovi Bibring, and Daniel Soukup, 7–28. Turnhout: Brepols, 2019.

Visi, Tamás. "Science and Religion in Ashkenaz: Berechiah Ben Natronai Ha-Naqdan and His Predecessors." In *Berechiah Ben Natronai Ha-Naqdan's Works and Their Reception*, edited by Tamás Visi, Tovi Bibring, and Daniel Soukup, 87–118. Turnhout: Brepols, 2019. https://doi.org/10.1484/M.BEHE-EB.5.117465.

Visi, Tamás, Tovi Bibring, and Daniel Soukup, eds. *Berechiah Ben Natronai Ha-Naqdan's Works and Their Reception: L'oeuvre de Berechiah Ben Natronai Ha-Naqdan et Sa Récéption*. Turnhout: Brepols, 2019.

Visscher, Eve de. "Hebrew, Latin, French, English: Multilingualism in Jewish-Christian Encounters." In *Multilingualism in Medieval Britain (c. 1066–1520): Sources and Analysis*, edited by Judith Jefferson and Ad Putter, 89–104. Turnhout: Brepols, 2013.

Vitz, Evelyn Birge. *Orality and Performance in Early French Romance*. Woodbridge, UK: D. S. Brewer, 1999.

Vitz, Evelyn Birge, Nancy Freeman Regalado, and Marilyn Lawrence, eds. *Performing Medieval Narrative*. Cambridge: Boydell and Brewer, 2005.

Vogelstein, Hermann, and Paul Rieger. *Geschichte Der Juden in Rom*. Berlin: Mayer, 1895.

von Bernuth, Ruth. "A Friend in Need Is a Friend Indeed? Friendship, Love, and Loyalty in the Yiddish Seven Sages of Rome." In *Medieval and Early Modern Jewish Romance*, edited by Caroline Gruenbaum and Annegret Oehme, 129–52. Kalamazoo, MI: Arc Humanities, 2023.

Wacks, David A. "Conflicted Identity and Colonial Adaptation in Petrus Alfonsi's 'Dialogus Contra Judaeos' and 'Disciplina Clericalis.'" In *Marginal Voices:*

Studies in Converso Literature of Medieval and Golden Age Spain, edited by Amy I. Aronson-Friedman and Gregory B. Kaplan, 69–90. Leiden: Brill, 2012.

Wacks, David A. *Double Diaspora in Sephardic Literature: Jewish Cultural Production before and after 1492*. Bloomington: Indiana University Press, 2015.

Wacks, David A. *Framing Iberia: Maqamat and Frametale Narratives in Medieval Spain*. Leiden: Brill, 2007.

Wacks, David A. "The Performativity of Ibn Al-Muqaffa's Kalīla Wa-Dimna and Al-Maqāmāt Al-Luzūmiyya of Al-Saraqustī." *Journal of Arabic Literature* 34, no. 1/2 (April 2003): 178–89.

Walters, Lori J., ed. *Lancelot and Guinevere: A Casebook*. London: Routledge, 2015.

Ward, Susan L. "Visual Environment of Jewish Learning in Twelfth-Century Rouen." *IMAGES: A Journal of Jewish Art and Visual Culture* 11, no. 1 (December 5, 2018): 43–56.

Weinraub, Eugene J. *Chrétien's Jewish Grail: A New Investigation of the Imagery and Significance of Chrétien de Troyes's Grail Episode Based on Medieval Hebraic Sources*. Chapel Hill: University of North Carolina Press, 1976.

Weiss, Shayna. "Frum with Benefits: Israeli Television, Globalization, and Srugim's American Appeal." *Jewish Film & New Media* 4, no. 1 (2016): 68–89. https://doi.org/10.13110/jewifilmnewmedi.4.1.0068.

Weissler, Chava. " 'For Women and for Men Who Are Like Women': The Construction of Gender in Yiddish Devotional Literature." *Journal of Feminist Studies in Religion* 5, no. 2 (1989): 7–24.

Wenzel, Edith. "Isolation or Symbiosis? Social and Cultural Relationships between Jews and Non-Jews in Medieval Europe." *Derekh Judaica Urbinatensia*, no. 3 (2005): 7–24.

Whalen, Logan E. *Marie de France and the Poetics of Memory*. Washington, DC: Catholic University of America Press, 2008.

Whetter, K. S. *Understanding Genre and Medieval Romance*. Aldershot, UK: Ashgate, 2008.

Wogan-Browne, Jocelyn, Ruth Evans, Andrew Taylor, and Nicholas Watson, eds. *The Idea of the Vernacular*. University Park: Pennsylvania State University Press, 1999.

Wolfzettel, Friedrich, ed. *Arthurian Romance and Gender: Selected Proceedings of the XVIIth International Arthurian Congress*. Amsterdam: Rodopi, 1995.

Woolf, Jeffrey. "Communal and Religious Organization." In *The Cambridge History of Judaism*, edited by Robert Chazan, 380–92. Cambridge: Cambridge University Press, 2018.

Yassif, Eli. *The Hebrew Folktale: History, Genre, Meaning*. Bloomington: Indiana University Press, 2009.

Yassif, Eli. "The Hebrew Narrative Anthology in the Middle Ages." *Prooftexts* 17, no. 2 (May 1997): 153–75.

Yassif, Eli, ed. *Me'ah Sipurim Ḥaser Eḥad: Agadot Ketav-Yad Yerushalayim Ba-Folḳlor Ha-Yehudi Shel Yeme Ha-Benayim*. Tel Aviv: Haim Rubin Tel Aviv University Press, 2013.

Yassif, Eli. "Oral Traditions in a Literate Society: The Hebrew Literature of the Middle Ages." In *Medieval Oral Literature*, edited by Karl Reichl, 499–519. Berlin: de Gruyter, 2012.

Yassif, Eli. "Sepher Ha-Ma'asim: The Character, Origins and Impact of the Collection of Stories at the Time of the Tosafists [Heb.]." *Tarbiz* 53, no. 3 (April 1, 1984): 409–29.

Yassif, Eli. *Sippurei Ben Sira Be-Yemei Ha-Benayim*. Jerusalem: Magnes, 1985.

Yassif, Eli. "Storytelling and Meaning: Theory and Practice of Narrative Variants in Religious Texts." In *Religious Stories in Transformation: Conflict, Revision and Reception*, edited by Alberdina Houtman, Tamar Kadari, Marcel Poorthuis, and Vered Tohar, 6–20. Leiden: Brill, 2016.

Yassif, Eli. "The Throne and the Queen: A New Version and Interpretation of the Romance of Solomon and the Queen of Sheba." In *Festschrift for Rella Kushelevsky*. Ramat Gan: Bar Ilan University, forthcoming.

Ziolkowski, Jan M. "Cultural Diglossia and the Nature of Medieval Latin Literature." In *The Ballad and Oral Literature*, edited by Joseph Harris, 193–213. Cambridge, MA: Harvard University Press, 1991.

Zonta, Mauro. "Medieval Hebrew Translations of Philosophical and Scientific Texts: A Chronological Table." In *Science in Medieval Jewish Cultures*, edited by Gad Freudenthal, 17–73. Cambridge: Cambridge University Press, 2012.

Zonta, Mauro. "The Zoological Writings in the Hebrew Tradition." In *Aristotle's Animals in the Middle Ages and Renaissance*, edited by Carlos G. Steel, Guy Guldentops, and Pieter Beullens, 44–68. Leuven: Leuven University Press, 1999.

Zwink, Julia. "Étude Lexicographique Du Traité Anonyme 'Fevres': Une Compilation Médicale En Ancien Français, Écrite En Caractères Hébraïques." *Panace@* 7, no. 24 (2006): 250–60.

Index

www.ingramcontent.com/pod-product-compliance
Lightning Source LLC
Chambersburg PA
CBHW030307100426
42812CB00002B/596

* 9 7 8 1 5 0 1 7 8 2 4 1 1 *